MY LIFE STORY

A COAL MINER'S SON

Bobby Whatley

Transcribed by Robert Alan Reed

NEWMAN SPRINGS PUBLISHING
320 Broad Street
Red Bank, NJ 07701

First originally published by Newman Springs Publishing 2021

ISBN 978-1-63881-644-7 (Paperback)
ISBN 978-1-63881-645-4 (Hardcover)
ISBN 978-1-63881-646-1 (Digital)

Printed in the United States of America

To my wife, Nettie Jo, whom I was married to for forty-eight years
To our four children—Carol, Teresa, Michael, and Cheryl

ABOUT THE COVER

The cover of my book was called Little Italy or Dago Hollow. When I was a young boy, I would cross over a little walkway with water beneath it to get inside a store building and buy candy from the Italian owner. They were very kind and polite people. This little community is no longer there since the Number 9 Coal Mines closed down in the fifties. I went to school with Augusteen and Jhonny Salvadore, who lived there on the hillside.

People no longer live in those houses. They have all rotted down and gone.

ACKNOWLEDGMENTS

I am most grateful to my uncle Morgan Lovejoy for taking up time for me and a lot of other young boys in Piper-Coleanor, Alabama.

I thank A. J. Wells for my first sand bucket, rake, and hoe when I was four years old.

I thank my grandson, Robert Alan Reed, for copying my book onto the computer.

I thank Marshall Goggins and Paula Fancher for some of the photos that appear in my book.

I have known personally all the people I have written about—Mr. Chism, my barber when I was young in Piper, Alabama; Mr. Harry Fulman, our road commissioner; Dr. W. E. Stinson who brought me into the world and, after I was grown and married, brought my first two children in the world; Harold Campbell; Betty Lovejoy Campbell; Brother George Colburn; Mrs. Sue Pickett; and Mr. Ed Perry, my income tax man.

I thank Renee Radner for suggesting that I write this book.

INTRODUCTION

B efore I start this autobiography, I would like to thank God for providing me a long and happy life. We all have a purpose. None of us is perfect. No one person is better than anyone else, regardless of what race or skin color we may be.

There is good and evil in people of every race and color. Some of us are lucky, some are unlucky. Some are rich, others are poor. Some people may have more formal education than others, but God created every one of us as equals. Jesus will forgive the sins and save the souls of those who sincerely want to be with him for eternity. He shed his blood on the cross so that our sins would be forgiven. God blessed me with a wonderful family here on this earth, and I hope that all our family will be together again in heaven with our Lord Jesus Christ.

Nettie Jo Whatley

This nonfictional biography is dedicated to my beautiful wife of forty-eight years, Nettie Jo Whatley (née Moore), and our four wonderful children: Carol Bethlyn (McKeown) Whatley, Teresa Lanett (Davis) Whatley, Michael Lou Whatley, and Cheryl Deneen (Nguyen) Whatley.

I am thankful that I have lived long enough to write this autobiography. According to the Bible, we are only guaranteed seventy years on earth. I am eighty-four years old at the time of this writing, so I am living on borrowed time. I leave everything in God's hands, and I believe that God is always one step ahead of me, planning my life in the way that he sees fit. Sometimes things bring me down, but God lifts me out of the hardships and into better days.

I think God kept me around this long to help raise some of my grandchildren. It is hard to imagine what might have happened if I had not been there for them. Sometimes things happen in life that we don't understand, but I know God has a plan for us all the time. We cannot see the wind, radio waves, or who knows what else in the sky; but we know these things are there.

Why then do some people think they have to see God to know he is there and has blessed us all by letting us live on this earth? We are a chosen few who have enjoyed that privilege.

I have come close to death on many occasions, but I have always been saved. I don't question why God has saved me; I just know that he was looking out for me all these years. I certainly have not obeyed God's will as I should, but he knows deep in my heart that I am thankful for his giving up his only Son, Jesus Christ, for all our sins. I am a true believer that, as said in the Bible, angels are around to protect us when we are in danger, even when we don't even realize the danger is there.

One day, completely out of the blue, my niece Renee suggested that I write this autobiography to leave my children something to look back on, in remembrance. Renee told me that she wished she had suggested the same idea to her father and my brother, James Roland Whatley, before he passed away. So I decided that I would do just that. I think James could have written his biography better than I can because he was very smart and could probably remember some things clearer because he was two years younger than me.

CONTENTS

CHAPTER 1

CHILDHOOD

My mother, Lula Mae Whatley (née Broadhead), and my father, Benjamin Franklin Whatley, picked cotton for $0.50 a day before they were married. Shortly after they married, my daddy got a job at Piper Number 2 Coal Mines, making $2.80 per day. That was big money back in those days, but the work was hard, and the conditions were unsafe.

My mother and father lived in a two-story boarding house in Piper, Alabama. They had five children, all boys, so you can imagine how difficult it was for my mother to keep six males (the five of us and my daddy) in line. She did a good job with all of us. She was a good and very decent mother. I only remember my mother wearing dresses her whole life, except for when she would go swimming at Brown's Dam on Little Cahaba River. She would wear overalls to swim, and we would be off to ourselves away from other people. The bottom of Brown's Dam was like a solid rock. We would usually get out of the water from swimming and have leeches clinging all over us.

My mother never owned pants or shorts for the entire eighty-nine years that she was alive. She just wore a plain old dress, many of which were made out of flour sack materials when we were young. My mother and father would go to bed at eight o'clock every night and get up at four o'clock every morning whether they had to work or not. They would get up and drink their coffee. It smelled so good, and I wanted to drink some, but I couldn't swallow it at all. To this day, I have never had a cup of coffee in my life.

My mother had blond hair, and my father had red hair. My oldest brother, Franklin Delonoy Whatley (February 12, 1934–May 1, 2015), was born in the Piper boarding house, with red hair like our father's. My parents later moved into a house on Lizard Road in Piper, just down the road from the boarding house. I, my brother James, and my brother Bennie Ray were all born in the house on Lizard Road. I was the second child and had blond hair like my mother. She said there was a bad snowstorm during the time that I was born, and Dr. Stinson had a hard time making his way to our house because of all the snow and ice. I probably nearly killed my mother because I was so big. I was born Bobby Gene Whatley on December 28, 1935, and weighed eleven pounds. James Roland Whatley (October 23, 1937–August 9, 2001), my parents' third child, was born with blond hair like my mother. Bennie Ray (January 24, 1941–April 18, 2002) was the fourth child, born with red hair like my father. We later moved to a house on Main Street in Piper, Alabama, where my youngest brother and my parents' fifth child, William (Billy) Crawford Whatley (June 23, 1942–January 1, 1986), was born with red hair like my father.

Top: Benjamin, Billy, Franklin, Lula Mae, and James Whatley
Bottom: Bobby and Bennie Ray Whatley

We never knew my father's parents because they passed away before I was born. My daddy never talked about his parents, and we never asked about them. Franklin was born about a year before my daddy's father passed away.

My father had a Ford Model B truck with a small bed on it when we lived on Lizard Road. When I was four or five years old, my daddy got into his old twenties Model B truck and started up the hill. I ran after him, hoping to catch him because I wanted to go with him wherever he was going. I was crying because I could not catch him. He was probably laughing. He did not want me to go with him that time, I guess.

We only had three churches that I can remember in our community: a Baptist church, a Methodist church which was next to a bridge going over the railroad tracks to Porter Town, and a Holiness church between Piper and Coleanor. Piper and Coleanor were communities together.

We were raised as Baptists, but we would go to all the churches. We went every Sunday morning, Sunday night, and Wednesday nights. Church was the only place that we had to go after dark. We had no television, no phones, and no air conditioner back then. The post office and store closed at 5:00 p.m.

Piper Post Office around 1914, Postcard. Courtesy of Tom Fanchi

Piper Post Office

We seemed to change girlfriends every week or two. We could walk them home, holding their hands, which was a big deal when we were kids. Every now and then we would get a little kiss. That was really romance, although short-term romance.

Arthur and Fannie Wallace lived across from the Baptist church, and Mr. Arthur was in church every time the doors would open. In church, women wore dresses and lipstick, and some wore hats with veils down over their faces. I can only remember three beautiful girls that wore slacks in those days because it was considered a no-no for decent women. The girls' father was an alcoholic, but one day he decided to be saved in church. He became one of the most dedicated parishioners that I have ever known, quit drinking alcohol, and became a true Christian.

Back then, the preachers seemed to have more spirit in their sermons. They worked in the coal mines all week and preached on Sundays. They did not preach for the money; it was for the love of Christ. We would take our nickel and put it into the plate when the ushers came by.

The church would post the amount of money collected on a board behind the preacher. Most of the time, the collections would amount to between fifteen and twenty dollars. That was a lot of money back then. When the preacher began his sermon, you would not fall asleep or get bored. He would shout and move around to keep your attention. They weren't very educated people, but they knew how to preach from the Bible. All we could hear was that the end of the world was coming.

The churches did not have air-conditioning or fans for the hot days or heating for when it was cold. I can remember the preacher's white shirt being soaked from sweat. Most of the churches had little handheld fans on the backs of seats near the hymn books for anyone that felt hot. We could hardly wait until vacation Bible school each summer so we could make our little crafts and learn about God and Jesus. We had a big bell in the church steeple with a rope hanging down low enough for us kids to reach. I would go to the church an hour early so that I could ring the bell really loud to remind people to come to church. The bell was so loud that you could hear it all over the coal mining community.

One thing that we looked forward to when we were kids was having dinner on the ground after church. Sometimes all the ladies would bring different dishes. Everyone would enjoy the food, and the kids would enjoy playing games.

Sometimes we would go to the Holiness church between Piper and Coleanor. There was a woman there who was the most dedicated Christian I have ever met. Everyone called her Aunt Dolly Warren, even though she was not our aunt. When the Holy Spirit would hit her, she would start dancing and jumping all around and speaking in the unknown tongue. She would rattle off so many words in such a short span that we could tell it was not fake. She was a great lady.

After the preacher would finish his sermon each Sunday, one of the families would invite him over to their house for lunch. We called it dinner back then.

We had a really good preacher in Piper named Brother George Coburn. He worked in the coal mines all week and preached on Sundays. My father only went to church about once a year because he was usually drinking by then, but he always made us go to church every Sunday with my mother. Even when we had company over, my father would make us go to church anyway and would say that our company could wait until we got back home. One day, I asked why he never went to church. He said, "You'd better shut up, boy!" And that was the end of the conversation. I knew to shut up. He always said that when he passed away, he wanted Brother Coburn to preach at his funeral. I think Brother Coburn may have passed away before my father. I don't know where he moved to from Piper.

My father had quit drinking years before he passed away and was baptized at West Blocton Baptist Church. He had cancer of the lungs, liver, and stomach. The doctors found the cancer too late and were not able to operate. My father had waited too long before going to the doctor. Once the doctors discovered the cancer, they gave my father about thirty days to live. He lived ninety days before he eventually passed away. His baptism was sadder than his funeral. The church was packed full to standing room only.

When I was about five or six years old, I was out in the yard one day, playing with my little car. I started to build me a little play coal mine in the dirt, but I had heard that the end of the world was coming so much that I thought to myself, "Why build a play coal mine if the end of the world is coming and it will all be destroyed anyways?"

When we were young, different preachers would come to Piper and set up tents. They would get sawdust, free from the sawmill, to put on the ground of the tents for people to walk on after the chairs were put down. The preachers would give us children pencils and twelve-inch wooden rulers to go around the neighborhood and give to people and to tell everyone to come to the church revival under the tent.

When I was seven years old, my mother talked me into going up to the altar with her to get saved. We did and later on were baptized at Bulldog Bend on the Little Cahaba River. I really didn't know what I was doing other than what my mother told me to do. Later on in life when I was nineteen, in the air force and stationed in Tripoli, Libya, in North Africa, I accepted Christ into my life again and was baptized in the Mediterranean Sea by an air force chaplain who was a preacher from Louisiana.

Baptism in the Cahaba River

I will admit that I hit a backslide after I got out of the air force, but I know my Lord will forgive me. He said once saved, always saved, but we have to repent for our sins before entering into heaven. God will be our judge, and no one on earth has that power. The Bible says, "Judge not, that ye be not judged." I think we all backslide one way or another. If not directly, then maybe indirectly. No one lives a perfect life. We have to forgive, but may not forget. Some people will say, "Look at that hypocrite going to church. Just to be seen." We don't go to church to judge that individual. We go to try and save our soul. That person has to deal with their own soul. We shouldn't say, "I am better off than he or she is." Only God can say who is better off when judgment day comes. Sometimes I think people just want an excuse not to go to church.

When we were small, my daddy managed to get a Santa Claus suit from somewhere, and he would just pop up around Christmastime wearing it. At Easter, we would go into the woods to find mulberry trees, and he would pick the berries off the tree and eat them. Mulberries looked like blackberries, but they were about an inch long and grew on big trees instead of briars. When I was about four or five years old, a little carnival came to town and set up all the rides between Piper and Coleanor. My favorite part was going around and around in this little red car that I thought I was really steering. I was really turning that steering wheel!

I enjoyed playing with paper dolls and coloring books. We would cut out paper dolls and put different outfits on boy and girl paper dolls. The coloring books really kept us busy. We only had a little box with maybe ten or fifteen different colors in it. They smelled so good. I loved playing with baby dolls, and I had one that was a little Black doll. After I got tired of playing with a doll, I would tear it open and take out the part that made the crying sound. I would play with the crying part, holding it in my hand and pointing it in different directions to make the crying sound louder.

We had good neighbors across the road from us at the house on Lizard Road. Their names were Loyce and Lois Reid. The people in the Piper community gave Loyce the nickname Lost John. They had three little children named Betty Joyce, Tommie Jean, and Don. My brothers and I would sometimes go to their house to play with the Reid children. All of us were between the ages of two and five years old at the time. Mrs. Reid would put a little pallet on the floor and give us cookies to munch on while she went next door to visit with Ms. Clara Bell Warren, but she was never gone long.

One day, my brother Franklin and I were outside playing in our yard. We looked down toward the Reids' house and saw it was on fire! Mrs. Reid was next door visiting with Ms. Warren. Franklin and I ran inside our house to tell our mother. Mrs. Reid ran inside of her burning house to try and save her children. She got Tommie Jean and Don, but she could not find Betty Joyce. After the house had burned, they found Betty Joyce's burned bones behind a door where she had tried to get out. Mrs. Reid was burned pretty badly herself from saving the other two children and had scars for the rest of her life. The scars were a reminder to her of the physical and emotional pain from that day. I still remember them putting Betty Joyce's bones in a tub and bringing them to our house. Those old coal company homes were built out of heart pine, and when they caught fire, they would burn up so fast it was like someone was pouring gasoline on it. Later on, the Reid family moved to Chicago, Illinois, for a few years before moving back to West Blocton. Tommie Jean still lives in West Blocton, but her brother Don was murdered in Chicago. Mrs. Reid passed away at the age of ninety-three.

We had a lot of good friends and kinfolks around us. Joe and Beatrice Hriber lived down at the end of Lizard Road, and they had four children: Jo Ann, Mary Sue, Johnny, and Carolyn. Johnny and I were really close friends and still are today. Johnny used to hang out on the riverbanks all the time, but he didn't know how to swim. That was very dangerous because he could have fallen in the river while he was by himself. One day, I tried to get him in trouble. Johnny got too close to a skunk and smelled like it, so I ran to his house to tell his mother. I thought she would whip him, but instead she just laughed. Johnny and I didn't have anything to do when we were fourteen or fifteen years old, so we would get on the road, which was all dirt back then. There was no pavement on those country roads. We would hitchhike about thirty miles to Calera, Alabama, to get a Coca-Cola and then turn around and hitchhike back home to Piper just for something to do. Our parents didn't know where we were; they thought we were just outside playing.

Another thing that I would do with my brothers at that age was order a big box of assorted fireworks from Ohio and sell them for twice what we paid for them. Then the government passed a law that fireworks couldn't be sent by mail anymore, so that ended our moneymaking venture.

Uncle Joe and Aunt Fannie Lovejoy lived just above us. They had fourteen children. One of their sons was my age and named Bobby, but everyone called him Boggy. Boggy, Johnny Hriber, and I were always doing something together. We had another good friend that lived down the road from us named Kate Edwards. Kate had a daughter named Eloise and a son named G. H. Edwards. One day, Mrs. Edwards came running up to our house saying that she just heard on the radio that there was a bus on fire somewhere and she was afraid that G. H. might have been on that bus, but we found out later that he wasn't.

I had hair as white as cotton when I was little. We would wear what were called sunsuits that my mother would make out of flour sacks, until we started school. She made all our sunsuits and her dresses with an old pedal sewing machine. She didn't have an electric sewing machine until later in her life. She would cut up different cloth scraps into squares and sew quilts by hand. Once we started school, we would wear overalls up until we got to high school.

My mother's mother, Mary Elizabeth Broadhead, and her father, William Broadhead, lived in Red Eagle, Alabama, between West Blocton and Centerville. They lived in the woods by a railroad track. Every time we visited, Grandmother Broadhead would give us a sack full of prunes to eat. On the way, we would pass Bulldog Bend and stop at a clear spot to get spring water to drink. There was always an aluminum dipper at the spring for anyone that wanted to drink. Everyone drank from the same dipper, and we always saw minnows swimming in the spring. One day, while we were visiting when I was about six, a train came down the track really slow. My daddy jumped on the last railcar, and it scared us. We thought our daddy was gone for good. After a while, he came walking back through the woods, and we sure were happy because we didn't want to lose our daddy. Another incident happened that day that scared me. Grandmother had a pretty deep stream in front of her house, and I don't remember how but I fell into it and nearly drowned. I was going under the second or third time when my daddy reached down and pulled me out.

My mother's mother was a very religious woman. She didn't believe that anyone should work on Sunday because it was the Sabbath, a day that everyone should rest. She would even prepare her meals for Sunday the night before. She passed away that same year at the age of sixty-eight. She was lying on her bed and told us that she could see the angels coming for her. Then she passed away. After my grandmother passed, my grandfather moved into our house with us for about seventeen years before he passed away at the age of ninety-one. He was a very smart and humble man. Before my grandmother passed away, we would always stop by a little store not far from her house and get candy and drinks. The building is still there, but it is not a store anymore.

Old store where we stopped for candy

We led a very simple life in the woods of Piper, Alabama. We didn't really know what was going on in the rest of the world. Piper had one barbershop, with a barber named Mr. Chism. He charged fifty cents for a haircut. A young lady by the name of Paul Gray

Fancher would come to his shop sometimes and sweep the hair up off the floor for him. Mr. Chism had a pretty wife and two sons. They were a very nice family.

Mr. and Mrs. Chism

Piper had one of the best doctors I have ever known, and he had a good nurse helping him. The nurse's name was Ms. Irmie. She wasn't married, and I don't know if she ever got married. Dr. Stinson seemed to know a little bit of everything, including how to cure people of their ailments and sickness. He would come to anyone's house to deliver babies or take care of them when they were sick. He had a doctor's office, but he would come to you if you couldn't get to him. Dr. Stinson delivered all five of my mother's boys for fifteen dollars each. After I married my beautiful wife, Nettie Jo, he also delivered our two oldest daughters, Carol and Teresa, at Alabaster Hospital before he passed away. My daughters cost a lot more than the fifteen dollars that he charged my mother.

Most people in the mining camp didn't have an automobile. They just worked in the mine and stayed home most of the time. Some Black people had horses. We had a bus that came through Piper, Marvel, Booth Town, Helena, and other small communities going to Birmingham every day. The bus driver's name was Mr. Henry Spears.

By the time the bus got to Birmingham, there was even hardly room to stand. His bus would be loaded every day. I remember going a few times with my mother, but I don't remember why. We would go to a movie on our visit and go back home the same day, on the same bus. There was also a man named Mr. Wilcox Randall that drove a gasoline truck, and I thought that was a dangerous job. I thought if he ever had a wreck, that gasoline truck would blow up. I didn't think about them maybe having safety valves to keep them from blowing up if it caught on fire.

There were about seven hundred houses in the Piper coal mining community, one post office, a large store, a barbershop, and a train station. We would get mail two times a day. The mail truck ran early in the morning and again in the afternoon. Stamps were only three cents.

Mining communities in Central Alabama

The store was like a Walmart and had groceries, tools, clothing, jewelry, and other items. The store had a front porch with spaces between the boards, and when people threw their cigarette butts down, they would fall between the cracks. We boys would crawl under the porch to collect the cigarette butts and any loose change that we could find. We would tear the cigarette butts open and make us a cigarette to smoke, hoping our mother wouldn't smell it on our breaths or else we would get our butts torn up. One thing that I am thankful to my brother Franklin for is for telling on me for smoking when I was sixteen years old. Two years before that, when he was sixteen, he said, "If you don't tell on me, I won't tell on you." The first time that I put a cigarette in my mouth, Franklin went to my mother and told on me. My mother said, "Bob, you aren't smoking until you are eighteen years old!" But by the time I turned eighteen, I didn't want to smoke, and I never picked up that bad habit. Thanks, Frank, for telling on me. Right before Mr. Jones sold the Piper community to a Mr. Tutwiler out of Birmingham, the big store mysteriously burned to the ground one night. The company rebuilt a much smaller store that only sold groceries, and Tom Jones and Mr. Eady worked there. We would tell Tom that we wanted a nickel ice cream, and he would stack the ice cream as high as he could. If we told him we wanted five cents worth of nuts, he would give us probably a half pound in a paper sack. We loved our Bazooka bubble gum too.

School Days
1946 - 1947

Edward Moore

Piper Store

We bought our little five-cent boxes of Cracker Jacks so we could get the prize out of the box. We would dig down in the box just to see what kind of prize we were getting and then eat the caramel popcorn.

When we were seven or eight years old, we started picking blackberries every year to sell. We could sell all that we could pick. We started out selling them for twenty-five cents a gallon, but then we raised our price to thirty-five cents a gallon. As we got a little older, people would come out from Birmingham to buy plums and blackberries from us. We knew where plum orchards were that didn't belong to anyone and we could get tubfuls. The people from Birmingham would give us three days' notice. We would have buckets, tubs, and pans full of blackberries and plums by the time they got there, and they would come back every summer. We could never get a gallon of wild blueberries because they were so good that we would eat them as fast as we could pick them. I was picking blackberries one day and Mr. Frederick came by selling watermelons and vegetables from his truck. Mr. Frederick was the uncle of Ira Fredericks, who married my cousin, Phyllis Lovejoy, later on in life. Mr. Frederick told me that he would swap me the largest watermelon on his truck, which was very large, for two gallons of blackberries, so we traded. Another time, I was picking blackberries by myself. I had four gallons picked and was walking down a path in the woods between Bulldog Bend and Piper. I was looking down at the ground, covered in sweat, and a big rattlesnake jumped up at my throat and missed. I don't know why he didn't strike at my legs. My good Lord was looking out for a dumb kid, I guess. I killed the snake, but if he would have bitten me, I probably wouldn't have made it home. It was over a mile away; no one knew where I was, and sweat was pouring off me.

Potbellied stove

I bought a straw hat to keep the sun and gnats out of my eyes while I picked berries. I was the champion blackberry picker when we lived in Piper. One summer, I picked sixty-five gallons and eleven gallons in one day. I sold some of the blackberries and gave twelve gallons to my aunt Myrtle and some to different neighbors. The fastest that I ever picked a single gallon was thirty minutes. I would put a drinking glass in both pockets, fill them, then dump them into a gallon syrup bucket. Uncle Morgan Lovejoy and my granddaddy

William Broadhead were the only people that could even come close to beating me at picking a gallon of blackberries. Of all the men that I have known in my lifetime that were good and honest men that I have tried to pattern my life after, the most notable were Uncle Morgan, Granddaddy Broadhead, Edgar Moore (my father-in-law), and Mr. Harry Fulman. They were all great and respectable men.

Harry Fulman

If anything caught on fire in Piper, including houses, people would just watch it burn because we didn't have a fire department. It seemed like every year a house would burn down either in Piper or Coleanor, and I would have a hard time going to sleep after seeing someone's house burn to the ground. People usually couldn't save very much before their house burned down. The houses were all made of heart pine with wooden shingles. Every house had a fireplace and potbellied stove with pipes running from the stove through the roof or the walls to the outside of the house. They also had woodburning stoves that we would put wood or coal in for heat in the wintertime. We didn't have electric stoves or heaters when we were young.

Sometimes the rooms would be front and back, and the fireplace was designed to go up the same chimney. The woodburning stoves are what the women used to cook on back then. The stoves had ovens over them to keep the cornbread warm and a little place on the end to keep water warm. After the stove got hot, it would cause the water to warm or get hot.

The stove had six eyes where we could put the wood and coal in to keep the fire going. We had a little joke about the stove. We would say, "What is the most important part of the stove?" The answer was the lifter, legs, and poker. The poker was used to keep the coal stirred so the fire would keep burning. The lifter lifted the eyes off the stove so we could put more wood and coal on the fire to keep it burning. We would use the poker to stir up the fire before putting the eyes back on. We would always get the fire started by using what we called splinters, which were the really rich pine with rosin on it. That would start the fire quick and easy. Then we would keep adding wood and coal in the stove to keep the fire from going out.

We would roast marshmallows on the fireplace after we got the fire started. Then in wintertime, we would crack our hickory nuts and walnuts on the hearth of the fireplace with a hammer. We would take a bobby pin that the women used in their hair to pick the "goodies," as we called it, out of the nuts that we cracked. There was also a smaller hickory nut called scaly bark. We would always pick up nuts in the fall to have plenty in the winter. Sometimes we wouldn't have anything to eat for breakfast except grease gravy, and it tasted terrible.

Bobby pin

When I was in the first or second grade, there was a dead tree close to our school that had some woodpecker holes in it. Sometimes flying squirrels would build nests in the hollow trees. Jack Seagle and some of us pushed the little tree over, and when we did, we found some little flying squirrels in one of the holes. I took one of them. They had just been born and didn't have too much hair on their bodies. I took it home with me after school let out that day. I put it in a little box and fed it milk out of a small bottle, like a medicine bottle. The next morning, before I left to go to school, I decided to put the baby flying squirrel under the woodstove to keep it warm. That was the wrong decision! When I came home from school that afternoon, the poor little thing was baked. I didn't think about how hot it would get underneath the stove. I imagine it was a miserable death.

When I was in first grade, Jack Seagle, who was four years older than me, would put me on his shoulders and run across the railroad trusses. That was dangerous because if he had fallen, we probably both would have dropped a hundred feet below. We were young, and that thought never entered our minds.

There was a swinging bridge down below our school going over the big hollow that the railroad truss went over. Sometimes we would cross over on the swinging bridge if we were going from Piper to Coleanor. We could see the swinging bridge from the railroad trusses.

In the woods close to the swinging bridge, we would dig up certain little plants with roots that looked like little jugs. The real name of the plant was wild cinnamon.

Swinging Bridge

When we went to school, we took our lunch in a paper sack or a little tin lunch bucket. Sometimes, all we had to put in our lunch was a fried Irish potato sandwich or a butter and sugar sandwich. I would give some of my lunch away to a friend, even though I wanted it, but I didn't tell my mother. She thought I was eating all of it. Later on, we got a lunchroom at the school, and we had some really good cooks. It seemed like all the women knew how to cook good food back then. We would have some of the best butter beans and hot dogs that I have ever eaten, besides my mother's naturally. One of my classmates' mother, Bessie Jones, was one of the cooks. Her son's name was Roy. Mrs. Turpo was another one of the cooks.

When I was in first or second grade, I got into my first fight. We had outside toilets at our grammar school. There was a long cement trench for three or four of us to wee-wee at the same time. A few of us were in the process of going wee-wee when the little boy next to me turned his tally whacker at me and peed in my face. We started fighting on the ground. I looked up on the bank and saw our principal looking down at us while I was on top of the boy, whipping his butt. We quit fighting, and I told the principal what happened. He took the boy inside and tore his butt up. So the boy got two whipping that day, one from me and one from the principal.

That was the first and last time that I had a fight with anyone other than my brother James. We got into a fight one time, and he bloodied my nose and hurt my feelings. I was ten years old, and he was eight, but he was bigger than I was.

Once we started school, our mother bought us three pairs of overalls and three shirts to last us the whole year. There was no middle school back then, so high school was from seventh to twelfth grade. Once we were in high school, my mother bought pants and shirts for us to wear. I remember when I was in twelfth grade, she made me a shirt out of flour sacks. The collar was one color, and the rest of the shirt was another color. I was ashamed to wear it to school, but I never told her that. She did the best that she could do. We were so poor that we could hardly pay attention!

The coal company would print out $7.00 sheets of money that could only be spent at the company store. The money was split into $0.05, $0.10, $0.25, $0.50, and $1.00. We could tear off whatever we needed. I still have a sheet of that money. Times were hard after the Depression and World War II. One dollar would buy a lot of food.

Tennessee Ernie Ford sang a song about coal miners which said, "You load sixteen tons. What do you get? Another day older and deeper in debt. Saint Peter, don't you call me 'cause I can't go. I owe my soul to the company store." That was about right.

Walker Fendley was the paymaster in Piper. The company would let him advance money to coal miner families, and by the time payday came around, they would have already spent their whole paycheck or most of it. When we were young, most of the men kept tobacco in little pouches. The pouch had drawstrings to close the bag after they got out whatever they needed.

Some of the men would smoke tobacco out of a Prince Albert can. After they emptied the bags or cans, we would use them to keep our change in, if we had any. My daddy had a little cigarette roller he used to roll cigarettes. We would lay the tobacco paper down in his roller and put tobacco on the paper, and the little roller would do the rest and make a perfectly rolled cigarette. If my daddy did get a little extra money, he would smoke a lot and drink bootleg whiskey. Sometimes he would have one lit and forget about it, then light another one. He would let the cigarettes burn so close to his fingers. The cigarettes made his fingers look stained yellow. A pack of camel cigarettes was $0.21 back then, and my daddy smoked three packs a day. There were times when I knew Daddy wouldn't be home all day, so I would sneak a pack and take them to my grammar school and sell them for a penny each.

Piper had all dirt roads. We had names for different sections of the community. We had Lizard Road, Silk Stocking Road, Old L, New L, Sweet Ridge, Porter Town, Black quarters behind White quarters, and Big Road, which someone changed the name to Crows Feet Road over the years. Big Road was wider than the average dirt road and was half a mile long.

I was six years old when my parents decided to move from Lizard Road to a two-bedroom house on Main Street. Every time a car would come down the road, the dust would come into the house because we kept the doors and windows open. We had to varnish dust off the furniture every day. My aunt Lid and uncle Crawford Lovejoy—we called them Big Mamma and Big Daddy—lived up on the hill across from our house.

I would go up to Aunt Lid's house and say, "Mamma, have you got a tater?" I always called her Mamma, and I was asking for a baked sweet potato. My mother got on to me one day and told me not to ask for a tater. So from then on, Aunt Lid would hide me behind that old coal stove and give me a cold sweet potato. She would keep some baked every day. I thought I was really hiding from my mother, and I bet they got a kick out of that.

Lid "Big Momma" and Crawford "Big Daddy" Lovejoy

There was another family in Piper that we used to visit when I was small named Smith. The man's name was Vernon, but I never knew his wife's name. I just called her Smith. They had three small children about our age: Junior, Lucille, and I forget the third one's name. I would do the same thing that I did at Aunt Lid's house. I would go up to her and say, "Smith, can I have a tater?" And she would always give me one. Everyone had gardens back then and always had sweet potatoes planted, and they usually had some baked. When work slacked off in the coal mines in Piper, they moved up close to Bessemer to another coal mining community called Blue Creek. When I got a little older, my mother would let me go visit them in the summertime for a week or two. One summer, I went to their house for two weeks. While I was there, a man by the name of Joe Rumore was advertising on the radio that anyone who brought a cap off a Hadacol bottle could get into the fair for free. Junior was the oldest, and he had a car. We would go all around looking in trash piles to see if we could find a Hadacol bottle to get the cap. Joe Rumore was getting paid to advertise for Hadacol, saying it would give you more energy. A lot of people bought the product, thinking that it would.

After I was grown and married, Joe Rumore would call out numbers on a one-dollar bill to give away different prizes. Everyone would save their dollar bills to try to win. I forgot which radio station he was on, but I heard he owned all or part of it. The radio station was on the road between Bessemer and Birmingham. I passed right in front of his radio station one day while I was going to work in Birmingham. The weatherman came on and said there was no rain in the forecast for today. All he had to do was look out of the window to see that there was an electrical storm and rain was pouring down.

Aunt Lid would go to South Carolina to visit her sister Laurel every year. I wanted to go with her so bad because I had never been farther away from home than Decatur, Alabama, which was only about a hundred miles away. I think she took Frank, James, and Bennie Ray at one time or another. I never knew why she took my brothers but never took me.

I didn't know where babies came from at the time my mother went into labor with her fifth son, William. She started screaming, and it scared me to death. I ran up the hill and told Aunt Lid that my mother was dying! Aunt Lid didn't get too excited because she knew my mother was having a baby. I couldn't figure out why she was acting like nothing was happening. William Crawford Whatley—we always called him Billy—was named after both my mother's father and my uncle Crawford Lovejoy. Billy was born dead, but Dr. Stinson kept switching him back and forth between cold water and hot water until he started breathing. It left him spastic, and he could never walk. Dr. Stinson predicted that he would only live maybe eight years. My mother took really good care of him, so he lived forty-four years before he passed away.

When Billy was six years old, my mother put him in a cripple children's school in Birmingham. He went to school until he was sixteen years old. That was the longest that the state would pay for him to go to school. They furnished his crutches, leg braces, and wheelchair. His legs eventually got so crooked that he couldn't wear braces. He couldn't use crutches. For the rest of his life, he either had to crawl around or use a wheelchair. He was very smart, but he couldn't speak too plainly. We would go visit him a lot of times on the weekends. He was homesick and always glad to see us.

As he got older, he lost all his teeth. He couldn't wear false teeth. If I was away from him for three or four months, it would be hard for me to understand him when he talked. If I said, "What?" he would just say, "Forget it." And then I would laugh. He would talk to women every day, and they could understand him. He would listen to the scanner every day and kept up with what was going on. If someone would tell Billy their name and phone number one day and he didn't see them until a year later, he would still remember it. He had a great memory. He might talk to ten women a day, but he would remember their phone numbers, and they would call him if they wanted to hear any gossip. Any time someone important came to town like the governor, they would always come by to see Billy.

When Billy was about three years old, my daddy was drunk one night and bought a solid white horse from a Black man for five dollars. The next day, my daddy had a picture made of Billy on that boney white horse. Billy had his braces on. My daddy took the horse back to the Black man and got his money back. The horse looks well fed in the picture, but it was nearly starved. I still have that picture.

Billy and Ben Whatley

Piper didn't have a fire department when we were young, but when Billy was forty-three, the West Blocton Fire Department made him honorary fire chief on August 15, 1985. It was very thoughtful of them. Billy passed away four and a half months later on January 1, 1986. Billy always sent birthday cards with one-dollar bills in it to people he knew. He sent Midge Rach, who was married to Gordon Rach, a birthday card on October 18, 1968. Midge still has the card and the dollar that Billy sent. Midge would write letters for Billy when she wanted to write something.

Billy was born the same year that World War II broke out. Times got really hard for people during the war. Everything was rationed because our government was putting everything into our armed services. There were a lot of things that the store manager couldn't sell. He could still sell bananas, black pepper, sugar, certain candy bars, lard, and a few other things. He would sell the things that were limited to his favorite customers until he ran out. He didn't know when he would get more in. I remember we couldn't get certain clothing with real buttons. The buttons were made out of hard cardboard. We couldn't get little toy cars with rubber tires. The tires were made out of wood because all the rubber went into the war.

My daddy could hardly buy gasoline or tires for his old Model B truck. When the gas tank would start leaking, he would put octagon soap wherever the leak was, and it would stop.

He would walk to the post office or to the store instead of riding. We loved riding on the running boards or straddling the headlights on the fender when we went down the road in that old truck. I was on the running board one day, about to jump off and go home, when my mother yelled at me from the front porch to look both ways. I looked and didn't see any cars, but when I leaned to jump off, Hershel McBurnette shot by in his car and barely hit my arm. He stopped about a hundred feet up the road. I guess it scared him and my mother. My mother tore my butt up because I nearly got killed.

I remember Aunt Lid and Uncle Crawford being worried that their son, Clarence, who was stationed at Pearl Harbor, was going to get killed when the Japanese attacked. He wasn't hurt or killed and got out of the army when he got back to the continental states.

After the war started, the Piper community started having bombing drills. We could hear the sirens all over Piper when they went off. The sirens would warn everyone to turn off their lights in case the enemy came over to bomb our community. Piper would be totally dark. Then people started building storm pits, and they would stock food in them in case we got bombed. Glover Lovejoy built one at his house in Wilton, Alabama, and stocked it mostly with canned goods. When the war was over, everything went back to normal. No more bombing drills, and everyone took the food back into the house.

Before the war was over, different movie people would come to Piper and show movies on the side of Doris and Bill Fritz's house. The Fritzes had six or seven children, but I can only remember Alton and Patsy. A man would come to our grammar school once a week and show different movies in one of the classrooms. Anyone could come, but it cost ten cents. They would always play a comedy, like *Bugs Bunny* or *Popeye*, before the main movie. I would be sitting there, holding my little girlfriend's hand. All of a sudden, the movie tape would break, and the teacher would turn the lights on real fast so he could repair it, and I would put my hands in my lap real fast until the lights went back out. Most of the movies we watched had Roy Rogers, Gene Altry, Tom Mix, and Lash Larue. We watched the *Lone Ranger*, *Red Ryder and Little Beaver*, and *Tarzan*. Every once in a while, we would see a scary picture or a war movie.

While Bill Fritz was overseas in the war, a man named Foots Lucas worked at the Piper store. He would come by Doris's house every afternoon and throw candy up to the porch to the children. Bill lost his legs in the war and was sent home. One day, I was at Bill and Doris's house, and Doris had a pistol in her hand. She thought it was empty and pointed it at me. I told her not to point that pistol at me because it might be loaded. She said, "Oh! It's empty," pointed it at the wall, and pulled the trigger. It was loaded. She was so scared that she ran to the door to see if her husband had already left to go to the store. He had just left. I don't know if she ever told him about it or not.

When I was in the first grade, I had a really pretty teacher named Ms. Langston. I would walk around holding her hand, pretending she was my sweetheart. I remember that I had two little magnetic dogs that I played with in class all the time. When I was grown and married, I would go by to see Ms. Langston at her house right below Harold and Betty Campbell's house in Six Mile, Alabama. Ms. Langston lived to be in her nineties. In grammar school, she would let us take a nap every day. There was a little girl named Helen Lumpkin in my class that liked me, and she would help me get my homework. She lived just two houses above ours, across the road from Bob and Glenda Allen, so I would walk to her house. We always swapped comic books with Bob and Glenda. That was seventy-two years ago. They would be worth thousands now. Bob and Glenda's grandmother raised them; I never knew why. She did a very good job. They were both very smart and disciplined.

We had a principal named Ms. Farrington. She had one good eye and one glass eye. She was a tall and manly-looking woman. She and Ms. Langston, who was very short, lived with each other until Ms. Farrington passed away. I think my daddy dated Ms. Farrington years before when he was single.

We got our first wagon when I was about seven or eight years old. It was made out of wood. Even the wheels were wood. We paid five cents for the wagon to a friend that made it himself. Then we decided to make our own wagons. There were a lot of empty company houses. Some were about to fall down. We would tear some of the boards off to make our wagons. I don't know where we got them, but we found some real wheels to put on our wagons. The wooden wheels were too bumpy. We made some of our wagons with steering wheels made out of broom or mop handles, and we made homemade brakes using two pieces of wood with two hay bailing wires hooked into the wood. We used our feet to push the wood in front to tighten the wood in the back against the wheels. We also made wagons with a box on it to hold the scrap iron that we picked up.

Mr. Calvin Jones from Birmingham owned all of Piper and Coleanor for most of the years that I was growing up. Mules pulled the coal out of the rooms to the main slope and then hook to the motor and cables to pull the railcars out of the mines. The cars would hold about a ton each. If a mule broke his leg, they would kill it, put railroad crossties on him, and burn him to ashes. There wasn't much safety back then. There was a siren that went off when a miner would get hurt or killed. I remember the siren going off a few times. The women would get frightened, thinking it may be their husband or son that got hurt or killed. I remember most of the coal miners drinking bootleg whiskey when we were growing up. It seemed like my daddy would take a little drink every day before he went to work. If the miners had a pint bottle, one would take a drink and pass it around to let everyone take a sip. Maybe they did it to settle their nerves, or maybe it was just to be sociable, but I saw what it did to some families. I said I would never fool with it, and I never have. I hated it so much that I thought about going to Birmingham to throw rocks through the windows of the liquor stores. I didn't realize at the time that they probably had insurance to cover the windows and I would have been in some serious trouble.

As a young person without much money, I sometimes thought about robbing a bank. But then again I would have been in so much trouble, and I had no idea where to begin with a bank robbery. That's how ignorant I was as a child. That was bad thinking, but times were really hard for us. I pulled a wagon around picking up scrap iron until I was in the eleventh grade. We could sell anything to men coming around to buy scrap iron during and after the war. Everything was made out of glass, tin, and iron back then. There was very little plastic. We would sell rags, tin, barrels of clear broken glass, old tires, scrap iron, copper, brass, aluminum, and Coke bottles.

Coke bottles and old tires would sell for a nickel, and scrap iron sold for thirty-five cents per hundred pounds. I remember Carly Harrison would pass us with our wagons to see if we had any scrap iron from the coal mines. The scrap iron man would come around often, if we had a big pile. He would guess how much we had. If we had five hundred pounds, he would guess three hundred. We finally got some scales to weigh our scrap iron. Then we would tell him the right amount after we weighed it ourselves.

He didn't like us weighing the scrap iron ourselves because he couldn't cheat us. We didn't see him as often after that. We could get a lot of scrap iron and copper because the mining company would throw a lot away. We would walk for miles to get the clippings out from under the telephone poles, where the linesmen would work the power lines and leave clippings all over the ground. We could get about fifteen to twenty-five cents a pound for copper and brass. We would find telephone poles that had guide wire running from the poles to the ground, after the mines shut down and the wires had been taken down. We would dig into the ground where the guide wire was connected. There would be a lot of heavy iron, such as mining cartwheels, holding the guide wire down, so we would dig it up and sell it to the scrapman. Only the power pole would be left standing there. We even dug up the old burn pits from where the broken-legged mules were burned to get the scrap iron off the crossties.

The electric company had taken most of the lines down after the mines had closed. People began moving to other communities. Someone started taking the main power lines down in Piper and Coleanor and sold whatever Alabama Power hadn't taken down yet. We had about a hundred pounds that we had collected at that time and were going to sell. My daddy scared us by saying the FBI was coming to Piper to find out who took the power lines down and that he would get rid of all the copper that we had collected. He told us that he threw it into the Big Cahaba River. We had worked hard and walked many miles to save that much. We found out many years later that he had swapped it for bootleg whiskey. I couldn't have done my children that way. He never told us who he swapped it with, but it was probably Dan Babb. Dan Babb was a bootlegger that lived in the woods close to the Big Cahaba River. He only had one leg and wouldn't open the door unless we identified ourselves as someone he knew.

When I was seven or eight years old, my daddy gave all of us chores to do. Once he told us what the chores were, we did not get a reminder. We would just get our butt whipped. My chores were to bring in the slop jar at night and take it out early in the morning. The slop jar was what we did our number ones and twos in so that we didn't have to go outside to the toilet after dark. We used the toilet outside in the daytime. Sometimes, we would have to move the spiders and cobwebs before we could sit down over the toilet hole. We used newspapers or Sears, Roebuck catalogs for toilet paper. We had to put lime in the slop jar to kill all the maggots. We would cut our wood and cross stack it so there was plenty of air between the stack to dry out. We would keep a pile of firewood behind the stove to stay dry. We would take coal inside with scuttle buckets and then use them to take the ashes out of the stove and fireplaces.

Slop jar

Scuttle bucket

Brother Coburn had a son the same age that I was named Bob. I think we were in the first or second grade and he was absent from school one day. When our teacher asked him why he was absent, he said he had eaten an apple, and the seed had grown a tree in his stomach. Now that is a preacher's son for you. We always heard preacher's children were the meanest, but I don't think they were any different than other children. Bob Coburn and Billy Rice were playing in the yard across from us; and Bob had a pick, digging a hole, I guess. He raised the pick up, not knowing that Billy Rice was right behind him and put Billy's eye out. Some of the kids and some grown-ups took Billy up to a neighbor's house that had a light hanging down from the ceiling. It was an old company house with twelve-foot ceilings, and the light cords would just hang down. We put Billy up next to the light and covered his good eye to see if he could see out of his damaged eye. He never could, so he had one good eye and one glass eye for the rest of his life. Billy didn't let that bother him at all. He was very smart in high school and became a successful businessman. He owned businesses in two states. Bob Coburn felt bad about what had happened for years, but it was just a freak accident, and Billy felt bad that Bob felt bad.

Around this same time, my mother started easing up on restricting us so much, and she would let us go to a friend's house for an hour to start with. We had to be back home in one hour, or we knew our butts would be torn up and she would put a stop to us going anywhere. We would get wood off the old company houses and build us a seesaw or a flying jenny. We could go up and down on the seesaw or go around and around on the flying jenny. We would bury a big post in the ground and use a big nail, about one foot long, to connect the wood to the post. We made our own wagons, rubber guns, and bows and arrows out of hickory wood and fishing string. We had certain kinds of wood for our arrows, and we sawed our rubber gun pistols and rifles out of three-quarter wood and tied knots on the rubber so they would shoot farther.

We would tie a clothespin to the back of the gun, put one rubber in the mouth of the clothespin, and then stretch two or three more behind the clothespin so we wouldn't run out of ammunition.

We would use our thumbs to push the ones off the back of the clothespin. When we got in a battle, whoever got shot had to drop out until the last man was left.

All tire tubes were made out of real rubber, which we used in our slingshots and rubber guns. Years later, they came out with the synthetic rubber tubes, which were no good for rubber guns and slingshots. We didn't like that very much. I had a cousin that got his eye shot out with a rubber gun. We tried not to shoot anyone in the face with the rubber guns, but sometimes it would happen by mistake.

We would always find something to do. We would cut little whatnots out of three-quarter wood that we would usually get off apple boxes. We would sell them in the neighborhood for thirty-five cents after we got them painted. People would hang them on their walls. People would buy them from us, just to help us make money. We used a coping saw to cut them out because we could curve the saw blade any way we wanted to easily. One day, we stopped at a store, and this man had a stack of apple boxes that he was going to burn. We were in my daddy's timber truck, and I wanted those apple boxes so bad, but I was too bashful to ask for them. I don't know why my daddy didn't ask for them because he knew that I wanted them and we could have put them on the truck.

When we were young, we would use a certain kind of hollow stick with a knot about every six inches to make our kites. We also used these hollow sticks to make our corn silk pipes, and we would insert it into a big acorn to smoke our corn silk. I haven't seen any of these big acorns in years. I think maybe a disease or chemicals may have killed all those kinds of trees. The stores sold kites and rolls of kite string for ten cents each. We made our own out of the hollow sticks and newspapers. We would mix flour and water to make paste and tear up an old sheet or shirt to make the kite tail. They flew as good as the store-bought kites. We would get the kites up and add three or four balls of string to it until the kite looked like it was a mile high. Sometimes, we would just tie the end of a string to a tree stub or a tree and let it fly all night. It would still be flying the next morning. Sometimes our kites would get way up high, and the string would break. We would go way back in the woods looking for them. Sometimes we would find them, and sometimes we wouldn't. Sometimes they would be lodged in a tree where we couldn't get them. Occasionally, a bird would bite on the string while the kite was flying.

We also had a yo-yo get-together where we would do different tricks. We would also throw washers and horseshoes for a pastime. We would get big washers off the railroad trusses that were left on the ground, dig holes about forty feet apart, and toss the washers in the hole, just like throwing horseshoes. If we wrung the hole, it was 5 points. A leaner on the hole was three points, or whoever got the closest to the hole got one point. Sometimes, if we couldn't find the store-bought horseshoes, we would just use the actual horseshoes that had been taken off horse hooves after they were worn out. They have commercialized that game into a game called cornhole where you take two built-up platforms with holes four inches round and throw beanbags or shelled corn at the holes. The boards are placed forty feet, the same as washers and horseshoes. Cornhole has the same scoring system as horseshoes, except in horseshoes you had to be within a horseshoe's length to the post for a point to count. Almost every year, one of us boys would get a football and a ball pump for Christmas. We would play with the football until the string holding it together and keeping the tube inside would wear out or break. Once the string broke, the tube would start coming out. Then we would get a sock, fill it with rags, and play football with that.

One day, we were playing out in the middle of the dirt road with a sock full of rags, and a Catholic priest came down the road and stopped his car. I guess he felt sorry for us. He told us he was going to send us a football and got our hopes up. We were sure he was telling the truth since he was a priest, but we never saw or heard from that priest again. Now, why did he have to stop in the middle of the road to tell us a lie? He could have kept on going down the road instead of stopping and deliberately telling us a lie. We will never know.

We would play baseball until we hit the ball so many times that we would finally knock the cover off. Sometimes we would put black tape on it or unravel the string just to get the hard center out of the middle of the baseball. It was a hard rubber ball the size of a Ping-Pong ball. If we didn't have another baseball, we would use a limb from a tree and a tin can for the ball.

When we were young, we could hardly wait until school let out for the summer. We went barefoot every day until school started again. We never went anywhere outside of the community, and our feet would get as tough as leather. After we got our feet toughened up, we would run and skip. We would run some and then skip some. We mostly just played ball in the dirt roads or went picking blackberries. We would get stone bruises on our feet every year from always being barefoot.

There wasn't much traffic back then since many people didn't have cars. Most of the traffic was from the coal trucks running coal up and down the road. Occasionally, trucks from out of town would come to Piper, such as the rolling store. The rolling store would have about the same amount of vegetables or food as a store, but everything seemed fresher. The rolling store would go down every road in Piper. One day, a milk truck came to Piper, and I saw his dolly fall off the truck. I ran over and got it. I sure would have liked to have had the good wheels off the dolly to make me some wagon wheels, but I stopped the milkman the next day and told him that I had found his dolly. He gave me a little bottle of chocolate milk. I asked him if he had one for my mother, and he gave me another bottle, which I gave to her. I liked chocolate milk and cocoa, so I learned how to make my own. I didn't like sweet milk, but I made my chocolate milk out of cocoa sugar and sweet milk. I made my hot chocolate out of cocoa pet milk and sugar.

Rolling store

I always tried to look out for my mother because she was such a good woman and worked hard tending to all of us men. I sold grit paper and seeds when I was little, and I would always get her a pot or pan instead of getting myself something. They didn't give us money for selling grit paper, but if we sold a certain amount, they would give us a prize.

When the war was over, we were able to begin buying little cars for thirty-five cents that were about two or three inches long with rubber tires. I took care of those cars as if it were a Cadillac because I knew I wouldn't get another one to play with until next year. Now children get little cars by the hundreds and don't take care of anything because we try to give them what we wanted when we were little and didn't have the money to buy. Now children have so many that they will be out in the yard, scattered everywhere. I got my first little car when I went to Birmingham to visit Aunt Myrtle and Uncle Morgan once school was out. We kids would catch a city bus to downtown and go to the different stores, then catch the bus back home. I guess the busses were running a certain route every hour. Betty and Bob Lovejoy knew how to show us around town. There were also streetcars in Birmingham like the ones still in New Orleans that ran on electrical wires, but they eventually quit using them.

Most of all the old company houses that we lived in were up off the ground on posts. We would play with our little cars under the house where it was very dirty and dusty. We would get way up under the house with our little cars as far back under the house as we could. Our heads would be between the ground and the lowest rafter, and we could hardly breathe. We would have to turn our heads sideways to get back out to keep from suffocating. It was scary, but we didn't realize how dangerous it was. Snakes could have been down there too. We sure would get dirty, but my mother never complained even though she had to use a rub board and a big black pot to wash our clothes.

Washboard and tub

She would hang them on clotheslines to dry. She had two kinds of clothespins, a straight pin and one that had a spring that would clamp tight. Later on, my mother got an electric washing machine with rollers, which was called a wringer. When she fed the clothes into the wringer, it squeezed the water out of the clothes. She had to be careful not to get her hands caught in the wringer. My mother would starch our clothes when we got them off the outside clothesline.

Old washing machine

We boys would sprinkle our clothes with water and iron them ourselves. Every once in a while, we would scorch our clothes with the iron on the ironing board if we weren't paying attention. If it was raining outside, we would hang our clothes inside the house to dry and then iron them. We usually had a place behind the woodstove to hang a few clothes to dry quickly, in case of an emergency. Sometimes we would see a rainbow in the sky while it was raining and the sun was shining. The older people would tell us that if we found the end of the rainbow, there would be a pot of gold there.

One day, I was outside in an old wooden garage playing with my little car. I pushed it up to a ground rattlesnake in the corner of the garage. They are very poisonous, and he was coiled up and ready to strike before I saw it. I was very lucky that I saw the snake before it did strike at me. I was about six or seven, but I got me a rock and killed it.

We were young boys when we learned how to play Go Fish with a deck of cards. If it was cold or a rainy weather, we would sit there all day playing Go Fish. We didn't have many other things to do. We would put puzzles together or play checkers or dominoes. We would play Chinese checkers, fiddlesticks, or Monopoly, which was put on the market in 1935 when I was born. I sure did want a little service station with cars for Christmas, but I never got one.

Most of the time, I would get a football, a pump, and a bottle of cheap red or yellow hair oil. One year, I got two cap pistols with scabbard and a belt with rolls of caps. I had a scabbard on both sides with cap pistols. We liked putting the caps on something solid and hitting them with a hammer to make them pop. I got some toy soldiers from somewhere, and I really enjoyed playing with them. I also had a navy cap that I wore in the summertime. I thought I looked good with that navy cap on my head.

We had no running hot water for baths. We always had to warm our water on the woodstove, get it boiling, then pour it into a number two or three washtub. We would have to add some to the cold water until it felt right. We took our baths in the kitchen in the wintertime because it was warm from the heat of the stove. My daddy always used a lather brush and soap to make shaving cream to shave in the kitchen because we had no bathroom and the kitchen was warm.

I was probably six or seven years old when I decided that I would see what a naked woman looked like since I had no sisters. Back then, you weren't warned not to do something that was wrong. We knew what was right and what was wrong. We always had a tablecloth on the kitchen table that would hang down really far. I got under the table, thinking my mother couldn't see me. She saw me under the table trying to see her out of curiosity. She yanked me up, told me to get in the next room, and tore my butt up. Nowadays parents are more lenient.

All they would probably do now is say to get out from under the table and go to the next room. They would not whip the child. When we did something wrong and we knew it was wrong, we knew it was a butt whipping. No excuse!

I remember one day while my mother was washing clothes, I got under the house and built a fire. The fire was touching the bottom part of our house, and my mother just happened to see it when she was walking back up the stairs. Naturally, I got my butt torn up because I could have caught our house on fire. When I was a young man, I was always playing with matches.

My youngest brother Billy and my granddaddy were cocking a BB gun one day, thinking it was empty and pointing it at each other's heads. Finally, a BB came out and hit my granddaddy right above his eye, but the BB just barely went under the skin.

My granddaddy would take us hiking about fifteen miles through the woods. He would always find a hickory tree to make us a whistle. He was good at whittling things. He was constantly sharpening his knife on a whetrock. I would go with him to get small cypress trees out of the swampy woods. He would make stools, swings, and chairs and set tees out of the cypress trees. And he would use the bark from the trees to make the seat on the chairs. He would make cedar caskets and whittle a little man to lay in it. When he pulled the lid of the casket back, the little man's privates would pop up. He made a little rocking man which stores have a patent on now. He made them out of wood, but the stores make them out of stainless steel. When I was in the air force in 1955 and stationed overseas, we would play battleship on a piece of paper. Now the stores have made a game out of that and have a patent on it. We made our own slingshots, or flips as we called them, and now the stores make different slingshots. In my opinion, the store-bought slingshots are not as good as the ones we made out of wood. Now they have a patent on the slingshots too. We would fill our pockets full of rocks to shoot in our slingshots until our pockets had holes in them. We would also have holes in the knees of our pants from getting on the ground to shoot marbles.

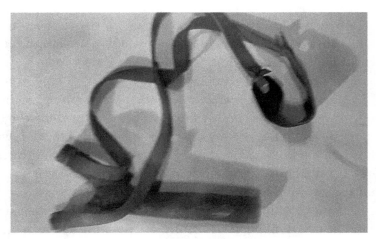

"Flip" slingshot

We had a really nice school in Piper that went to the twelfth grade at one time, but by the time I started school, it just went to sixth. My granddaddy was the janitor at our school. We had good radiator heaters at the school, and my granddaddy would keep putting coal in the furnace down in the basement. Sometimes I would help him shovel the coal into the furnace. He cleaned the floors every afternoon after we got out of school. He would put sawdust with some kind of oil in it, and that would really make the hardwood floors shine and smell good. I would stay after school sometimes to help him finish. He gave Harold Campbell, who married my first cousin Betty, his first job helping in the afternoons.

In third grade, I had a good teacher named Mrs. Herron. She wouldn't let anyone play for keeps in marbles. If she caught someone playing for keeps, she would take their marbles away and put them into her fishbowl. She would only let me and Bobby (Nootchie) play for keeps. She would take marbles out of her fishbowl to give to Nootchie, then stand over us, and watch us play. I would win all the marbles. We would play for keeps at home, and sometimes we would play lag marbles.

We would line up about ten marbles in a row, get back thirty feet, and throw our marble or steel ball at the line of marbles. If we knocked one or more marbles off the line, we kept shooting until we missed. Then the next man up would do the same and so on until all the marbles were gone. We would also draw a line in the dirt and throw coins at it. Whoever got closest to the line won the coins from everyone else, usually pennies and nickels. We didn't seem to ever have much money. While I was in third grade, I went to a rodeo in Birmingham and had a really good time. I remember a cowboy lassoing a calf around its leg. It broke the calf's leg about at the knee, and its knee was just dangling loose. I went back to school the next day, and Mrs. Herron let me tell the class about the rodeo.

I did not enjoy going to the fair in Birmingham too well after I got a little older. First of all, I won a little horse clock, and this old lady said that I didn't win it. Then I caught them cheating on another game. They would give you three balls to knock three dolls completely down to win a prize. There was a crack in the curtain separating the two games. After someone knocked two dolls down, they would slide a board out so that the last doll wouldn't fall down completely. When I saw them cheating, someone in the back said, "We have a Peeping Tom." I said, "I see what you are doing." And I drew the ball back as if I was going to throw it hard. The man grabbed my arm and said, "No, you don't." So I walked out with the ball in my hand. They closed the curtain so no one else could see what they were doing. It's a shame that the fair has to cheat children out of their money. Our authorities should not let that kind of thing happen. That is, if they even know about it. I did enjoy a side show where this Black man, who was missing some of his teeth, was in a place with a bunch of slimy bullfrogs. He would put the bullfrogs in his ears and one in his mouth and had slime hanging out of his mouth. A Black lady and her son walked in to watch him, and the lady frowned. When she frowned, the man picked his nose and ate a booger. Then she and her son both left with a frown on the lady's face. Later on, I saw the man from the show out in the crowd wearing a suit. I guess he had finished his shift.

When we were young, we would go out and pull pranks on people on Halloween. I just went along and watched. I remember my brother Franklin and some of the other boys would turn outside toilets over and shoot out porch lights with BB guns. Jody Clinner told me that they picked Mr. Walker Fendley's new car up and set it in between two trees. He said he didn't know how Mr. Fendley got his car out. I remember helping Glover Lovejoy pick his toilet up to set it upright. Another mischievous thing that I remember myself and two other boys doing happened as we were coming back from a movie at the Piper grammar school. We got up on a bank with a handful of gravel and threw it at some men in a convertible. Three men got out of the car and came looking for us, but it was after dark. We were scared to death and ran through the woods. The men were from out of town, and we didn't know who they were, but they didn't catch us. If our parents would have known about what we did, they would have torn our butts up, and we would have deserved it. That was dangerous. When I was fourteen years old, my mother said, "You boys will see the day that I didn't whip you enough." So I decided that day to keep up with how many whippings we got that summer. I swear I am not lying, but I averaged four whippings a day for a solid three months that summer.

I thought my name was Robert until I was sixteen years old. When I went to get my driver's license, my mother informed me that she had intended to change my name from Bobby to Robert, but she never did it for some reason. My two brothers, James and Franklin, would call me Robert because they knew I didn't like it. I would say, "Momma, they called me Robert again!" And she would whip who- ever called me that. Now, why didn't my mother tell me my name wasn't Robert? It would have saved my brothers from getting a lot of whippings. If we just touched each other on the arm or leg, we would say, "Momma, he touched me!" and she would whip whichever one of us who was guilty. I would tell my mother about all the whippings after I was grown, and she would just start laughing about it. We may not have gotten a whipping but two times one day and six the next day, but it averaged out to about four times daily. My mother said we would get whippings as long as we were under her roof.

My mother would let us hike to West Blocton, which was about seven miles from where we lived, to see a movie. Mr. Philpot owned the movie theater in West Blocton, and his wife collected the admis- sion fee. The movies cost ten cents up to age eleven and twenty-five cents for anyone twelve or older. I was small for my age, but old stupid me was so proud to be twelve years old. I told her, "I'm twelve now!" And she said, "That will be twenty-five cents please." If we got there and didn't have any money, Mr. Philpot had a wooden door in the back of the theater. So we had a little place where we would sit on the ground, whittle with our knives, and watch the movie through the back door. We always had pocket knives in our pockets when we were young, and we were always whittling or cutting something. Sometimes we would go a little early and let Mr. Ebb Carr pick us up with his little finger. He liked showing us kids how strong he was when we were about twelve to fourteen years old.

Bully Harris's barbershop was next door to the movie theater. The pool hall was up behind Bully Harris's barbershop. One Saturday night, another boy and I hitched a ride to West Blocton to see a movie, but we didn't catch a ride back home until 2:00 a.m. There weren't many cars on the road back then, and we never knew who we were getting in the car with until we were actually in the car. We had a little mining car beside the road at Number 9 Coal Mines, and we would sleep in it until we hear a car coming. In the wintertime, we would take the oil rags out of the railroad car axles and make a fire to warm by until a car would come. We didn't realize that those oil rags were there to keep the axles on the railcar oiled. My mother met me at the door when I got home and said, "Son, if you are ever out this late again, you will get torn up!"

Well, guess what! The very next Saturday, it happened again. I and whoever I was with couldn't get a ride until about 2:00 a.m. This time, my mother met me at the door, whipping me with a piece of firewood. She said, "Son, this is hurting me more than it is hurting you!" I said, "Oh no, it isn't!" My mother wouldn't just whip us and say nothing. All the time she was whipping us, she would be going around and around with her mouth going the whole time. The sermon was worse than the whipping. I didn't want the sermon. My daddy didn't whip us, except maybe once a year, but when he did, we knew it would be bad. He had a mining belt about four inches wide. He would put our heads between his legs and pull our britches tight, and he didn't know when to stop whipping us. My mother would usually step in to stop him from beating us. He had usually been drinking when he got us. I saw my mother pick up a kitchen knife one time and threaten him if he didn't stop. My mother would usually whip Franklin, James, and me altogether if anything happened. And she thought we weren't telling her the truth. She said she would whip all three of us to make sure she got the right one. I remember one time when we were young, my mother whipped Franklin, but not James or me. Franklin got under the bed and started crying. I felt sorry for him, so I got under the bed and started crying with him.

Bennie Ray was a little curly redhead that could get away with anything. I don't ever remember him getting a whipping. He was four years younger than me. One of our neighbors would get him under our house and teach him curse words. My mother would just laugh at Bennie Ray. If it would have been Franklin, James, or me, we would have gotten our butts torn up. I remember one time during World War II, my mother came home and told my daddy how a crazy bunch of soldiers was over Bennie Ray on the bus from Birmingham to Piper. I think my daddy thought the soldiers were looking at my mother and not at Bennie Ray. My mother was a tall, blond-haired woman who still had a pretty good shape after having five children and was still in her late twenties at that time. I remember Walker Fendley and his wife talking to my mother one day, and Mr. Fendley told my mother that she was the prettiest woman in Piper. It didn't seem to bother Mr. Fendley's wife. He wasn't flirting. He was a good man and had a very pretty wife himself.

We just had a two-bedroom house with no air conditioner, no television, and no telephone. We did have a big radio, about four foot high. I remember women coming to our house and dancing with one another when the men weren't around. I remember Franklin used to lie on the floor and listen to the creaking door on the radio. Five of us boys slept on the sagging beds in one bedroom, and my mother and daddy slept in the other bedroom. We kept all the doors and windows open in the summertime because it would get so hot. We had screen wire over the windows and doors so the bugs couldn't get in. We never locked our doors or took the keys out of our automobiles. We would even sleep on the front porch sometimes because it was cooler than being in the hot and muggy house in bed. Everyone in the coal mining community trusted one another, and most everyone was very poor. We didn't have all the mess and meanness that goes on these days. The people in the coal mining communities looked out for one another and would help one another if they could any time there was a need.

We always had so many different animals around our house and an abundance of houseflies. There were holes in some of our screens on the house, and the flies would get in. We would take turns swinging a towel around the rooms to shoo the flies back out of the front door. Shooing flies could take hours, and we had to do it every day. Some of the holes were made by us kids from chasing one another and running into the screens. We used a lot of flyflaps and hand-pumped insect spray to kill the flies.

We had big old iron railings at the heads of our beds. Sometimes at night, we would stand up on the railings and do belly flops onto our beds. Our beds were about worn out and swayed in the middle, but we slept good. Our mother would holler and tell us to go to sleep. If we kept on belly flopping, we would see her head peep around the corner. We knew it was butt whipping time whenever we didn't mind our mother, and she had to get up out of bed. Then we would go to sleep after we got our butts torn up, but having all that fun was worth the butt whipping. We weren't mean kids. We just liked to have fun.

My mother made all our quilts on our beds. In the wintertime, we would put three or four quilts on us to stay warm. Women would use a thimble on the end of their finger to push the needle through the quilt. My daddy would bank the fire in the fireplace to try to keep the house warm, but the fire would usually go out some time through the night. The next morning, he would get up and rebuild the fire. After he got the fire going well, he would come over to our beds, yank the covers off us, and holler, "Get up!" We had to get up or freeze. We usually slept in our long johns. I remember one time, my daddy had a stick of dynamite, about as round as a baseball and two feet long, under my bed. If anything would have made that explode, we would have all been dead and the house would have been turned into splinters. He had gotten the dynamite from someone when they were stripping coal in Piper. I don't know why he had it, but one day it disappeared, and I was relieved. He may have sold it to someone. He didn't need it. I had a black cat when I moved back home after I got out of the air force before I was married, and I would come home after a date and let the cat sleep on my bed. My mother would holler, "Get that cat out of the bed!" But I wouldn't listen. One day, the cat disappeared just like the dynamite. I assume my daddy took it off somewhere.

Another thing about those old company houses was they had flat locks on the doors about four inches wide and six inches long. The key to the lock was about four inches long, and if it wasn't in the lock, we could look through the keyhole and see into the next room. My mother and daddy would go into their bedroom sometimes during the day, close the door, and have sex. We knew what they were doing, but we didn't dare to let them know that. I would peep through the keyhole to try and see them, but they always got under the covers before taking their clothes off so I couldn't see anything. No wonder I got so many whippings. I was very inquisitive.

Some of the women would help one another wallpaper the rooms in the company houses rather than painting them. They would find different colors of print for the paper. To me, that was prettier than painting because the wallpaper had different designs and colors. They would mix flour and water to make the paste and cover all the wallpaper to paste it to the walls. It would take two people to do it. Those old company houses had twelve-foot ceilings, and the wallpaper came in two—or three-foot-wide strips. The paper came in rolls, so the women would cut off the length that they needed.

My mother had three brothers and one sister. Two of her brothers had passed away before I was born, so I never met them. One of them was killed when a log fell off a truck and landed on him. The other was riding a bicycle and had a wreck where the handlebars went through his stomach. The third brother, Charlie Broadhead, had mental problems and rode a bicycle all his life until he passed away at the age of seventy-five. Charlie stayed with Mr. Jones on the outskirts of West Blocton in an area called Lowerytown. When we lived in Piper, he would occasionally ride over to see us and usually bring a whip that he made out of long snakeskins with him. He could really pop a whip. He would show us his play badge that someone had given him and tell us that he was working for J. Edgar Hoover and the FBI, and he always had a dip of snuff in his mouth.

My mother's sister and her daughter, Margaret Burns, also dipped snuff. My mother pretty well had to keep close contact with all them, and they all passed away before my mother did. My mother also took care of my brother Billy for forty-four years before he passed away.

Charlie, Lilian, and Margaret are all buried at Cahaba Valley Baptist Church by the Little Cahaba River. The church was built in 1817, and they still have church service there every week. I think it is the oldest church in Alabama. My daddy had two brothers and no sisters. Uncle Curry married a lady named Mary, and Uncle Eddie married Mary's daughter, Delores. Delores was thirteen years old, and Uncle Eddie was thirty-eight when they married. Uncle Eddie didn't know what the words "I'm sorry" meant. He lived with his father after his mother died, when he was young. From what my mother told me, Uncle Eddie's father was the meanest man on earth, and I think some of that meanness rubbed off on Uncle Eddie. After he came home from World War II, he was a bad alcoholic and was also a diabetic. He got a young lady in Centerville, Alabama, pregnant but didn't marry her. She had the baby and named him Jimmy Ray Whatley. In the early seventies, a bunch of us men would play tag football, and Jimmy Ray would play with us. That was the first time that we had met. I was told that Uncle Eddie had left Centerville because Jimmy Ray's uncles, his mother's brothers, had threatened to kill him.

When I was a small boy, I remember him coming to our house drunk and falling asleep with a lit cigarette in his hand. He burned holes in whichever couch or chair he was sitting in, but he never said he was sorry. Uncle Eddie worked at Hayes Aircraft in Birmingham and was still drinking every day when his wife reached the age of nineteen. They began to have marital problems, and she told him that she wanted a divorce. He told her that if she ever tried walking out that door with their two children, Eddie and Ronnie, he would kill her. She got the children and started out the door. Uncle Eddie got his gun and shot her through the heart, killing her in front of their two children. Then he shot himself under the chin. The bullet went out through the roof of their home. The Birmingham news showed where the round went through the roof. Then Uncle Eddie cut both of his wrists, but he still managed to live.

Uncle Eddie's wife, Delores, was a tall and beautiful little woman. Everyone knew the marriage wouldn't last because they knew my uncle would never change, but she was blinded by love. I didn't have any use for Uncle Eddie after he killed his children's mother. Like always, he was only thinking about himself. He wasn't thinking about the other people that he was hurting.

My daddy started collecting money from anyone who could donate to get the best lawyer in Birmingham. The lawyer told him that if he could come up with two thousand dollars, he would take the case. Two thousand dollars was a lot of money in the early fifties. The lawyer did what he said he would do and got my uncle off on a light sentence of twenty years for cold-blooded, premeditated murder. My uncle only spent six years in Kilby Prison before he was released for good behavior. The Bible says an eye for an eye. What has happened to our civilization? I went to visit Eddie one time while he was in prison in 1957. I was in my air force uniform, so the guard didn't frisk me, and I had forgotten that I had a knife in my pocket unlit I got back outside to go home.

Once Uncle Eddie got out of prison, he always counted on someone else to take care of him. My uncle Morgan Lovejoy let Eddie live with him in his home over the years. My brother Bennie Ray also let him stay with him for years. Eddie had stayed with Bennie Ray before as well when Eddie was younger and had no job. Then my brother was always saying that Eddie was stealing his money. He was just plain sorry his whole life, causing people trouble and never appreciating anything or anybody. He seemed to think people owed him something. He lived to be eighty-four years old and died in an assisted living facility in Centerville.

Uncle Curry and Aunt Mary had to raise Eddie and Delores's children. I was about their age, and one summer, I spent two weeks at their house. But I wished my mother had just kept me at home. I had poison oak all over my body, so Mary had to treat me. She put coffee grounds and pet milk all over me to try to cure the poison oak. When I went to bed with all that stuff all over me, it messed up her sheets, but she never complained. I never knew why, but Mary walked with a limp. Uncle Curry developed leukemia and suffered a lot before he passed away. They would give him blood, but it would just pass on through his body. I remember Aunt Mary knowing how to cook deer meat real tender before Uncle Curry got sick. She would soak the meat in vinegar all night before cooking it the next day. That tenderized the meat and kept it from getting tough to eat when it was cooked. Uncle Curry and Aunt Mary lived near Birmingham about forty miles from where I lived. We didn't have deer back home until about ten years after I left for the air force. We would have given anything for deer meat. We just killed rabbits and squirrels or raised a hog to eat.

We would always be barefoot when we plowed our garden. The soft dirt would feel good and cool to our feet, squashing between our toes. My daddy would lay out the rows, as they called it, with a horse pulling the plow. After he made the rows, we would help him plant everything. When we planted our sweet potatoes, we would tote tubs of water from the house to the garden to add to the vine and give the potato a jump start if there was no rain right away. Irish potatoes were supposed to be planted by February 14, but sometimes a frost would kill them after they came up. Then we would have to replant. We usually planted a little of everything. We would raise peanuts and all kinds of vegetables. We would plant corn in one place, and if we raised popcorn, we had to plant it four or five rows away because the corn would crossbreed.

Women back then canned every year in mason jars. They would make fig preserves, which my daddy was crazy about. They canned blackberries and made pickled peaches. We would plant about an acre, which kept us busy. All we had were hoes and rakes. No modern equipment. We would plant about three pieces of corn to make sure it would come up. If two or three corn came up, we would let it get about a foot and pull the shortest stalks up to let the largest one grow faster by itself. While the garden was growing, we were not allowed to play baseball on Saturday unless the garden was spotless of weeds and starting to produce. After the garden was producing, I would load my wagon up with corn, tomatoes, lettuce, turnip greens, and other vegetables to take over to the Black quarters to sell and make some extra money. Once our sweet potatoes were ready, my daddy would borrow a mule from a Black man and plow them up. We would follow behind him, barefooted, picking up all the sweet potatoes. We would keep the big ones to cook or fry. We called the little ones "scrubs," and we would bake those. Sometimes the plow would cut some of the big potatoes. We would dig the Irish potatoes up by hand with a straight fork. We would pick poke salad in the summer for my mother to cook. It would grow wild, and if we pulled it when it was two or three feet high, my mother would wash it a few times and cook it. Poke salad tasted identical to spinach, but if it got five to six feet tall and had berries, it was poisonous and we couldn't eat it.

My mother cooked a lot of butter beans on our old coal stove. She was a great cook. She could cook anything: candy, pudding, pies, cakes, apple pies, squirrels, and rabbits. We would go rabbit hunting in the daytime, and we would ride down the country roads on the front of the car at night. We would shoot the rabbits as they crossed the road in front of our headlights, even though that was against the law. We would also hunt birds at night. We would shine our flashlight up in the trees or in the bushes and shoot them while they were sleeping. Glover Lovejoy and I would go coon hunting at night, but we never did find any to kill. Our main meal was butter beans and cornbread when we were young, and we were lucky to have them. Times were hard. This is still my favorite meal today, with some boiled okra mixed into it.

When I was six or seven years old, we had good neighbors with two daughters and a son. One of the daughters was in my grade. My mother told me the neighbor would let her son go down to the store in the summertime, stay around the men, and report back all the latest gossip to her. The little girl next door would tell the other kids not to eat at the Whatleys. "All they have to eat is beans and cornbread." Sometimes when we had a big rain, I would roll my britches up and wade in the water barefooted going down the ditches. My mother told me not to do it because I might step on a piece of glass. Guess what! The next big rain, I was wading in the ditches again. The little girl next door had heard my mother tell me not to do it again. So she ran to my house and told my mother, and my mother tore my butt up. I went outside and saw the little girl by their wooden gate. I was mad at her for telling on me, so I picked up a brick and threw it at her. She jumped on the gate, and the brick splattered. I didn't realize at the time what it would have done to her if the brick had hit her. I didn't care. There again, I would have gotten my butt torn up again.

When we were young, we had to take our baths on the back porch in the summertime. Usually, four of us boys would get in a number two or number three tub at the same time. We had a closed-in back porch, but anyone on the front porch could look through the bedroom window to the back porch. If this same little girl knew we were taking a bath, she would come up to our house and walk back and forth on the front porch, watching us naked in the tubs. We always had to get on our knees beside the tubs to wash our hair. The little girl would put her tub by the faucet beside her house where we could see her from our porch. She would fill the tub with water and get naked. All of us boys would be at the end of the porch looking down at her. She would stand up naked, turn around, and sit back down. My mother would say, "Y'all quit looking down there at her!" But we kept looking anyway.

We would sit on the front porch in the summertime because it was so hot in the house with no air conditioner. We had a fence wire across part of our front porch. We had cud zoo vines growing on the fence to keep the sun out of our eyes. Mosquitoes were bad in those vines, so we would put rags in a bucket and set them on fire to keep them from biting us. Mosquitoes can't stand the smoke. Part of our porch had bannisters, so we would get tin cans or old pots or buckets to put on them to plant flowers. We would get clippings from other people's flowers to grow our own. We had all kinds of flowers.

A friend of mine got me in trouble with the little girl next door's mother. I was up on my closed-in back porch using a grease gun to suck in water and then shooting it out at a long distance. The little girl's mother was sitting on her front porch, and my friend told me to squirt the water out and holler out, "This is the way Mrs. Champion pees!" I filled the grease gun up with water and peeped around the corner of the porch. The little girl's mother looked up and saw me as I squirted the water way out and hollered what my friend told me to say. The next afternoon, I was walking home from school, and I saw my mother on the neighbor's porch. I said to myself, "Oh Lord, I've had it again!" My mother called me over to the porch and made me apologize to the lady and told me to go on home, and she would be there in a few minutes. I knew right then that my butt was going to get torn up again. My mother came right home, like she said she would, and tore my butt up. After she whipped me, she said that she wished she hadn't because the little girl's mother was down there crying because of it. I also wished she hadn't because my mother knew how to use a switch.

A little while later, our neighbors moved into the house where Dr. Stinson lived after he moved out. The husband decided to open a small coal mine between our house and the school. The big company mines had shut down by that time. I was fourteen years old and wanted to work for him in the mines, but I was too young. The coal miners would send coal cars out of the mines to dump into the coal bin. Sometimes they would send the cars out with rock that they dumped outside. Sometimes there was a mixture of rock and coal together. My brothers and I decided we would stay out there and pile up the coal that we sorted from the rock and sell it for five dollars a ton. I think some of the miners saw what we were doing, and they "accidentally" started putting more coal in the rock cars so we would have more coal to sell. About a year or two later, our old neighbor decided to shut his coal mine down.

Another couple moved into our old neighbor's house. Their names were Erskin and Clara Belle Warren, and they had five children about the same age as us boys, so we always had a good time together. They had one daughter that was a few years older than us, and she dated a boy with a convertible Chevrolet. She was a little wild, so my mother told my daddy that she had better not catch him looking down at that floozy. When I was in the first or second grade, the sister of the boy who was dating the floozy (as my mother called her) told us all about the birds and the bees. When we were young, in grammar school, we seemed to swap girlfriends every other week, and we could hardly wait until Valentine's Day so that we could give pretty valentines to the girls that we liked the most.

Erskin and Clara Belle's oldest son was named Erskin Jr., but we called him Laney Boy. He would get mad at his daddy about something, run down into the woods in front of their house, and say he was running away from home. His parents would just laugh at him. If we would have laughed at him, we would have gotten our butts torn up. Erskin Jr. wasn't afraid of getting whippings, so he did as he pleased. Even though he was only fourteen or fifteen years old, he would make scuppernong or muscadine wine and drink it. Erskin Jr. had three sisters and one brother. His brother, Billy, was the same age I was, and we always had something to do for a good time. When we were in grammar school, Billy and I liked the same girl. When the girl grew up, she married another friend of ours and turned into a very beautiful lady. They later divorced.

Billy, the little girl two houses down and I were down in our cow barn one day. We told the girl, "If you let us see yours, we will let you see ours." After we all grew up and Billy's family moved to California, Billy and I kept in contact with each other until about two years after I joined the air force. We wrote each other letters for a couple of years but eventually lost touch with each other. We haven't seen each other since we were kids. Mr. Erskin Warren was a skinny man, and he had a lot of big blood vessels showing in his arms. I was young and asked my mother why he had all those blood vessels showing on his arms, but she said she didn't know. We lived next to the Warrens for a few years before Tutwiler started stripping coal. As long as there was no rain, we all stayed outside doing something, whether it was summer or winter.

I remember the first chicken that I had was little biddy that I gave Jim Brantley eighty-five cents for. I wanted it so bad. I could have bought a full-grown chicken for the same amount. Eighty-five cents was a lot of money back then. Jim had a brother named Harris and a sister named Nell. Nell Brantley married my cousin Jack Lovejoy. When we were coming up, everyone's animals just ran wild. We had some Black people living behind us, and their chickens would lay eggs in the bushes in the ditch. If we found a nest with eggs in it, we would take them home and boil them. If we didn't find a nest quick enough, they would hatch a bunch of biddies.

I don't remember where or when, but I got two bantam chickens. The bantam chicken is smaller than a regular chicken, and they lay smaller eggs, but they taste the same. The hen laid some eggs and hatched them out. The biddies got grown and kept producing more biddies. I wound up with about thirty-five bantam chickens in a hurry! We would build them nests with apple crates in the barns, but they would still go somewhere else to lay their eggs. Sometimes when my mother wanted to fry a chicken, we would just go out, catch one, wring its neck off, and clean it. We would try to watch where the bantam chickens were laying their eggs, if not in the barn. We would put wooden or plastic eggs in the nests, and that would make them keep laying eggs in their nests for some reason. I guess they thought the fake eggs were theirs too.

If for some reason we couldn't find where their nests were, the bantam chickens would hatch more biddies. Sometimes they would hatch in the wintertime, and I didn't bother taking care of them because I already had enough chickens. Most of the ones that I didn't care for just froze to death. Most of the chickens that we killed were roosters. We didn't buy chicken feed. We let them run wild and live off the land. The chickens always stayed around the house. They knew where home was. In the summertime, we would get us a gallon syrup bucket, fill it with water, and put bricks on it out in the yard. We would put eggs in a bucket and build a fire underneath it to boil some eggs. It was a lot of fun.

Billy Warren, next door, had a big white duck that laid big white eggs. I would swap him two bantam chicken eggs for one duck egg. Duck eggs taste the same as chicken eggs. One day, I got mad at Billy's duck because she was up in my yard. I picked up a piece of coal about the size of a baseball, threw it at the duck, and knocked it out cold. It scared me to death. I picked the duck up and took it down to the cow barn and tried to hide it where my mother wouldn't find it because I knew I would get my butt torn up. I put the duck underneath a tub in the barn. I just knew it was dead. I went back to the barn later that day to check on the duck. Lo and behold, she had come to. Man, I was one happy little boy to see that duck up and walking under the tub. I never mentioned that to anyone. I would have still gotten my butt torn up for knocking the duck out, even though it didn't die. My mother was switch happy, but I guess she had to be to keep all of us boys in line.

We kept cow and hog feed in that barn. My daddy would castrate the male hog and fatten them up before the wintertime. We also had big ole rats hanging around, ready to eat the feed. We would find big holes in the ground where the rats had made tunnels. We would fill the holes with water to flush out the rats. When they came out of the holes to keep from drowning, we would be ready to kill them with a stick. We kept fifty-five-gallon barrels outside to catch the rainwater. We would tote five-gallon buckets or tubs full of the water to put on our garden when the weather was hot or dry. Sometimes the big rats would fall into the barrels of water and couldn't climb out, so naturally we would kill them too.

Everyone would let their cows run wild in the community. Most of the time, the cows would come back home in the early afternoon. We would put cowbells around their necks so that if they didn't come home, we could go looking for them and hear the bell around their necks. If a cow was pregnant and had the calf who knows where, we would have to go looking for them because the mother would not leave her baby to come home. Sometimes the cows would eat a weed called bitterweed, and it would make their milk taste a little bitter. The weed would grow in clusters about two feet tall with yellow flowers on it. We would milk our cow every day to make sure we had plenty of sweet milk. We would let some of the sweet milk clabber, churn it by hand, and make our own butter and butter milk. I didn't like sweet milk, so I would use pet milk in my cereal whenever we could afford it. Sometimes we would see a big red ant about one inch long, and we called them cow ants.

When I was eight years old, my mother bought my first bicycle from Jack and Mary Ethel Lemley. It was a twenty-eight-inch bike that had belonged to her son, Jackie. The bike was a little big for me. I had to pedal down one side and then the other just to ride it, but that was okay. I was just glad to have a bike. I couldn't even sit to pedal. My mother paid $8 for the bike, which was a lot of money back then. Mary Ethel Lemley married my cousin Clarence Lovejoy after he got out of the army. Mary Ethel had a brother named Doug and a sister named Eleanor Ann. Eleanor Ann was my little girlfriend on and off when we were in grammar school. Most of the time, she was William Mason's girlfriend. One day, Franklin was pedaling our bicycle down the hill real fast, coming from the schoolhouse on the dirt road. I was on the handlebars, and James was on the back of the seat. James's foot got caught in the back-wheel spokes, and the bike flipped over. I was the first to hit the ground, and I got a little skinned up, but it knocked the breath out of both Franklin and James and tore up their watches. Roy Jones was up on the hill. When he saw us wreck, he started laughing. James and Franklin got mad at him because they didn't think it was funny. We got the bicycle up and went on home. The bike was fine. I had a J. C. Higgins bike, and after riding for a while, the brakes would stop working. I learned that if I poured water on the rear brakes, they would start working again. We would spruce up our bikes by putting reflectors and mud flaps on them. We also put a light on it so we could see at night. Sometimes we would put a basket on the front or back so we could haul things, like groceries, in it. Sometimes we would put Coke bottle tops on the spokes so it would make a noise while we were riding. We knew how to work on our bicycles completely. If something broke, we could and would fix it because my daddy didn't get involved at all. We knew how to tighten the spokes on the wheel without warping the rim. If it wasn't tightened just right, it would warp the rim, which would cause your tire to rub the bicycle frame.

One day, I was going real fast down a hill on a dirt road on that J. C. Higgins bike when, all of a sudden, I saw two cars parked up in the middle of the road facing opposite directions. My brakes wouldn't hold. I yelled for help when I got to the cars because I just knew I was going to wreck and I knew I would get hurt pretty bad as fast as I was going. I guess the people in the car didn't know my breaks weren't working, but with a little help, I squeezed between the cars. I was so embarrassed that I just kept on going.

The only animals that people put in pens were the hogs. We built hogpens out of slats of lumber from the sawmill. Back then sawmills would cut slats off the trees which still had bark on them, and they would just keep the best lumber with no bark. They would burn the slats or give them to anyone that wanted them. Everyone was so poor that the hogpens were all made from the slats given to us by the sawmill. We would make feeding troughs from two pieces of wood and put slop, hog feed, or scraps in it for the hogs to eat. We also used the slats to build little sheds in the hogpens to get under on sunny summer days. We would keep water in the pens for the hogs to wallow around in to stay cool. We kept the drinking water in a tub. Most people kept the hogs behind the house to fatten up and kill in the winter or fall for food. If a family didn't have a hog, they would save us their scraps, and when we killed a hog, we would give them some of the meat. White people didn't eat chitterlings, but the Black people did. So we would give them to whoever showed up first. We had a fifty-five-gallon barrel that was tilted to put the hog in after we shot it in the head. The barrel had water in it, and we would build a fire underneath to get the water scalding hot, which would make it easier to pull the hair off the hog. After cutting the hog up, we would use a little hand grinder to make sausages, and we put the lard in five-gallon cans. The best eating was when we cooked the sausage when it was freshly made with homemade biscuits and syrup. Big Daddy Lovejoy (Uncle Crawford) had a big hog that was over eight hundred pounds. I can remember that hog had six piglets at one time. Big Daddy had a smokehouse, and when he killed a hog, he would hang it from the rafters, which he called curing the meat, and would put salt on the hog to keep it from spoiling.

We would wear what we called hand-me-downs. If one of us outgrew our clothes, we would pass it down to the next child. The neighbors would pass clothes around if they didn't have a child that would fit in them. Shoes were the hardest to hand down. They usually just wore out. If you wore pants with a hole in them or a girl wore a dress above her knees, they were considered poor. Nowadays people pay lots of money for that look. This generation wears it to be popular; we were considered poor.

I guess one or two women in Piper may have had a job working somewhere else, but I don't remember who it might have been. Most of the women had children to raise, and their husbands worked in the coal mines. The women would stay home cooking, cleaning, and raising the children. They would do a lot of canning foods from the garden in the summertime. We always had a big garden. We would save the cow manure all year to put on the garden for fertilizer. Cow manure would make a garden grow bigger and faster than store-bought fertilizer. We didn't raise any ribbon cane, but Mr. Fancher always had a big field planted. He charged five cents for a stalk of it, but sometimes we would sneak down to his field and steal a little of his cane.

We always had animals around. Besides the cows, hogs, and chickens, we also had dogs and cats. If one of us boys got a dog or cat, the rest of us would get one. We didn't take care of them. We just let them do the best that they could on their own. We never heard of a veterinarian. If our dog got the mange, we would tie them to a tree and put burnt motor oil on the mangy area. Burnt motor oil would cure the dog of the mange. We would pull big white ticks off the dogs and smash it while it was full of blood. The dog would smell its own blood and start slobbering out of its nose and mouth. If there would have been animal cruelty laws back then, we would have been put under the jail. We were brutal to the animals, and as young kids, we didn't think much of it. We learned it from our daddy and other people. Right or wrong, that's how life was. We would tie two cats together, hang them over the clothesline, and watch them fight. We would use our cats to train our squirrel dogs out in the woods. We didn't give it a second thought because we had seen our daddy do it.

I was really small, and I saw a turtle going across the yard. I grabbed an axe and hit the turtle with the sharp side and split it wide open. As I got older and started driving cars, I would try to hit rabbits, turtles, squirrels, snakes, opossum, or anything else that was in the road just for sport. As I got older still, I realized how precious life is, and I couldn't hurt animals anymore. I try to keep from killing it unless it was a poisonous snake, like a rattler or water moccasin. I know most snakes, and if it isn't poisonous, I don't kill them. If I catch a bug inside the house, I will take it outside and turn it loose rather than killing it. I remember when I was young and on my way to school, I saw a black racer, which is not dangerous, with a frog in its mouth. I thought I was going to scare the snake, but when I went toward it, I guess he thought I was after his frog. He started coming at me. I got scared and started running myself away from him.

Sometimes I would be walking down the road barefoot and see a small snake. And I would step on it behind the neck, then reach down, and pick it up. Snakes can't strike backward. They have to coil up and spring forward. I would take them home to show my mother when I caught one. Mother told me not to be catching snakes, or else one day I was going to get bitten.

Sometimes on a creek bank, I would see a snake going into a hole, and I would grab it by the tail and jerk it back out. I was just seeing if I could outsmart them. One day, I reached down to grab a rattlesnake behind the head, and he threw his head back with his mouth wide open. The back of his head hit the back of my thumb. That scared me a little, so I stopped trying to catch snakes.

Smoking frog

Sometimes we would catch a frog, put a cigarette in its mouth, and light it. The frog couldn't spit it out. So every time it hopped, it would be taking a puff from the cigarette. We would have to pull the cigarette back out of the frog's mouth. I caught a whip-poor-will in the woods and took it to school. It had a really large mouth. I think it was sick because it died shortly after I caught it.

One day, my dad was behind somebody moving, and their baby goat fell off the truck. My daddy got it and brought it home to us. As the goat got larger, it grew horns and would headbutt us (playing with us). If I was walking down the road and whistled, the goat would come running to me just like my dog would. Someone told my teacher how it followed me around, and she couldn't believe it. The next morning, I went to school with the goat following me. But when I got to school, the teacher made me turn around and take it back home. Later on, when he got larger, he started eating our clothes that we kept on the back porch to be washed. So my daddy sold it to a man for five dollars.

When we were kids, we would catch lightning bugs in the summertime and put them in a Coke bottle to watch their bodies light the bottle up yellow. We would also catch June bugs and tie a string to their leg and watch it fly around while we held the other end of the string. We caught daddy longlegs, as we called them. I guess they were kin to the spider family. They had long legs and small bodies. I'm not sure if they just didn't or couldn't bite us, but none of us ever got bit by one. We watched doodlebugs bury themselves in the dirt under our house. We would catch honey bees in our hand and let them sting us. Then we would let them go, just for something to do. I stopped doing that when a bumble bee got between my toes and stung me. We would put a stick with a string tied to it under one side of a tub and put corn under the tub. We would hide behind a tree, and when a bird would go under the tub to eat the corn, we would jerk the stick out to make the tub fall and trap the bird. We would then lift the edge of the tub and catch the bird with our hands. We would also throw rocks at the chimney sweepers just to watch them dive at the rocks. They were bad about getting in our chimney and building nests, which made the chimney a fire hazard. We were so bored at night we enjoyed watching airplanes fly over even though it was miles and miles high. We would watch them until they were completely out of our sight. A man from Montevallo had a Piper

Cub plane that he would fly so low over Piper, Alabama, that his wheels would clip the leaves on top of the trees.

I don't remember how many times or how long my mom and dad would separate, but one time I went with my daddy, and my brothers stayed with my mother. My daddy was always drinking. I don't know who my mother stayed with one night, but I went home with my daddy. And we stopped on the Big Cahaba River bridge, and he let me shoot his pistol into the river. I was small and thought that I would hear the bullet splash into the water. We went home, and I made some dough, thinking I was cooking biscuits. But I left them in the oven too long and burned them to a crisp. I know two or three times my parents separated for a week or two, and I would see my daddy walking down the road in the distance. I wouldn't say anything to him, but it hurt me, and I never mentioned it. So I don't know if my parents ever realized that it hurt me. I said right then that I would never divorce my wife for any reason because I would never want to hurt my children like I was hurt. My daddy was pretty rough on my mother at times. Sometimes he would leave on Friday, and we wouldn't see him again until Monday morning. When he got home, he would go back to work in the coal mines. Sometimes they would get into an argument, and my daddy would slap my mother down. We three older boys—twelve, fourteen, and sixteen years old—went to him and told him that if he ever hit her again, all three of us would jump him. That was the end of him hitting our mother. Daddy knew we were serious, but he had no hard feelings about it. My daddy made home-brewed whiskey when we were young. I remember yeast went into making it. He had the bottles to put it in, sort of like Coke bottles, and he had a bottle capper to seal them. Sometimes he would run out, and we would go to two or three different women's houses to borrow money so he could buy bottled whiskey. It was hard on my dad trying to provide for my mother and five of us boys and my grandfather when the mines were down or on strike. He didn't know anything else, except for bootlegging. There wasn't any government assistance back then.

We had a black-and-white dog named Skipper. He was the best squirrel dog we ever had. Skipper would go after everything. One day, I saw Skipper and another dog playing tug-of-war with a snake in their mouths. The snake broke in half, and three eggs fell out. Skipper saw a ground squirrel go into a hole in the ground, and he started digging like crazy. After a few minutes, he threw the squirrel between his legs, and the squirrel ran off. Skipper loved getting into the 1940 Chevrolet with my dad to ride the roads. Sometimes when my dad was drinking, he would put Skipper on top of the car, and Skipper would stand like a statue. Skipper knew that if my daddy saw someone, he knew that he would hit the brakes and he would bounce off the front of the car. He never got hurt, thank goodness. Skipper liked riding in the cab with his head hanging out of the window. One night, someone came into Piper and stole Skipper and about four other squirrel dogs from their owners. Back then people wanted good squirrel dogs so they didn't have to train them. Sometimes when we were squirrel hunting, we would see bushes with berries the size of huckleberries. The berries would turn black when they were ripe, and we would put those and sweet shrubs into our pockets because they smelled so good.

In the wintertime when the leaves would die, we could find the prettiest Christmas trees, and we could cut them down for free. If we ran across a whiskey still in the woods, we would just keep on running and never tell anyone. One time, I was squirrel hunting by myself early in the morning, still hunting as we called it. That is when you sit under a tree and wait for a squirrel to come in sight and you shoot. I saw a fox squirrel run into a hollow tree, so I set the leaves on fire in the bottom of the tree. The squirrel ran out and went up into a taller tree and was wiping his eyes from the smoke. I had a .22-caliber rifle and shot him in his mouth. After picking the squirrel up, I went back to the fire that I had set and urinated on it to put it out. A few hours later, Freddie Lovejoy asked me where I had been hunting. I told him, and he said that a bunch of men had gone into the woods to put out the fire (that I had started). I didn't realize that the fire had started back up again.

We used to build our own swings with a wooden seat or just tie a knot at the end of a rope. On occasion, we would use a small car tire for the swing. We could always get steel cable if we didn't have rope available. We made all the swings on the Cahaba River out of the steel cable that the miners would use to pull the coal out of the mines when they quit using mules. We would twist the cable and take turns using the swing while it untwisted, which would make us very dizzy. We made the swings and diving boards at Bulldog Bend on the Little Cahaba River. We would build a ladder on a tall tree, run a long mining cable from high in the tree, and connect it to another tree lower to the ground. The trees would be about seventy-five to two hundred feet apart. And we would hold on to a tire rim, ride it down the cable, and hit the ground running. We would get a steel wheel rim from a horse buggy or an old bicycle to play click and wheel. We would push the rim with a stiff stick, like a broom handle, and guide it, running behind it so it wouldn't fall.

Bulldog Bend

Railroad tracks were fun. We would walk for miles balancing on the rails without falling off. Of course, as children, our feet were smaller. Just for fun, we would climb to the top of a young pine tree and lean until the pine tree would lean over, and we would jump off to the ground. After a while, the tree would break in half. We enjoyed fighting wasps in the old houses. If you laid flat and didn't move, they wouldn't sting you. But if you moved at all, you would get stung. Yellow jackets built their nests in the ground. We had to be careful when mowing the grass because they would swarm and sting us before we even saw them. If we found a nest in the ground, we would pour gasoline in it to kill them. Baby wasp and wasp nest are very good bait for catching brim fish.

Bobby Whatley

We would make sleds out of barrel slats or two-by-fours to slide down a hill covered in pine straw. We would sharpen the wood because it wouldn't slide with a blunt edge. We also used cardboard to slide down those hills. Cardboard was also good for steep dirt hills. We would pull our wagons up the hills and ride it back down, then repeat over and over again until we were worn out. If the wheels on the wagon hollowed out, which they did at times, we would put an extra washer on the axle to keep the wheel from wobbling. We would put plenty of grease on the wheels to make the wagon go faster. Slinky was one of our toys, and we would watch it walk down the stairs over and over.

When spring would come, we enjoyed seeing everything in bloom. The honeysuckle was pretty, and the buttercups were little and had pollen. Buttercups were used to smash pollen in our friend's faces after asking them to smell it. We played jacks with a small ball and star-shaped spikes made of pot metal or aluminum. We also played paddle ball with a little rubber ball attached to a paddle. We would count to see who could paddle the ball more times than the others. When the buttercups were blooming, there was another weed that would bloom called milkweed. The stem would bleed milklike fluid if we broke it in half. Dandelions had a fuzzy top that we would blow off. Mushrooms would grow wild, and when they died and turned black, we would hit them with a stick to watch the black dust fly out. We called that dust "devil's snuff." We didn't know at the time how dangerous that was. We would get into the old company homes with our BB guns and shoot one another from one house to the other. My granddaddy bought me a pump BB gun that would shoot really fast. We also used slingshots with chinaberries to battle one another in those houses.

At night, we would play hide-and-seek. If I tagged you before you reached the base, you would be out and have to count next while the rest of us hid again. We played hopscotch and attached two empty cans with a string to play telephone and talk to each other. We made wooden stilts from the wood that we got from the company houses. The lights in the company homes hung down so low that we could reach them. For the fun of it, we would unscrew the bulbs and stick our finger in the socket for an electric tingle when we got older. It is a wonder that we never got electrocuted. When a fuse in the main fuse box went out, we would replace it with a penny, which served the same purpose, but it could have shorted out and cause the house to catch fire.

When we were young, we would dig a ditch about fifteen to twenty feet long and use wood to place over the ditch. We would pour dirt onto the wood to make a dark tunnel, and we would take a lit candle with us, even though we didn't have to. There was a sawmill in Piper that had mounds of sawdust that would get packed hard, and the heat from the sun would cause it to smoke. Sometimes we would bury one another up to the neck in sawdust. Bluebirds would build nests in the birdhouses that we made, and martins would build houses in the gourdes that we hung.

We had an electrical line running from the house to the outhouse. One day, when I was walking back to the porch from the outhouse, a hummingbird lit on the line. I didn't know what a hummingbird was back then. I didn't know that they come around in the summertime and fly farther south in the winter. I keep four hummingbird feeders up at my house every summer and feed them. We can count as many as fifteen to twenty humming birds eating out of the feeders every day. Humming birds eat the pollen out of flowers. Everyone grew flowers and didn't know about the hummingbird feeders when I was a boy. Aunt Lid raised a lot of big sunflowers, which were good for the hummingbirds.

My daddy bought an old secondhand army truck after World War II was over. It was a straight shift truck with gears in the floorboard. The only heat in the truck came from the motor and blew through the floor. The steering wheel was so loose that my daddy had to keep turning it back and forth to keep it on the road. Sometimes Daddy drank and would not be paying attention to where he was going. He would be looking off somewhere and start running into the ditch, so I would yell at him, and he would jerk the wheel to get us back on the road. He always had to pump the brakes and sometimes shift to a lower gear to stop. We were always having to add brake fluid. We always had to double-clutch those old straight shift trucks to change gears without grinding, and we didn't have power steering back then. My brother Franklin was twelve years old when my daddy bought the army truck. The windshield had a half-moon shape to it. Franklin learned how to drive the truck, and he was going down the road one day toward the store and could barely see out of the corner of that windshield. Someone thought the truck was coming down the road by itself. We could see his little redhead sticking up. We had a sheriff or constable in Piper, but he didn't care about driver's licenses.

I was also twelve years old when I learned how to drive, but I didn't get my license until I was sixteen and had to go to Centerville, Alabama. We were going down the road, and the man testing me asked how long I had been driving. I answered, "Since I was twelve." The man said, "Turn around and let's go back." And he gave me a hundred on my driver's test. One day, we were going in the truck to Bulldog Bend to swim. My mother and daddy were fussing about something as we went out of Crows Feet Road, and my daddy turned while going too fast, and the truck went up on two wheels. If we had flipped over, it probably would have killed some of us because the cab and canvas top were very flimsy. I'm not sure if it was true or if Daddy was pulling my leg, but Daddy said he lived at Bulldog Bend when he was a child and owned a big white bulldog. That and because there was a bend in the river was how he said it got its name. My daddy made a lot of money with that army truck. The Black people would hire him to take them to the ball games or parties if they were out of town. Daddy would also move people to different houses or out of town for a price. Three of us boys would go into the woods with him to haul rich pine to people so they could use it in their stoves or fireplaces. Daddy would take the canvas off the back so we could fill the truck up with pine from all over the hillsides. He would get $15 for a truckload. We boys didn't get a penny, but we didn't expect anything. Daddy taught us boys to be hard workers, and we didn't have anything else to do anyway. We would be going up a steep hill, loaded with pine, and Daddy would tell us to be prepared to jump if the truck stalled because he didn't know if the brakes would hold. One of us boys always rode on the running boards so we were ready to jump, but fortunately we never had to.

My daddy was a coal miner, but if the mines weren't open, he would find other ways to make money. He would haul workers from Piper to Marvel to work in the mines when the Piper mines shut down. We would cut the timber for the coal mines that was used to hold the mine up from collapsing. Daddy had a gasoline saw, and he would give us a crosscut saw and pay us $0.05 for every six-foot timber that we cut. Using a crosscut saw could be very difficult if both people on either side of the saw didn't know how to use it. We were too small, and it was too dangerous for us kids to use the gasoline saw. When the pine rosin would stick to the blade of the crosscut saw, we would have to pour turpentine on the blade teeth to make it easier to cut the timber. We kept the turpentine in a Coke bottle with pine straw stuck in it. The most money that I ever made in a single day's work was $2.85. Fifty-seven timbers in one day was a lot of hard work. We were glad to get the money, and it was a day out of school. Our dad didn't give us money; we had to work for it. My mother would slip me $1 after I was in about twelfth grade, but she always told me not to tell my daddy. Mother got her driver's license in the lumber truck and only made one mistake. In reverse, she backed over the line a little bit. There was this old man that lived by himself, and he knew that we needed money, so he would let us wash off his porch and pay us $0.50. Fifty cents was a lot of money for such a small job. We liked playing in the water, so we enjoyed doing that job. Sometimes I would clean a big yard. I would stay and clean all day and tell the people to just give me whatever they wanted. I did one yard for Glover Lovejoy, and he paid me a pack of firecrackers. I wanted money, not firecrackers.

I was about fourteen years old when I started helping Glover Lovejoy. I was glad to get any kind of work, so Glover hired me to clean all the bricks that came out of these three houses. I cleaned bricks for about two months in the summertime, and he paid me $15, but I was glad to get that. Anything was better than nothing, I thought. Glover would always cut our hair when we were really young, and I don't know if my daddy paid him for that or not, but I hope he did.

My daddy decided to move up the road from where we lived, across from Alex Hayes's house where Billy Rice had his eye put out with a pick. Alex and his wife had two sons, Gordon and Jimmy Hayes. Jimmy is deceased, but Gordon still comes to the Marvel reunion every year at Pea Ridge, Alabama. We had good neighbors on both sides of our house: Rip and Ruth Romager on one side and Uncle Morgan and Aunt Myrtle on the other side. Mr. and Mrs. West lived diagonally across the road from us. The Wests had five children about our ages that we were raised up with. Junior, Sara Nell, Douglas "Ducky," Jenny Faye, and Ellen were their names. Mr. and Mrs. West were good Christian folks. One summer, Mr. Alex rounded up a bunch of us young boys and took us to pick corn all day at a man's house. The man paid us $0.50 for picking the corn and fed us all dinner. We sat around a long table, and the dinner was so good.

Harold Campbell had a brother named H. T. Campbell who had one leg that was shorter than the other. H. T. had to wear a special shoe with a thicker sole. He sold cars for Wood's Chevrolet in West Blocton when it was a booming town. The Number 9 Coal Mine was up and running. My brother James worked there for a while, but he quit because he did not like working in the coal mines. My daddy wanted to buy a car. So every afternoon, H. T. would bring a different car to the house so my dad could look at it. I wanted every car that he brought, especially this old Packard. My daddy ended up buying a 1940 Chevrolet, but I don't remember if he bought it from H. T. or someone else. I don't remember what he did with that old timber truck either. He had stopped hauling timber to the mines in Marvel and didn't need it anymore. I wanted to date girls, but I was too ashamed to take them out in the 1940 Chevrolet. It didn't have a driver's window, so we would put a sheet over the door and slam it shut to cover the window.

When we were teenagers, we would do a lot of fishing. We lived one mile from Big Cahaba River and three miles from Little Cahaba River. We kept trotlines in Big Cahaba River most of the summer. We would keep a minnow basket out in all the branches close to Piper and seine different ponds around the Number 2 Coal Mines to catch crawfish. We used minnows and crawfish on all our lines. There was a big swampy pond above the Number 2 Coal Mines where we would seine for crawfish, but we also got turtles and snakes. The water was so muddy and murky that we would mar up in the mud. It is a wonder that we didn't get a snakebite. I know the Lord was looking after us crazy kids. I was fishing in the same pond one day catching small bass. I didn't tie the rope to the tree very tight, and all five fish swam off together. There are about nine species of fish in that river that are nowhere else in the world and a species of lilies that bloom in the river every May. That is the only place in the world, with the exception of maybe two or three other places in South Carolina and Georgia, where those lilies grow. We have a lily festival each year in the town of West Blocton.

Cahaba lilies, photo by Keith Boseman

My brother James's wife, Willa Dean Jordan, nearly drowned in the Big Cahaba when she was about three or four. Willa Dean's father jumped off the river bridge with her on his shoulders. He never came up, but Willa Dean floated to the top. And when her brother, Archie Jordan, saw her, he jumped into the river and pulled her onto the bank. Mr. Jordan's body was found hours later.

Most people that went fishing in the Big Cahaba or Little Cahaba rivers would just tie a rope or chain to their boats with the other end attached to a tree, but they didn't lock them. Back then most men would make their boats out of twelve-foot-by-three-quarter-inch wood and would put tar in the cracks to seal them so the boat wouldn't leak. No one had motors on their boats. There were too many shoals to go over to use a motor. Everyone just used paddles. If we wanted to use someone's boat, we would just use it and then put it back the way we found it. Everyone trusted one another to do the right thing back then. Sometimes we would have to go through a lot of woods to get to the river to fish. We would mark trees on our way to the river just in case we wanted to come back before daylight and not get lost.

Sometimes the Big Cahaba River would get up real high when it rained hard for a long time. It would wash people's boats down the river and lodge them against the pillars of the bridge. We boys would let ourselves down on a rope, get into a boat, and ride down the swift river a couple of miles to get it to the bank and tie it to another tree. One day, we went out on the bridge and saw a boat lodged against the pillar, so we let ourselves down the rope and got into the boat, but it had a big hole in the bottom. A tree had punctured it. This was in January, and we didn't have the strength to climb back up the rope, so we had to swim to the riverbank. We were so cold that we were pink. We had to run back to the bridge to get our rope and then run home because we were freezing.

Sometimes we would hang limb hooks from the trees in the Little Cahaba River. We had to watch for snakes on the limbs because, a few times, we had snakes fall into our boats.

Sometimes we would put a cowbell on the end of the line. That way, we could tell if there was a fish on the line because the bell would be ringing. We would make our lead sinkers by melting big pieces of lead. We would put double ends of wire in a hole in the sand for the size we wanted and then pour the hot lead into the hole. It would cool in a hurry, and then we had the sinkers the size that we wanted. We had a lot of rich and damp soil in our backyard that we could dig big wiggler worms up to use as bait for catching catfish. We would also sell the worms to Freddie Lovejoy by the quart. We put the worms in a jar with no dirt and sold the jar full solid with worms for thirty-five cents. After a light rain, we would go into the woods and collect ground puppies which the catfish really liked. We would turn over logs and rocks, and they would be underneath. We had to watch out for snakes when looking for ground puppies. They looked sort of like a lizard. They could be black or brown and slick look-ing. One time, my brother James turned over a log, and a dangerous snake jumped into his clothes. We never saw clothes come off any-one so fast! We looked around for the snake, but we couldn't find it. James put his clothes back on after shaking them out really good. As we started walking off, our dog Skipper found the snake and killed it.

Mr. Harry Fulman had a farm connected to the Little Cahaba River. He owned land on both sides of it. We would go down there at about 7:00 p.m. and gig us about half a tub of fish in three or four hours. That was against the law, and the game wardens swore that they were going to catch us, but they never did. My daddy would take blasting caps in a half stick of dynamite, throw it into a deep blue hole in the water, and then touch both ends of the wire connected to the blasting cap to a flashlight battery. It would blow up the dynamite, and the fish would be stunned and float to the top. We would be right below, down in the river, ready to catch all the stunned fish before they came to. That was also illegal. We also did what we called phone catfishing in the Big Cahaba River.

River redhorse fish

The thing that we called the phone was a magnetic piece with a handle connected to it. It comes out of a transformer, and you hook two wires to it, then put the other end of the wires into the water. When you turn the handle really fast, it paralyzes the catfish. It doesn't bother fish with scales, and it doesn't hurt them, but it is illegal. We did river redhorse fishing in the middle of April every year. The redhorse is kin to the suckerfish, and they are really boney. We could not fillet redhorse fish. We would pick the bones out because they are good to eat. They bed in both the Big Cahaba and Little Cahaba rivers. When we were kids, we enjoyed bursting the double bubble inside of them, which is their lungs. All the females would have a sack of eggs inside their body. I was in Mobile several years ago and saw a report on TV that said the redhorse is nearly extinct. They said they could only account for about eight left, and one was in a lake in Georgia. I didn't catch the phone number, or I would have called them to tell them to throw away their extinction calculations. I could show them hundreds in the middle of April. I took my wife to the Little Cahaba River one year and showed her forty-two redhorse on their beds. I don't ever remember one being caught on a hook. The only way that we knew how to catch them was to have a long fishing cane with about four feet of cord hanging from the end, then tie a thin copper wire to the cord to make a round noose with a piece of lead on the bottom of the loop. You drag the loop on their bed, and when it goes over their head, it tightens up. Then you throw them onto the bank without any slack in the line. Otherwise, they would slip out. Just like when you catch a cow, it scares the others; when you catch a redfish, it would scare the others off. They would come back to their beds after about five minutes or so. My daddy caught 103 in one bed. There is a picture of these fish in the *Tributaries* book (issue number 9, 2006) in Montgomery, Alabama, by Jim Brown. If you call Montgomery *Tributaries*, they will send you a copy of the book free of charge. They bed in the same place every year, whether the river is muddy or not. They bed in shallow gravel in the water.

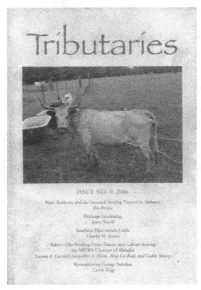

Tributaries, issue number 9, 2006

My daddy built us a twelve-foot boat using three-quarter-by-twelve-foot boards with tar on it. We never had a motor on the boat, so we used paddles to move up and down the river. We would set a trotline every now and then after we built that boat. My daddy, we boys, Raymond Jones, and his two sons, Rick and Roy, would go to the Jerico River to fish. The last trip when we went was a disaster. Both men were drinking; the game warden came out to check us out. We had two seines that were twenty feet long, which was against the law. The men had two gallons of moonshine whiskey. The game warden took one of the seines and one of the gallons of whiskey. They didn't see the other seine or the other jug of whiskey, so we were still able to use the other net without getting caught again. There were a few big holes beside that river where we would seine for bait. The river would get up whenever it would rain, and a lot of fish would get trapped in those big holes when the water went back down. We would seine for bait fish but also catch turtles and snakes sometimes. If we caught a lot of fish, we would sell them for fifty cents per pound without cleaning them. About the time that we got our lines ready to fish, Raymond got terribly sick. I guess from drinking too much moonshine whiskey. We had to get our lines out of the water and get him back to the house. So that trip was ruined.

When I was about fifteen years old, my mother would let us go to Bulldog Bend to swim during the summertime. We had to hitchhike everywhere we went. We had a shortcut through the woods on the way to Bulldog Bend. If we started through the woods and heard a car going down Big Road (Crows Feet Road), we would run through the woods to get back to the road before the car had time to get there. Whoever was in the car would always pick us up if they had room, and they would take us to Bulldog Bend. Most of the time, that was where they were headed anyways. Most men and women would get to the river before changing into their bathing suits. The men had one place in the woods to go change, and the women had another. Some of us young boys decided to build a fort close to where the women would undress so that we could see them. One day, one of the women yelled out, "Some boys are over there watching us undress!" So we took off down to the river as if they didn't know who we were. Everybody knew everybody back then.

A lot of days, we would go to the river in the morning and go home by lunchtime. We would eat lunch and go right back to the river again to swim. Most people swam at Bulldog Bend. The Big Cahaba had places to swim, but they weren't as good as Bulldog Bend. Sometimes a bad storm would come up, and we would just stay in the water. We would go under the water and look up at the lightning. We weren't thinking that the lightning could strike the water and kill us and we would die in that electrical storm. God's angels just looked out for us dumb kids.

I didn't know what poison ivy or poison oak looked like back then, so I caught my fair share of poison oak, and I was really allergic to it. One summer, I had to wear shorts and roll around in a wheelchair a lot of the time because of it. I would put calamine lotion on me. Then I tried coffee grounds and pet milk combined. Finally, I started taking poison oak shots. For a while, the shots worked, but then they stopped. When I was thirty-five years old in Nashville, Tennessee, a man by the name of Jim told me what would cure poison oak. He said he would get into the bathtub with water and Clorox mixed. I tried that, and it didn't work. So I decided that I would scratch the poison oak until I would bleed and then put Clorox directly on where I was bleeding. That seemed to be the remedy. The next morning, the poison oak would be all dried up. It burned when I applied the Clorox, but it was worth it to keep from going crazy from itching all the time. If the poison oak was runny and I touched any other part of my body, it would spread to wherever I touched. My doctor said that if I just got in the wind near poison oak, I would catch it. I didn't have to actually touch it.

When Piper was booming, had plenty of work for everyone, and was shipping a lot of coal out by truck or train, a statesman was in town under a big oak tree in front of our house, counting all the automobiles going up and down the dirt road. He was trying to determine if the road had enough traffic to pave it. My daddy got into his truck and just rode up and down the road as if the man couldn't recognize what he was doing. The man was probably laughing, knowing what my daddy was trying to do. Trying to make it look like there was more traffic.

When I was about fifteen years old and Jody Seagle was about sixteen or seventeen years old, he had an old car that we ran around in. We didn't have any money most of the time. We would find any old tire in a ditch with mud in it, clean it up, put a boot in it, and run it until it blew out. We would put fifty cents worth of gas in the car, and sometimes we would run out of gas and just walk home to try to get more gas from somebody. Sometimes we would go down to Harry Fulman's farm on Little Cahaba River in Jody's car late at night and gig for fish. Jody went to New Orleans one time when he was young and brought a Cajun girlfriend back with him. She would iron his clothes and try to help Mrs. Seagle around the house, but Mrs. Seagle told him that the girl had to go. So he took her back to New Orleans.

I enjoyed dating girls that wore dresses and lipstick. They seemed more ladylike, and I liked tasting lipstick. It let everyone know that you got some sugar if we had lipstick smeared on our lips. Now it seems like girls don't wear dresses or lipstick, but I think it is beginning to come back. I was fourteen or fifteen years old when Sherry Moore would have a wiener roast party on Smith Hill where she lived. I would hitchhike over there from Piper, about six miles away, to go to her parties. We would play spin the bottle to see who we were going to go walking up the road with. Naturally, we would try to make it point to the person we wanted to walk with or kiss. Sherry was in the same grade with me at West Blocton. Any time we went to West Blocton, we would get Huey Frederick to make us a cheeseburger at his restaurant. He could really make a good burger, and we would usually play music on the Rock-Ola that he had in his restaurant.

Right after I got my driver's license, William Mason and I were riding around in Piper. We came up in front of our house and saw that William's brother-in-law was drunk and fussing at my daddy, trying to fight him. He was mad because my daddy wouldn't sell him bootleg whiskey. I had a shotgun over the seat in our 1940 Chevrolet. I have never told anyone about this, but if he had started fighting my daddy, I was going to grab that shotgun and shoot him. I would have been in serious trouble, but I wasn't thinking about that at the time.

I didn't tell my daddy at that time or anyone else after that what my intentions were.

Every Wednesday night, we would load the 1940 Chevrolet with as many people as we could and would go roller-skating in Centerville. I got to where I could skate pretty good, I thought. When I went around the curve at the end of the rink, my feet went out from under me, and I hit the floor, which broke both bones in my left wrist. I went to three different doctors, and they were afraid to fix it because they thought my hand would grow downward. I broke my wrist at 7:30 p.m. and didn't get it set until 3:00 p.m. the next day in a hospital. It happened at the end of the school year, and I couldn't take my final typing test, so my teacher gave me a written test. I passed the test, and I have never had any trouble with my wrist since then.

There was a girl in my grammar school class named Betty Jones. She had a brother named Harold and a sister named Ann. They lived in Hawkinsville, about two miles from Piper. Betty had to study by candlelight or kerosene lamp because they had no electricity there. The power lines did not go that far. The iceman would come around daily to deliver ice for them to put into their icebox on the back porch. They had well water on their back porch also. A man named Hershel Day owned the property, and every time we went there to pick blackberries, it seemed like he would always be watching us. For some unknown reason, we were sort of scared of him, but he never said anything to us. We found out years later that he was a schoolteacher, but not at our school. He always came to the Piper reunion, but he passed away a few years back. I guess he still didn't know that we were scared of him when we were kids. He was a good Christian man. His son, James, is a history teacher at Montevallo College and has written a book called *Diamonds in the Rough* about the coal mines. It took him twenty-five years to write it, but he only worked on the book for a total of fifteen years.

When Mr. Tutwiler bought Piper, we had no idea what he was going to do with it. He put in a program right away to try to get all the houses and yards looking good, and he would give $100 to who-ever got their place looking the best. People started cleaning yards and whitewashing fences if they had one. After a while, we figured out that Mr. Tutwiler bought Piper to start stripping the coal from under the houses. A few months after he bought Piper, he started selling the houses for $50 per room so that someone would buy them. Then they would tear the house down and start stripping the coal where the houses were. He sold all the houses, except for the two that the bosses lived in back in the early fifties, and those houses are still there. Some families still live in those two houses. Tutwiler had big draglines brought in and all sorts of tractors and Caterpillars to remove all the dirt off the coal. We stayed in our house a long time after he started stripping the coal. He got rid of all the houses in Coleanor first and started stripping for coal there. My brothers and I would go to Coleanor in the summertime and weekends to get any coal that the draglines threw away in a dirt-and-coal mixture until they got down to the solid, clean coal. We would pile it up and sell it for $5 a ton. We didn't have anything but time on our hands anyways. My mother would fix us lunches to take to work and put us some Kool-Aid in mason jars. We would take for the crane operators something to drink, and they would make sure that we got a little extra coal mixed with the dirt.

After the draglines would get all the coal out of one strip pit, they would go farther down the road and start clearing off more coal. We would get a lot of coal out of the banks of the coalpits that the equipment would leave, and we made some pretty good money by the time that school started again. Five dollars a ton was a lot of money back in the late forties. When they closed all the mines in Piper, my daddy started working in the mines in Marvel for Mr. Ben Roden's coal company.

Marvel water tower facing north

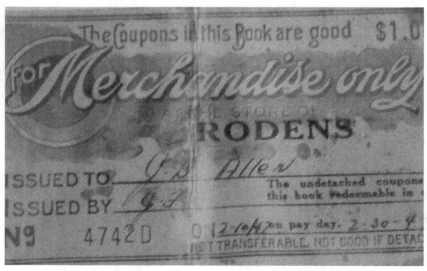

Roden Coal Company store voucher, 1947

Marvel was six or seven miles from Piper, but we stayed living in Piper while my daddy worked in Marvel. My daddy got paid sometimes in Roden Coal Company checks where the money could only be spent in the Roden Coal Company store in Marvel. Sometimes when my mother needed something from the store to cook, she would let me hitchhike to Marvel to get a few groceries. Sometimes Bobby Quinn would pick me up in the bread truck. The truck had a sliding front door, so he would let me stand up in the doorway. I saw a devil's food cake on his dash one day that sold for five cents back then. I guess it was the one he was taking back to the bakery, and I wanted to ask him for it, but I was too bashful to ask. I'm sure he would have given it to me if he knew that I wanted it. One day, I caught a ride to Marvel to get some groceries, and afterward, I bought me an ice cream to eat while I was waiting for a ride back to Piper. A Black man had a car full, but he stopped and gave me a ride. He was drunk and just going all over the road talking about airplanes, not watching where he was going, and I was afraid that we were going to wreck. I was so concerned, watching the road, that I forgot about my ice cream. It had melted all over me. I sure was glad when I got home and got out of that car. Although I did appreciate him giving me a ride.

I would also hitchhike to West Blocton every Saturday to play dominoes under John Langston's store. I was the only young person playing with all older men. I would get a pack of potato chips and an orange drink for my dinner. We would play for five or six hours every Saturday.

I had a fifty-cent coin that I had for fifty years, but I gave it to Marshal Goggins when I went to the Marvel reunion in 2009. The reunion is the first weekend of June every year. The fifty-cent coin was made out of brass about the size of a quarter and had an R punched out in the middle, which meant it could only be spent at the Roden company store in Marvel. They keep a lot of pictures and other things at the center in Pea Ridge where we meet every year, just to remind us of the old days and to see folks we haven't seen in a year.

Ben Roden

After Tutwiler sold all the houses in Piper, we finally had to move to Marvel where my daddy was still working in the coal mines. He rented a house on Broadway for us to move into. We would ride the school bus from Marvel to West Blocton. I was in tenth or eleventh grade by this time and made a lot of new friends.

Home in Marvel (second house on the left)

Ben Roden owned the community of Marvel. The coal mining towns were each owned by one man. They owned the houses, the store, and everything in the town. The stores would have saddles and everything to put on horses and plows. A lot of people had horses instead of cars, and no one owned their houses. All the houses belonged to the coal company. Everyone usually paid five to ten dollars for rent every month (a lot of money back then), and they only made about two dollars per day, digging for coal. That was still better than the fifty cents my parents were making per day picking cotton. Mr. Henry Fulman was the road commissioner when the mines shut down. He was put in charge of distributing commodities to the families in the community that needed help. The food was locked down in the basement of our church. There was cheese, rice, beans, and a few other things to eat. We would tell Mr. Harry that we needed something to eat. He wasn't supposed to, but he would give us the keys and tell us to get whatever we needed. I don't know if he did the same thing for other families or not. I finished high school just as the mines closed down, and I couldn't find work for myself. That is when I decided to join the air force. My father went to a new coal mining community called Blue Creek close to Bessemer. That is where my family moved to after I joined the air force. Mr. Roden started selling all the houses to individuals like they did in Piper, but the people stayed in their houses, so they didn't have to tear them down like they did in Piper. The Roden people were good people. I heard later on that Mr. Roden died of a heart attack in an airplane while traveling.

Roden Coal Company store

We would get bored with nothing to do and nowhere to go, except church on Sunday and Wednesday nights, so sometimes Billy and Bobby Little and I would hitchhike to Montevallo to get a milkshake at the drugstore and then hitchhike back to Marvel. It was about fifteen miles from Marvel to Montevallo. We would hitchhike there to see a movie and come back after dark. That road happened to be paved part of the way, but very few cars came by after dark. We would lie down in the middle of the pavement until we heard a car coming. Then we would get up and hold our thumbs out. That could have been a dangerous thing to do, but anyone would pick us up. Most everyone knew and trusted one another back then. People would hardly pick up hitchhikers anymore. I did for a while because I said I would always pick up hitchhikers after I was grown. My wife, Nettie Jo, didn't like me picking up the hitchhikers after we got married, and I finally stopped because there was so much meanness in people now. It wasn't like the good ole days anymore. What a shame.

A bunch of us boys went to church one night. Bobby and Billy were seventeen at the time; they were twins. They were always comical. The twins, someone else, and I were in church; and my brother Franklin was with some other boys outside the church, looking in the window. The song "You Got to Have a License" had just come out, and every time the preacher would say something during the sermon, the twins would always say, "You got to have a license." We would all get tickled every time they would say it and couldn't stop laughing while the preacher was preaching. The preacher finally told us boys that we had better behave, and then he continued preaching. The deacon went outside after Franklin and the other boys, so they took off running. If my mother had found out about that incident, we would have gotten our butts torn up.

While I was in the twelfth grade, Billy and Bobby worked for Mrs. Roden, the wife of Mr. Ben Roden who owned the Marvel mining community. They told me Mrs. Roden would hire me for fifty cents an hour, so I went to her house and asked for a job. I was out in the yard when she came to the door, and instead of me walking up to her and asking for a job, I just hollered and asked if I could work for her. She asked who my father was, and I said Ben Whatley. She said, "Okay, just start cleaning the yard." I worked every Saturday from then on until I finished school. She was a really nice woman. She lived in the largest house in Marvel, across from the big store and the post office near the railroad. The train came really close to her house. Most of the coal in the mines was shipped out on the railroad cars every day. The company would leave empty railroad cars to be put under the tipple every day until they were loaded full. Sam Stano was releasing the brake on one of the railroad cars one day in Piper, and the car got loose. He was running down the track, telling everyone to get out of the way. Finally, that railcar hit another one that was being loaded, and it stopped. Sometimes if we didn't have much yard work to do, we would bring the coal and firewood into her house. She had carpet on her floors and told us to make sure our shoes were cleaned off before we came in. Sometimes our shoes wouldn't be clean enough, and we would leave tracks on her carpet. She would give us baking soda and tell us to clean the track off the carpet. If there wasn't much work to do outside, sometimes she would let us help her bake a cake. She would make us completely clean the pan to put the icing on the cake. She didn't waste anything. After we helped her bake the cake, she would pay us for helping and then give us the cake.

Firewood

The mines shut down, and the people didn't have much food or money, so the county sent in commodities to help out until they could find work somewhere else. Marvel had two mines going at one time, and they both shut down. One incident happened before the mines closed where a Black man was running around with his friend's wife. His friend found out and decided that he was going to shoot him when he came out of the mine one afternoon. Another man found out about this plan, went into the mine, and told the first man what was going to happen when he came out of the mine. He handed him a pistol in case he needed it. When he came out, the two men involved with the same woman had a gun battle, and one of them was killed. I don't remember which man died. There was a cement wall outside of the mine, and one of the bullets hit that wall.

Marvel mine: scene of the shooting incident

The store and post office closed at 5:00 p.m., which left us with very little to do at night, except go to church. Sometimes a few Black people would come to our church, and we were always glad to welcome them in. They were good people. We would walk our girlfriends home, holding hands at times. A girl by the name of Dot Clark began to like me a lot, but I was never serious about her. Sometimes we would get on the bus in West Blocton and just stare at each other's faces until we got to Marvel for about fifteen miles. We were just trying to see who could outstare the other person. That was sort of stupid, but sometimes we did stupid things. One day, we were coming from West Blocton on the school bus, and there was a real steep hill that we had to go down before we went across the Big Cahaba River. The bridge was just one-way. If two cars approached from different ends, one car would have to let the other cross the bridge before they could cross. Back then they would let high school students drive the school busses, and one of our teacher's sons was driving ours. One afternoon at the top of the hill before going down the steep hill to the bridge, the brakes went out on the bus. The young driver did some quick thinking and took the bus over to a dirt bank until it stopped. If he had gone down the hill, we would have been going really fast, and if there was another car coming across the bridge, there would have been a terrible wreck. It probably would have killed some of us, so his quick thinking damaged the bus but probably saved our lives.

Big Cahaba bridge

When we lived in Marvel, some of us boys had BB guns, and we would go bird hunting. A box of BBs only cost a nickel, so we would kill every bird, no matter what kind it was. A lady would give us a nickel for each bird because she ate them. We had some good friends that lived four houses above us on the same side of the road named Fendley. They had four children close to our ages: Nettie Jo, Edward Lee, Bruce, and Donna. I liked Nettie Jo and dated her a few times when I came home on leave from the air force. I was fortunate that she would date me because I got her and Faye Fulman in trouble when we were in high school. We were going home on our school bus one day, and I got their lipstick and marked the back seat of the bus pretty bad. The bus driver reported it to the principal, Mr. Zeanah.

We had to go to the office, and I lied, telling him that Nettie Jo and Faye did it, and he believed me. He made both of them clean all the lipstick off the back of the seat. Nettie Jo and Faye would not talk to me for a long time after, but eventually they did. Before we had BB guns, we would use slingshots and rocks to kill the birds. One day, two birds were flying in the air about thirty feet apart. I shot at the bird in front, and instead of hitting that one, I hit the bird that was thirty feet behind it. Another time, I shot at a blue jay in a tree, missed, hit another one, and killed it.

Church at Marvel

Before I went into the air force, Bruce Fendley and I were on the side of the road one afternoon. And Bruce put a .22-caliber rifle shell on the ground, put the BB gun next to it, and shot, which made the .22-caliber round go off. Something ricocheted back and hit Bruce in the leg. He was bleeding a little but wouldn't go tell his mother. So I went and told her because I didn't know how bad it was.

Coal cars in Marvel

Later, we found out that the bullet didn't hit him; part of the shell did. Mrs. Fendley was a real nice Christian woman. We had some other good friends on that road, Mr. and Mrs. Opel and Aubrey Woods. They had three children named Jimmy, Jerry, and Guyen. We have a family picture that we took in the early fifties on our front porch at the house in Marvel and didn't realize until later that Jerry was in the background. We had a certain boy in Marvel that was mischievous and got into trouble sometimes. There was a ladder on the community water tank that you could climb to the top. This boy told us that he climbed the ladder and did a number two in our water tank. The tank had a big hole right on top so rainwater could go into it. He probably did that, but we never mentioned it to anyone because he probably would have been in serious trouble. We had a little train, called a dinky, just below the water tank that would pull little mining cars up and down the track. I had a chance after the mines shut down to buy a house near the dinky track for $1,100 for $25 per month, but I didn't buy it. I wish I had a lot of times. I remember seeing the first diesel train come to Marvel, and I didn't like that. I enjoyed watching the fireman throw the coal and seeing the smoke bellowing out of the smokestack in the old steam engines.

Piper water tank

We had some good friends on Broadway named Bobby and Pleze Allen. We would go up to their house and play dominoes. Pleze had to look at his dominoes sort of sideways because there was something wrong with his eyesight. He loved playing dominoes, and he was good at it. There was another Allen family, but I don't know if they were kin to Bobby and Pleze or not.

The other Allen family had children named Ruth, Jean, Paul, Oneata, Mary, and Jack. Mr. Allen had a small truck with a bed built onto it, and he let Paul drive it all the time. Paul was a good mechanic. If someone had automobile problems, they would get with Paul. And most of the time, he would be able to fix it, unless it was something major. We got a load of people in his truck one day to go swimming at Bulldog Bend, and he wanted me to drive. I was about seventeen years old at the time, so I drove. When we got to the bottom of Sand Pit Road and were going around the curve—there was a place in the dirt road where it had washed out—I was going a bit too fast when I hit the washed-out part and almost flipped the truck over. I had six or seven people in the back of the truck, and I was young and not going as slow as I should have. If we had turned over, it probably would have killed someone.

When we finished the sixth grade, we transferred to West Blocton High School for seventh through twelfth grade. We got either an S (satisfactory) or U (unsatisfactory) grades on our report cards in grammar school all the way through sixth grade. Once we got to high school, our grade system changed from S or U to A, B, C, D, or F. Back then, the schools used the same books every year. If we finished second grade, we could sell our books to someone else who was going into the second grade. It was the same way in high school.

I always wanted a guitar to play when I was young, but I couldn't get one. When I started high school in West Blocton, they were getting a band started. The band leader let me try out a horn and showed me how to blow into it. He said it would cost $113, but my daddy said he couldn't afford it, so I never played in the band. My parents didn't get interested in school like we did. They really didn't seem to care if we made an A or an F. If we failed a subject, we would have to take it over again. I failed science in the seventh grade, but no one caught it, and I never mentioned it. I was supposed to take science over again when I got to eighth grade. When I was in the tenth grade, I told our principal, Mr. Zeanah about it, and he got mad about it. He wanted to know why I never took science over, but he just let it go and never made me retake it. I was glad because I hated science. I liked history the best. We had a good history teacher named Mrs. Keys who would give us a test and walk out of the room. When the teacher wasn't in the room, we would shoot spitballs and make paper airplanes to sail to one another. She would come back in and ask, "Who cheated?" Some students would be truthful and raise their hands, but I would cheat and not raise my hand. I was very bashful in school. If a teacher asked me a question, even though I knew the answer, I would say, "I don't know," just to keep from talking. There were only three boys in the twelfth grade that we knew who drank a little. Mrs. Keys warned them that they would eventually get into trouble. Sure enough, one of them went to Mississippi one day, stole a policeman's car, and tied him to a tree.

He didn't hurt the policeman, but I don't know what happened to him after that. That is when General Eisenhower was running for president. Mrs. Keys said Eisenhower was a great general, but he would not make a great president, and she was right. I was in the air force in 1955 and sent to Tripoli, Libya, in North Africa, and our officers told us not to get put in jail there because Eisenhower made an agreement that the US government would not intervene. I mostly just went to school to look at girls and throw horseshoes, in that order. But later in life, that came back to haunt me. I should have studied more. If I made a D, that was as good as an A to me. I still have my tenth-grade report card, and it is straight Ds all the way down. The only As that I made were in conduct and physical education. That was terrible. When I got out in the real world, I realized that I couldn't cheat anymore. Going from grammar school to the high school in West Blocton was like going from high school to college. It was a big change. I never took my books home, and my parents didn't push education, so I stayed on the D honor roll. My goal back then was just to finish high school.

School Days
1942 - 43

School Days
1945 - 1946

SCHOOL DAYS
1953 - 1954

We had two study room classes a day, and if I didn't get my homework assignments, I would just get it from someone and copy theirs. I didn't realize at the time that would come back to haunt me. We had the largest homeroom when I was in high school. There were eighty students, and we had to use two rooms. At that time, there was only about five hundred students, across seventh through twelfth grade, in West Blocton High School. I never got a whipping in grammar school or high school because I knew it would be double when I got home. I wasn't interested in making good grade. I just went to school to have a good time. I enjoyed doing things, like throwing balls against the auditorium walls or shooting basketball on the half court. I had just enough strength to shoot from the half court to the basket, and I could ring it most of the time. I never tried out for the basketball team though. I was only 5 feet 3 inches and 117 pounds when I finished high school, and that wasn't tall enough to play basketball. Sometimes, if it was raining, we would have our physical education class inside the auditorium. Our teacher would tell the girls to grab a boy and start dancing to some music. I was very bashful and didn't want to dance, but our teacher would make us. My brother Franklin was a good dancer. I used to love to watch him dance. He was rated the number 3 best dancer in Birmingham.

Sherry Moore Franks

Sherry Moore, Betty Jean Province, and me would sit close to one another and copy off one another's papers. And we did good to just get a passing grade. Sherry failed a grade so that she could be with her boyfriend, Bobby Jo Franks. Later on in the years, they got married. Bobby Jo went to college and became a football coach, but he passed away at the age of forty-one due to a heart attack. They had three children: Donna, Diane, and Tony.

Franklin and James took school more seriously than I did. James stayed on the A and B honor roll in high school. They say he was a great football player in high school, but I never got to watch him because I had already joined the air force. The principal and Coach Higgonbottom said he was the best end that the school ever had. Franklin and James both went to the University of Alabama for a year and a half. James quit school and married Willa Dean Jordan and had three children, Renee, Lisa, and Greg. Franklin finished at Montevallo College. He married Beaula Collins, who finished school at Montevallo as well. They had two children, Frankie and Kareen. Bennie Ray and I weren't thinking about college. Bennie Ray went to work in the coal mines and I went into the air force. Billy couldn't work due to his disability. Bennie Ray married Linda Pickett and they had three children, Keith, Crystal, and Ray. I married Nettie Jo Moore. We had five children. Apart from the four mentioned earlier, our first child, Kathy Jean, was stillborn.

CHAPTER 2

MILITARY SERVICE

I graduated from West Blocton High School in 1954. I tried to find a job, but it was a lot like it was in 2012, pretty hard to find. In 2012, I saw a news report saying that there were twenty-four million people out of work. My cousin, Glover Lovejoy, was also out of work at the same time. Glover and I went over to the Westinghouse plant between Montevallo and Calera, to no avail. It was the same old story, not hiring. The receptionist said that I looked about fourteen years old. I did look young, and I wasn't shaving yet, but I was eighteen at the time. We went up the road to a rock quarry and got the same story again. Glover needed a job bad because he was married and he and his wife, Emma Lee, had three children. Their children were Phyllis, who was about my age, and Mitchie and Jimmy who were the two youngest. Phyllis was dating Ira Frederick at the time, and they got married later on. Mitchie was dating Ira's friend, Pete Lucas, and they got married later on as well. Jimmy married a lady by the name of Wanda Langston. I didn't know Wanda back then, but I found out later that I worked with her father, Bill Langston, at O'Neal Steel. I decided that I would go to Tuscaloosa the next day to find work. I don't know why because I didn't really know anything about Tuscaloosa. I went to the bank even though I had no knowledge of banking. The banker said he would hire me as a runner for $1.25 an hour, but I would have to wear a suit every day. That was out of the question because I didn't have a suit, and I sure didn't want to wear one every day, so I didn't go back for that job.

I decided that I would join the air force. My mother begged me not to join. She said she would buy me a new watch if I changed my mind, but I didn't let her talk me out of it. It was the best decision that I have ever made, and it changed me from a boy into a man in a hurry. I was like a mosquito lost in the jungle because I had never been farther than a hundred miles from home in my life up to that point, and that was to Decatur, Alabama. We got ready to go to Bessemer in our 1940 Chevrolet to be sworn in. I was the driver. My mother was in the front seat with me. My father and Billy were in the back seat. My father was drunk in the back seat and had put a pint of whiskey under the front seat earlier. He asked me to get it out from under the seat and give it to him so that he could take one drink. It was understood that he would take one drink and give the bottle back to me. I told him, "Okay, one swallow and then I want it back." But he decided that he wouldn't give the bottle back to me. That just broke my heart and made me very angry because he didn't keep his word. I got out of the car in front of the air force recruiting office at Bessemer and told him that he would never see me again. I was so tired of him drinking every day and treating my mother the way he did.

I was going away from home for the first time in my life. I was so small and a little scared because I didn't have anyone with me and I didn't know anyone. As I was going upstairs in the recruiting office to be sworn in, I didn't know my father was behind me. He saw me crying a little, and I guess that got to him. When my mother got back home, she poured two and a half gallons of whiskey down the drain and told my father that I did it. He told her that he didn't blame me and quit drinking cold turkey that day. He was sober for the rest of his life. We had tried every way we could think of to stop him from drinking in the past, and nothing else worked. I guess it was a blessing the way it happened.

That same day, several other boys and I left Bessemer on a bus headed to Montgomery, Alabama. We got our shots and then went on to San Antonio, Texas, for thirteen weeks for basic training and were issued our air force uniforms. We were to stay one night in Montgomery before getting on a train to San Antonio. There was a man that had gotten out of the air force after one term, but he was going back in. He made it to sergeant in his first term but had been busted down to airman first class (A1C) because of his smart mouth. He started arguing with the sergeant in charge right away, being a smart aleck. The sergeant then said for us to go to sleep because we were going to ship out the next day by rail. Some of the boys got rowdy and started throwing pillows and acting up. The sergeant made all of us get out of bed at 2:30 a.m. to pick cigarette butts up off the ground for about an hour. The next day, we got on the train to go to San Antonio. It took us about a day and a half to get there. It was an interesting trip. We could go from car to car, and we were seeing the backsides of towns rather than the front. During the day, there would be some people, mostly girls, at the railroad crossing waving at us. Some of the city boys jumped off the train when it was going slow to get to the pretty girls. The air force police came on the train and found out that they went absent without leave (AWOL). The police went back to get the boys, so they were in trouble from the start before we even got to basic training. I never did hear what happened to those city boys, but I never saw them again. We got to Lackland Air Force Base where we were to be issued our clothes, but my dumb butt didn't know what size I wore because my mother always took care of that. The people issuing the clothes did a great job at guessing my size since I had no idea what it was. From that point, I knew I had to change from a dependent boy who didn't think for myself to a responsible man that had to think for myself. I was all by myself in a big world that I knew nothing about. I was dumb to the real world. We were born in the woods, and we stayed in the woods. We knew nothing about life outside of the woods. There was a world of difference between the city boys and the country boys. The Northern boys seemed to be more educated and knew more about the world, but I think we had a better life just being plain and simple country boys. I talked to one boy that was eighteen years old, and he said he had never seen a real cow before.

I had water in my knees when I was in the twelfth grade. I went to see Dr. Stinson, and he told me to run a lot and it would work itself out. I would run about thirty yards, and it would really hurt.

I didn't think Dr. Stinson knew what he was talking about. When I got to basic training, they didn't want you to talk or complain; they just wanted you to train. The first thing they would tell you is "I'm not your mother, and I'm not your daddy." We started marching and kneeling down a lot, and that nearly killed me, but I didn't dare say anything or complain. Sure enough, the pain eventually went away, and I never had any trouble with my knees anymore. I guess Dr. Stinson knew what he was talking about all along.

I started writing to my mother; my girlfriend, Tommie Ruth Mowery; and Aunt Myrtle and Uncle Morgan every day. I wrote to them every day for four years while I was in the air force just to let them know what I was doing each day. I would give all the details and even tell what I ate that day. We didn't have much else to do, except sit around and wish we were back home. I missed seeing everyone and had a lot of lonesome days. I started reading my Bible every day while I was in the air force. I averaged about one and a half chapters a day and read it from the front cover to the back cover. I finished reading the Bible when I was on the Atlantic Ocean coming back to the States from Tripoli, Libya. I had been over there for eighteen months. I also read a lot of material written by Billy Graham and Oral Roberts.

There were a lot of things that I didn't like to eat when I went into the air force. I didn't like sweet milk, but I did like chocolate milk. I didn't care for turnip greens or tomatoes. The cooks in the air force put everything on your plate, whether you liked it or not, and the plate had to be cleaned when we were finished eating. If they gave us sweet milk, we had to drink it. After a few times, I loved drinking sweet milk. I guess that is why I went up in height and gained thirty-five pounds. I had a balance diet. I gained thirty-five pounds just in basic training. I was 5 feet 3 inches and 117 pounds going into the air force. And by the time I got out, I was 5 feet, 11.5 inches tall and 165 pounds. I had grown 8.5 inches after four years and after the age of eighteen, which is unusual. Another man told me that the same thing happened to him. He grew 8 inches taller. I had to be issued more clothes because the original uniforms didn't fit anymore. When I went into the air force, I had a baby face and no hair on my legs or face. I didn't even have to shave before I went into the air force. The sergeant asked me one day if I had shaved. And I said, "No, sir." He said, "Tomorrow, you start shaving." I said, "Yes, sir!" even though there was nothing to shave, except for peach fuzz.

It was really hot in July and August during basic training. We had to do a lot of marching every day because there was a competition between the other platoons on Saturdays to see who was the best. I thought I was really good. The training instructor (TI) sergeant would yell, "LEFT...RIGHT...LEFT...RIGHT...LEFT FACE... LEFT FACE!" One day, I turned right like a right-face call when he was yelling left face. I had half the men following me the wrong way while the other half was going the right way. The TI came to me and started screaming in my face. There was spit flying everywhere, and I was scared to death. That taught me to pay more attention to what he said from then on.

We had to get up early for Reveille every morning. When the sergeant yelled, "GET UP!" everyone bounced out of bed in a hurry. We got dressed and were out in the road, ready to march in just a few minutes to go to breakfast. After we finished basic training, we didn't have to get up for Reveille anymore.

We had to take an aptitude test in basic training to see what we were qualified to do. It seemed like everyone wanted to be an auto mechanic, but that field was full. We really didn't have a choice for what we wanted to do like they do now. Whatever we did best at on the test is what they would train us for. I said, "Oh Lord, here I am in trouble again!" They would give everyone around us a different version of the test, and I was used to copying off someone else's paper in high school. Now everyone around me had a different test, and I was on my own. I couldn't count on anyone else. They gave us an international Morse code test, and I did pretty well on it because I had taken typing in the twelfth grade and enjoyed it. They told me that I would be going to school for international Morse code for seven months in Biloxi, Mississippi, and I liked that because it was close to home. We went into the air force making $63 a month. We weren't paid much like they are now. When we finished basic training, we had to march up and salute three officers and a chaplain to get our last basic training check and be promoted to an A1C. That meant we were getting our first stripes and a raise in pay. We were all real nervous. We had to march in, take a right face, march up to the table, and salute the three officers. They would have us scared to death and made us hard-hearted and ready for battle, if need be. My turn came, and boy, oh, boy, was I nervous. I marched in, turned right for the right face, marched up to the table, and saluted. My hand would not straighten out level like most people because my knuckles would stick up when I straightened my fingers out. One of the officers said, "Straighten that hand out!" And my hand started trembling. I couldn't stop it; I was so nervous. He said, "What are you doing? Looking for a place to shit?" Then I was really scared and trembling. The chaplain got up and got my hand (if my knuckles went down, my fingers would go up and vice versa). The chaplain said, "Sir, his hands are deformed." I started to do an about-face to turn around to leave, but I was so nervous that I got my feet tangled up. The officer said, "What's wrong? Your feet deformed too?" But I got my stripe and raise anyway.

We left San Antonio, and my next stop was Biloxi, Mississippi, to learn international Morse code for eight hours a day, five days a week, for seven months. We were going through Houston, Texas, and one of the boys hollered at this woman, asking her if "it" was good. I was so dumb that I didn't realize until years later what he meant. The woman was pregnant. Something else I remember seeing in Houston was a woman walking down the street with a pint bottle in her hand, staggering and drunk. I was wondering why the police didn't arrest her, but maybe the police just didn't see her. After we got to Biloxi and settled down in our barracks, I decided to call a friend of mine in Birmingham. I was eighteen years old and had never talked on a phone in my life. I went to what we called a dayroom where everyone congregated and talked. I didn't realize that I had to get a phone where there wasn't any noise since that was the first time that I used a phone. I got aggravated because there was so much noise that I couldn't hear her talk. So I told her that I was just going to hang up and write to her, so I did just that.

Airman First Class Bobby Whatley, United States Air Force

I enjoyed going to school to learn Morse code, although the noise that you hear in while you are racing to see how many words you can send or receive in a minute nearly drove some of us half crazy. People that didn't like it were ready to commit suicide one way or another. One man climbed up on a water tower and was ready to jump to his death, but they talked him out of it. A lot of fights broke out while I was there because of disagreements about the civil war. A few of the Northern boys who were holding a grudge would pick a fight with a Southerner. Every time, the Southerner would whip the Northerner's butt. One time, somebody really beat one of the Northern boys so bad he could just barely see out of one eye. There was a big investigation over that incident, and our company commander nearly lost his job over it. We were glad they kept him there because he was a good person and a good commander. The Northern boys would talk about going to Mardi Gras in New Orleans. I had never even heard of Mardi Gras even though I grew up pretty close to

New Orleans. I didn't know where it was, and I was fifty-seven years old before I realized how close we were to New Orleans.

I was sending my money home to help my parents. I kept just enough to get by and see all the movies in the air base theater. It only cost $0.25 to see a movie on base back then. I enjoyed learning Morse code. There are one to five dits or dahs to make one number or letter. For example, an A is dit and dah. We had different ways of learning it. B is dah, dit, dit, and dit, sounded like "My, this is it." The number 2 is dah, dah, dit, and dit, sounded like "Grandpa did it." J is dit, dah, dah, and dah, sounded like "The darned old jay." C is dah, dit, dah, and dit, sounded like "Daddy got it." Out of the thirty people in our class, three others and I graduated at the top of the class, passing thirty words per minute receiving and eighteen words per minute sending Morse code. You either got a zero or a one hundred on a test. If you missed one character, you would get a zero. If you didn't miss a single character, you would get a hundred. I was in school one day and got really sick to my stomach. We had eaten scallops for dinner, and I thought that they tasted kind of peculiar. I asked my teacher if I could leave to go to the doctor. He said yes, but he wouldn't take me. I had to walk about two miles, all bent over. When I got to the doctor's office, there was about five other people in there for the same thing. One man was hurting so bad that they had to put him on a table to be rolled out. I told the doctor that the scallops we had eaten tasted bad. He looked at me like I was crazy, but later he found out that was the cause of our sickness. We had food poisoning. I couldn't look at fish for about five years after that escapade.

Sometimes we had marching drills on Saturdays, but the cadence caller was a friend of mine. He would put down that I was marching, but I was really on my way back home for the weekend. About four or five of us would go home for the weekends without anyone knowing where we were. It is a wonder that we didn't get killed going ninety to one hundred miles per hour on the way back home. We had one driver that would scare me to death. He would play chicken, driving on the wrong side of the road, and would jerk the car over to one side at the last minute. If the driver of the other car had jerked his car the same direction, we would have hit head-on. We could have easily been killed or killed someone else, but that's stupid smart-aleck young people. We were going ninety miles per hour one time and got pulled over by a policeman. One boy got smart with the policeman, and we told him to shut up before he put us all in jail. That's what the policeman told us he would do if the boy smarted off at him again. The policeman took us to a justice of the peace and charged us $100. That was a lot of money in 1954. They probably split the money between them because he never wrote us a ticket. We would always make it back to the base on Sunday night. We couldn't go through the guard gate because we weren't supposed to be out. The one driving the car was allowed to go through the gate because he had a sticker on his car that let him go in or out of the base anytime. The rest of us would have to climb over an eight-foot-tall fence below the guard shack to get back on base. I remember one time this chubby boy couldn't climb the fence. I had to help him get over, and then I climbed over after him. I didn't realize that I had cut my hand until I got back to my barracks. I was so scared of getting caught.

We had old-time barracks to live in with stalls for each one of us in a big open bay. If we put our shoes next to our beds, sometimes people would steal them. Other times you might go to get into your bed and find out that someone had short-sheeted you. "Short-sheeting" is when someone would fold your sheet back halfway. We had this one little guy in our barracks that was always wanting to wrestle me. One day, I accommodated him. I was pretty strong for my size. We got to wrestling in our barracks, dragging our feet with our shoes on, and we left marks all over the floor. Neither one of us won and finally called it a tie, but he had to clean all the marks up. I found out later that he was a wrestler in his high school. I had him around the neck, and he never could get out. He was a good friend of mine. I had a lot of good friends in the air force. Most of them were from Ohio and Pennsylvania. I hate to say it, but the Northern boys were more educated than the Southern boys as a whole. One area where they weren't so smart is when five Northern boys robbed an old White man down on the beach in Biloxi. They got $2 off the old man, and they got caught. One of those boys was just a trouble-maker. He would get two or three of his buddies to go beat up one person. He would spend all his money and then call his grandparents, and they would send him more. He got five years, and the other four boys got five years or less for robbing the old man, and they were all given dishonorable discharges.

We had United Service Organizations shows come to our base to entertain the troops. We had Bob Hope and some others, and one night, a guy was coming to hypnotize people. I asked my platoon leader if I could go watch the hypnosis show. The platoon leader was talking in a room with three of his buddies and having a good time, and he told me no. He said we were on restriction because someone had done something wrong and he was taking it out on all of us because he had the authority to do so. I slipped off and saw the show anyways and didn't get caught. It was a good show.

We finished the international Morse code school, and we all got our assignments for the duty station we were going to next, after we took thirty days of leave. While I was on leave and visiting home, I went to see my cousins Phyllis and Mitchie Lovejoy in Wilton, Alabama. They introduced me to Tommie Ruth Mowery. She was just fourteen years old at the time, and I was eighteen. Every once in a while, we would both date other people, but I didn't care for anyone else at that time like I did for her. I guess it was just a case of lonesomeness and being apart. She called my feelings "infatuation," but I knew I loved her. She was so beautiful and also a very good girl. I dated her nearly every night while I was home on leave. My mother said that I only stayed with her three out of the thirty days that I was home at nighttime. After my leave ended, I shipped off to my next duty station. I wrote to her every day, and I missed her so much. She started winning beauty contests, and she was a dedicated, churchgoing girl.

While I was home on my leave, my daddy and I went to Little Cahaba River to see if we could find some redhorse fish. I spotted some across the river and showed him. He caught 103 out of that redhorse bed that week.

Of all the places that the air force could have sent me, they decided on Tripoli, Libya, in North Africa. Everyone told us that was the worst place in the world that we could go, apart from Saudi

Arabia. I had to get on a plane in Birmingham to go to New Jersey for two weeks before going overseas. I got on a big six-motor plane (not a jet), and it was the first time that I had been on a plane in my life. After we were in the air, I could see fire coming from the motor onto the wing, and that sort of scared me. So I asked the lady sitting next to me, "Is that normal?" And she said yes and that it was nothing for me to worry about. She probably thought I was pretty dumb since I was in my air force uniform but didn't know anything about planes. We made a stop in Washington, DC, for some reason. I didn't know if we were allowed to get off or if we were supposed to sit still. I got off just to walk around in the terminal. I nearly got left behind, and I would have been in trouble if I had. As luck would have it, I just happened to see the pilot going toward the gate, and I got my butt back on the plane in a hurry.

When we got to the base in New Jersey, we had to get extra shots before going overseas to help us from getting diseases that we weren't exposed to in the States. New York City was just over the state line from us, so this alcoholic friend of mine wanted to go to the city one night before we shipped off to Africa the next morning. I told him that I would be glad to. First, we decided to go into this high-class restaurant where these petite people went with their fancy spoons, forks, and napkins. They were all about etiquette, so we decided that we were going to show our ignorance by ordering chicken, eating with our fingers, and being really messy. Everyone was looking at us like we were fools, and I guess we were looking back on it, so we got up and walked out laughing and being stupid.

We then went to a nightclub on Broadway. As we were standing outside the club, this girl came up to me and wanted me to go with her. She was a street girl, and I guess she saw how innocent looking I was. I told her that I had to stay with my buddy and, if she took me two blocks away, that I would be lost because I knew nothing about big cities. A navy guy told her that he would go with her, and she told him, "I don't want you." We then went into the nightclub, and three more women picked us up. One of them bought me a beer. I told her, "I don't drink," and I left it on the bar. All three of the women were about thirty-five years old, and I thought that was old at the time since I was only nineteen. The lady that I was with said she was married to a sergeant and had a seventeen-year-old daughter. My buddy was now drunk, and the three women wanted us to walk down Broadway at 2:30 a.m. We were shipping out the next morning at nine thirty. The lady asked if I would put her little fur around her neck. I said sure, and I put the fur around her neck. Then she asked if I would walk her down Broadway, and naturally, I said yes. As we were walking down Broadway, she took my hand and put it on her breast. I looked back, and my buddy was kissing the woman that he was with, and they were both pretty drunk by then. My buddy had lost his bus ticket and wet his pants. They all piled in a taxi, and I told them I wasn't going anywhere in a taxi, so they all got back out. The woman I was with asked if I was going to take her to another bar, and I told her, "I guess not. I am getting on the bus and going back to the base." I told my buddy that I was gone, and he said okay. The next morning, he got to the base thirty minutes before we shipped out overseas. He said four more women had picked him up, but he was $40 short. They brought him back to the base. He was an air force policeman. I heard after we were overseas that he got busted down to "slick sleeve" with no stripes, probably from drinking.

We got on our ship in New York and passed by the Statue of Liberty. Once we left New York, it was eight days before we saw land again. That was the Azores, and even though we didn't stop there, I was just glad to see land again. It was going to take us eighteen days to get to Tripoli, Libya. There was this really pretty red-haired woman on the ship with us that was on her way to see her officer husband in Turkey, and she was caught in bed with some of the soldiers. All the soldiers were put in the brig, like a jail on the ship, and they called the woman's husband to tell him that she would be going back to the States. They told me to guard her room on the ship and not to go into the room for any reason. She asked me to come into her room because she said the heater was acting up. I could hear it making a noise, but I said, "I'm sorry, ma'am, I can't come in there." So I don't know what happened after that.

We were in a couple of bad storms. We were on a nine-hundred-foot ship, but the rough seas threw us around like it was a toy boat. We were all given certain responsibilities. Mine was cutting butter into small pieces in the kitchen. After you cut butter and put all the Irish potatoes in the peeling machine all night, you are ready for bed. I was sick of smelling like butter. To keep from getting seasick in the rough seas, we had to eat apples or cookies to keep our stomachs full. Even a navy man got sick, and he was supposed to be used to the rough seas.

The civilians were on the upper floors, and the soldiers were on the lower decks, sleeping down under the waterline. That ship would creek and crack like it was going to come apart. If you tried to climb the stairs in the rough seas, about the time you would take a step up, the ship would rock. And if you weren't careful, you would skin your shins. When we were out on the deck crossing the sea, I thought I saw baby whales swimming along the sides of the ship. The navy men told us that they weren't whales but huge sharks.

We finally got to Tripoli after eighteen days on the ship. We got on a bus that took us to the air base. There was a stink in the air. I mean it smelled bad all day long, seven days a week, for the entire year and a half that I was there. I guess they were just used to the smell over there. I didn't see any Black people when I was in North Africa. It was an all-Arab country. I didn't care too much for Alabama until I got over to Libya. Since then I love Alabama. I said, "Get me back to Alabama." We sometimes don't appreciate what we have, but we still have the best country in the world.

A couple of times, there were swarms of locusts in the sky of Tripoli. There were so many millions of these locusts that the sky would be black. They would come down and hit our car, and they would be all over the road and desert. We would run over them by the thousands with our car. We were told that pesticides are put out to kill the locusts, but they lay their eggs in the sand.

One day that I was over there, the heat factor was 147 degrees Fahrenheit. If we walked out of the barracks in the middle of the day, we would have to put our hands across our face and spread our fingers until our eyes could adjust to the brightness. Otherwise, we would be blinded by the sun and the glare from the desert. There would be huge piles of salt, the length of a football field and about twenty feet high, on the air base that were pulled out of the Mediterranean Sea. The Arab people wore a lot of clothes. You couldn't see anything but heels and maybe one eye on some of the women. If you went downtown and saw a woman on the corner with her veil pulled open, it meant she was a prostitute. When they pulled their veil down, it meant they wanted you to circle the block, and then they would hop into your car and go with you. Not all the Arab women wore the full coverings. My roommate was from South Carolina and had an Arab girlfriend that wore Western clothes. He had his motorcycle over there, and he could ride it really well. The girl thought that he was going to bring her back to the States, but he didn't.

Two boys and I rented bicycles to ride. We were stupid enough to ride out into the desert one day. After a while, all the sand dunes look alike, so naturally we got lost. Some of the Arab people were hiding out in the desert, thinking World War II was still going. Back then, in the fifties, they told us two-thirds of the Arab people were either uneducated or had some kind of disease. All wars seemed to go through Tripoli one way or another. Some of the women would poke one of the eyes out of their newborn babies or punch a hole about a quarter of an inch through the front of the baby's head to keep them from having to go to war when they were grown. After being lost all day, we just happened to come out of the desert to another American installation that we didn't even know was there. We had ridden about forty miles from our base. They made us some milkshakes and took us back home. We were very fortunate. Some of the mean Arab people could have killed us out in the desert, and no one would have ever known it. Even though it was peacetime while I was there, we were on alert because we were about to go to war over the Suez Canal.

Tripoli, Libya, 1955

We had a little problem over there one time when we couldn't get anything to eat every day but beef stew. The officers across the base were eating steaks. So we decided to strike, even though we were in the air force and not allowed to strike. We told them we weren't working until they got us some decent food. One boy lost thirty-five pounds. He would go on shift and go to sleep instead of typing Morse code. The officers would see him sleeping, but they wouldn't say anything because they knew the situation. They finally got us some better food, and then we started caring about the work again.

We played a lot of cards. One game that just about every person in the service played was double pinochle. We also played battleship on paper, and now that game has been commercialized. I had never heard of pizza in my life until I got to Africa, but the town boys knew all about it and would bring pizza into work. I had never seen a bowling alley until I got to North Africa, but we had one on our base. A Northern boy asked if I wanted to bowl on his team. I told him I would try. My first two games, I bowled a 135 and a 137, but I don't remember what my third game was. We went on to win our league by one pin. The Northern boy was a good bowler, and to win the trophy, he had to strike out in the tenth frame, and he did just that. We were playing battleship at work one night, and the boys wanted me to smoke a cigar. I didn't smoke myself. I smoked that cigar just huffing and puffing but not inhaling because I couldn't inhale without feeling like I was being strangled. They kept giving me one cigar after another. We were on the midnight shift, and the next morning, I could see green.

We would take chances on a football raffle every week. Back then I kept up with who was the best on all the teams. One time, I won the raffle, and the winner was supposed to go to this sergeant's house for supper. I had my platoon sergeant with me. The sergeant's wife gave me a glass of hot tea. I didn't like hot tea, but she kept coming around and filling my glass up. I was bashful and didn't want to tell her that I had had enough. I was nearly sick when I left there. I didn't ever want hot tea again without any ice in it.

I had a good time riding camels while I was in Africa. I had to be careful because the camels would bite you if you didn't watch out. In 1955, gasoline in Tripoli was $2.85 per gallon. It was only $0.18 a gallon in the States. Just about everyone over there had bicycles or motor scooters, or they just walked. Some had cows that would pull two-wheeled carts. They would not kill cows there because cows were sacred to them. Eating pork was against their religion, and they claimed that over one million people died from eating pork at one time. They probably really died from food poisoning. They had trading places out in the open, called bazaars, and they would have meat hanging down from the ceilings, out in the open with flies swarming around and on the meat. They would eat it anyway. They had outside toilets along the roadside. You could see a person's legs or head if you rode by on the street. Any time we walked down the streets, we would see eight to ten men on the side of the road cooking strong tea or coffee in a tin can. If we walked down the streets in town to buy something from the merchants, some of the lower-class Arabs would come up to us and stick their hands in our pockets or try to take our watches off our arms. We weren't allowed to do anything to them because they knew if any of us got thrown in jail, the US government wouldn't get us out. The store owners would come out to our rescue and run them away from us because they knew we were coming to buy their commodities. I never felt like hurting another human being until I got over there. I could really hurt those thieves and not think anything about it. Just for the reason that they knew they could take advantage of us and they knew we couldn't do anything about it because of certain things that I am not allowed to talk about. I guess you have those kinds of people in every country. Bad people that prey on good, innocent people.

I started pitching softball in 1955 while I was still in Tripoli. I pitched on one to three different ball teams for fifty-three straight years all the way up to 2008. I still pitch once a year in West Blocton on a team that is all fifty years or older. It's called the Old-timers' Game. I was just fooling around, throwing the ball behind my back. Then someone asked me to play in a fast-pitch tournament with them. I played in the tournament, but every pitch was thrown from behind my back. I didn't know how to throw fast-pitch in the front. Later on, I learned how to fast-pitch in front, and when I played, I would throw some in front and some from behind. That way, their timing was off. The best game that I ever pitched was in Birmingham, Alabama. I pitched a two-hit shutout on the Fourth of July. I let two runners get on base in one inning. The men later on went to slow-pitch, and the women went to fast-pitch ball. When we first started playing in the fifties, if someone said "slow-pitch," we would say, "That's a girl's game!" And we would go back home. It changed in the seventies or eighties to men playing slow-pitch and women play-ing fast-pitch. I have a DVD where the news in Mobile came out and did a story on me when I was sixty-nine years old, playing with young people in their twenties. I was the oldest man in Mobile still playing on a ball team. All I could do in high school due to being so little was going out on breaks to throw horseshoes and look at girls. It all paid off eventually. I won a horseshoe trophy in Tripoli in 1955. I put ten straight ringers on, and the man that I beat had nine ringers on top of mine. We were both good, but I went on to beat him.

While I was in North Africa, I fell out with a certain group that was always wanting volunteers to help them or donate something to them. One of the air force officers had a baby that died over there, and he wanted to borrow $1,000 from this organization to send his baby back to the States to be buried, but the organization would not loan him the money. I went to that baby's funeral. They had to bury him in a pine box out in the desert. On another occasion, an airman tried to borrow $300 from the same organization to go to his grandfather's funeral in the States. The same thing happened; they did not help. After that, I decided I would not volunteer to help that group. If they needed volunteers, which they were always asking for, I wouldn't help.

Another sport that I was good at was table tennis or Ping-Pong. I was in a Ping-Pong tournament, but I had to ship out back to the States before I could finish it. I could play Ping-Pong as good as Chinese people. I played an average of thirty games each day for the last two months that I was in the air force, and I only lost twice. I would spot some of the men nineteen points and still beat them twenty-one to nineteen. They wouldn't get a point the entire game. I had a terrific slam on the ball. I would hit the ball hard like it was going to my left, and the opponent would jump in that direction, but the ball would go to the right. I could slam and return slams. I would kid with them and tell them that they weren't any good. A sergeant got mad at me one day, started to throw his paddle at me, and told me he would never play me again. He didn't.

I had never been on a golf course in my life until I was in Tripoli. Two of my good Black friends tried to teach me how to play, but I could just never play golf very well. My friends were pretty good golfers. There were so many palm trees on the golf course that it seemed like I couldn't miss hitting the trees, but it was still a lot of fun.

I think every young man that is physically able should have to serve at least one year in one of our armed services. Just to get them away from mamma and to learn some responsibility. We were playing horseshoes one day in Tripoli after I had already worked my shift, and our sergeant sent a man out to tell me to come back to work because someone didn't show up. I told him that I had already pulled my shift, and then I went back to my barracks and hid in my closet. I told my roommate that if they come looking for me, say he didn't know where I was. Well, they did come looking for me, and he told them he didn't know where I was. The sergeant said that if he sent after anyone else, they had better come or he would bust them. That old sergeant was an alcoholic too.

When I first got to Tripoli, Johnny Cash was there. He left three weeks later and said that he was going back to the States to make him a million dollars. He did just that and more. He went back to the States, got out of the air force, and then got put in jail for some reason. I heard that June Carter had helped him get out. I don't know if she was still married to Carl Jones or divorced at the time, but she later became Johnny Cash's wife.

I went to church every time the doors were open while I was in Tripoli. I read the Bible every day and a lot of stuff from Oral Roberts and Billy Graham. We had a good chaplain, which is the same as a preacher, and he was from Louisiana. I got saved while I was there and baptized in the Mediterranean Sea with several other troops, all by that same Louisiana preacher. We could catch a plane in Tripoli and go to the Holy Land in Jerusalem for $25. Just as I had decided to go, some man raped a girl there, and they cancelled the trips for some reason. I never found out if the man was a service member or not. I never tried to go to Jerusalem again after that. We would get with the Christian missionaries who were trying to teach the Arab people about God. They would give the people simple medications if and when they needed it. The Arab people loved aspirin, and they would tell you anything to get it. One lady told one of the missionaries that she had been pregnant for two years and needed an aspirin. The Arab men and women wouldn't let the missionaries treat them in the same room, not even if they were married. The curtain always had to be pulled.

I led a good, Christian life the best I could while I was in the air force. I stayed away from a lot of the temptations for three years and nine months before I got out. I dreamed one night that I saw Jesus up in the sky, and then he just disappeared behind some clouds. Later, I dreamed that I saw Jesus walking on water and, another time, that I was walking on water. Not many people are fortunate enough to have good dreams like that. Maybe later on, after I pass, it won't just be a dream. After I got out of the air force, I went somewhat astray, but I hope my God will forgive me for all my wrongdoing. He says once saved, always saved, but we have to atone for our sins. No one is perfect, and he will judge us when the time comes.

I went to Benito Mussolini's plantation in Tripoli. Someone was keeping it up real nice, and there were fruit trees all over the plantation. It was a tourist attraction. He had already passed away. I don't remember how or how long before. I spent the worst year and a half of my life in Tripoli. I guess part of it was from being so lonesome and so far from home. I was sure glad to get back to the good ole USA. We had a choice to go back to the States on a plane and get there in twenty-four hours or to take a ship and spend twenty-one days. I took the ship because as a Morse code operator, I had copied down transmissions from planes that had gotten out over the water, had trouble, and had to come back. I didn't want to chance a plane crash after being in that undesirable place for eighteen months. Just as we were shipping out, they caught six of the officers' wives running around with the motorcycle gang on the base. They were going to send those women back to the States also. Back then, people seemed to have higher morals. They wouldn't even allow the radio stations to play the song "Behind Closed Doors" by Charlie Rich because it insinuated something viewed as bad. Back then, if any dirty word, such as "s———t," were said, they would be beeped out because some child might hear it. Boy, things have changed, and for the worse. We might hear or see anything nowadays on the TV or radio whether children are present or not.

I was given orders to go to Michigan, which I was dreading because I hate cold weather. Luckily, they changed my assignment at the last minute and said I was going to Tampa, Florida, for my last year and a half of service. Boy, was I glad. On the way back to the States, we took some bus tours in some of the towns that we went to, and some didn't have signal lights at the intersections. They would have policemen directing traffic, and sometimes the bus driver would just go up and bump the pedestrians crossing the street. Then the pedestrians and the bus driver would start fussing and cursing each other out. We stopped in Rome, Italy, and Athens, Greece. In Athens, we took a tour bus, and they showed us a lot of ruins, including the beds of prostitutes, which back then were made of cement. We also went to Pompei and Naples, Italy. We saw where a volcano had erupted and came down a hill. It looked like a paved road where that lava came down. It covered a man up and just turned him into a statue, standing up. I guess he didn't run or get out of the way fast enough. I wanted to see the Leaning Tower of Pisa, but it was raining at night when we got there, and we were shipping out early the next morning. We went on a tour in Istanbul, Turkey, and saw a cannonball lodged into a castle door. It didn't go all the way through. We also went into a church that was built in either 500 BC or AD 500. It had dirt floors and old chandeliers hanging down. The walls were built out of different kinds of river rock, and if you stared into a certain part of the wall for a few seconds, the form of the devil would appear with horns and a pointed, forked tail. They said it just happened that way. They didn't know how to explain it.

Map of the Mediterranean Sea

When we got back to New York, I was one happy man. I caught a plane to Birmingham with a stopover in Atlanta. I had thirty days of leave before continuing on to Tampa, Florida. My parents were living in a coal mining community called Blue Creek at that time. I landed in Birmingham at about 2:00 a.m. and got a taxi. I asked the taxi driver if he knew where Blue Creek was, and he did, so he took me to my parents' house. I didn't let my mother know what time I would be coming home. I got out of the taxi and knocked on the door, and my mother came to the door with a pistol in her hand because she didn't know who was knocking on her door in the middle of the night. I let her know it was me. I said, "I went to Arab country and stayed safe, and now I come home and nearly get shot by my own mother." Then she laughed and hugged me. Out of the thirty days that I was home, I only stayed at home for three days. I spent most of the time on the road in our 1958 Buick, going on dates with my girlfriend Tommie Ruth. I took her to my house in Blue Creek one day, and we went walking in the woods. I had bought my daddy a .16-gauge pump shotgun straight from the factory while I was in Tripoli, and I don't remember why but I took it with us. I had it behind me, and Tommie Ruth told me to be careful with it. I told her that I had the safety on, and I thought I did, so I pointed it in the woods and pulled the trigger to show her. Guess what? Bam! I didn't have the safety on like I thought.

My daddy was working in the coal mines in Blue Creek. The road ran beside a creek or a river, I don't remember which, but it would be so foggy at night that I could hardly see the road. I just straddled the yellow line in the middle until a car was coming from the other direction.

After my thirty days of leave was over, I went on to Tampa for my last year and a half in the air force. Tampa has some beautiful beaches. There were a lot of divorced women on the beaches having a good time, looking for men with money. I had a friend that had a car, and we always went places together. We met two twins named Rio and Rita, and we would go places with them, just as friends, to have a good time. They were in high school, and we didn't call ourselves dating. They were just friends of ours that showed us different places in Tampa.

We were stationed off base next to a swamp. The snakes and mosquitos were terrible. One man caught twenty-eight rattlesnakes out in front of our barracks in one day. He got three dollars per foot for them as long as they were alive and not dead. That was still a lot of money in 1957. My buddy and I decided that we were going to catch some to make some money. We wrapped our legs with rags and went out into the swamp, but all we caught were two king snakes that were about five feet long. The mosquitos were so bad that if we went from one building to another, we had to run. They would swarm around us like gnats. These were the big brown mosquitos, so they would just cloud around us. They weren't scared like the little black mosquitos. One day, a friend of mine was changing a tire on his car. I went out to him and killed 358 mosquitos in five minutes. That is how bad they were. We could kill two or three at a time with the way they would swarm us. They didn't seem to bother us after nightfall.

The air force base was about a mile away from our post. Some of us would walk that far at night to see a movie on base, then come back. It usually took about twenty minutes to trot two miles. One day, we found a beehive in a five-gallon can. We managed to tie a rope around the can without getting stung. Then we rolled the car windows up and closed the doors, except just enough space for the rope tied to the can, and we went up and down the road, dragging those bees. They were really mad and trying to get into our car.

One day, a friend got sick with pneumonia and had to go to the hospital. I called, making fun of him, and took him a bunch of weeds. I told him that I brought him some flowers. The next day, I was feeling bad and went to the hospital. Guess what! I had pneumonia too. I wasn't allowed to go get my clothes, and they admitted me into the hospital for three days. Making fun of my friend had backfired on me. I wasn't making fun anymore.

We had a school bus off base, where we worked. Two other boys and I had a license to drive the bus so that we could use it to go eat on base. The best food on base was at the hospital. We were all top-secret soldiers, and we had a fence separating our barracks from a branch next to the swamp. Some of us drivers would come back from lunch and drive toward the fence pretty fast, hit the brakes, and slide to see who could stop the closest to the fence without hitting it. I slid a little too far one day and hit the fence. So our captain put up a sign saying, "Don't park close to the fence." He was a good ole guy and turned down a promotion just to stay there with us. If he would have taken the higher rank, he would have been moved to somewhere else. The air force offered us to get out three months early, but if we stayed in, they would promote us and give us more money. I wanted to get out for some reason, so I turned down staff sergeant to get out early. I wanted a family, and I didn't want to have to travel around. But the way my life turned out, I traveled more than I would have had I just stayed in the air force.

I worked in the coal mines for one year. Then I worked in the steel business for thirty-three years at different locations. I had a lawn care business for twenty years and built condominiums in Gulf Shores, Alabama, for three or four months with a friend of mine named Carlton Yarborough who was from Decatur. I ended up working in Birmingham, Alabama; Knoxville, Tennessee; Nashville, Tennessee; and Mobile, Alabama.

To let you know how dumb I was, being raised in the woods, I didn't know what tipping a waitress was. One day, before I got out of the air force, four of us servicepeople went to a restaurant to eat. I saw some money lying on the table where we were, and I thought someone had forgotten their change, so I put it into my pocket. I didn't realize that someone had left a tip for the waitress until one of the boys told me. I had no idea that you were supposed to leave the waitress a tip. That was embarrassing for me.

CHAPTER 3

THE COAL MINES

Before I got out of the air force, I would take a Greyhound bus from Tampa to Piper every weekend for the last five weekends that I was in the service. My father had lost his job in Blue Creek and moved the family back to Piper. I went back to see my girlfriend Tommie Ruth Mowery, and she had the prettiest lips of any girl that I had ever been with. She just lived about fifteen miles from my house in Piper. She was a very beautiful and talented girl. She was from a very poor family, like mine, and her parents were really nice people. I got out of the air force, and Tommie Ruth thought that I had been saving money for us to get married. I told her that I had been sending money home to my family to help my parents because I thought they were having a hard time. After all, they had taken care of me for eighteen years. That led to a bit of an argument, and we broke up after dating for four years. I found out years later that she had finished in the top 10 for a Miss Alabama pageant while she was in college at Montevallo. She finished school and became a teacher.

I met another girl in Aldrich, Alabama, about four or five miles from where Tommie Ruth lived. Her family were avid churchgoing people. I asked the girl if I could have a date with her, and she wanted to. She asked her daddy, and he said she couldn't date me because I had an uncle that killed his wife. That had nothing to do with me, and I don't know why her father was judging me because of my uncle. I didn't even have a use for my uncle after he killed his wife.

My father had decided to open his own coal mine when they moved back to Piper from Blue Creek. He did it just to survive, and that was about all it was, just survival. I moved back in with my parents after I got out of the air force and started working with my daddy in the coal mine for twelve hours a day, six days a week, for a year with no pay. I was drawing unemployment checks anyway. All four of us boys worked every Saturday for my daddy for free, just to help him make a living. Sometimes, I would have to work by myself down in the coal mines when we first started. Later on, he hired a man named Bill, but I can't remember his last name. Bill quit, so then my daddy hired another man by the name of Earl Booth. Earl was a very hard worker. My daddy paid him for each ton that he pulled out of the mine each day at $6 per ton. If Earl worked all day and only produced one ton, he only got $6 for that day. This was in 1959, and it was just survival for my daddy and Earl. Jobs were hard to find for coal miners back then because most of the mines had either shut down or laid people off.

This in Carbide Lamps we used coal mine—If light went out that meant (black drought) no oxygen in air. You had to get out in a hurry or you would fall asleep and die.

We just had carbide lamps to see how to work. If we were working way down in the mine and the flame on the light went out all of a sudden, we had to get out in a hurry. That was called black drought.

That meant there was no oxygen in the air, and if you didn't get out, you would fall asleep and not wake up. You would die. We had one man die in our mine, and my father found three more asleep but got them out in time. We also would play with carbide when we were young. We would get a baking powder can with a lid on it. We would put a nail hole in the bottom of the can. We put three or four pieces of carbide in can, then spit on carbide, and put the lid back on the can. The carbide built gas up. We would strike a match and touch the nail hole on bottom of the can, and that would blow the lid off the can.

All we had to get the coal out was blasting caps and dynamite. We had what we called a hand auger that I would use to drill a hole into the coal a foot deep. Then I would put a cap on the dynamite which had a fuse on it. We would light the fuse and hide behind the wall until it blew up. Then I would put a twelve-foot-by-three-inches board where I shot the coal. I had to put a timber under one end of the board, rest the board on my back, and put another timber under the other side of the board before it had a chance to cave in. Sometimes, we would have to shimmy between the timber and the board to make it tight. The smoke would be so bad that I couldn't see anything, so I would just feel around for the coal to put into the railcar until the smoke cleared. Everything was done by hand, pick, and shovel. We had no modern equipment. The dynamite powder would give me a terrible headache. Even when I got off work, it felt like there were drums playing in my head, and it would hurt so bad.

Some days, I would be working by myself if Earl didn't show up to work. My daddy would be outside to pull the coal out whenever I got the one-ton car loaded. I would touch two electrical wires together to make the buzzer outside ring to let him know when to pull the car out to empty it. He would empty the car into the coal bin and send it back down for me to load again. The top of the mine was so low that I would load the coal in one end of the car, then get on the other end of the car, and pull the coal to that end with a rake. Then I would go back to the other end of the car again and start over. It was so low that I couldn't stand up all day. We would turn a room to the left side of the main mine shaft, then go thirty feet deeper, and turn a room off to the right of the main shaft. Every time we shot the coal, we had to put timbers in to hold the top up. Sometimes the top would put so much pressure on the timber that it would break a foot from the top, rather than in the middle. I also had to dig an air course down beside the main shaft to keep the air circulating. I dug the air course with a pick and shovel, and I made it so small that the top would be four inches above my face when I was lying on my back. I would have to shovel the coal beside my body. There were always little mice in the mines, and if we saw one coming up the shaft, we would get farther out because the mice always seemed to know when the top of the mine was going to cave in. I wouldn't dare let my son work in a mine under those conditions, but my daddy worked like that for forty-seven years and thought nothing of it. I didn't realize at that young age how dangerous it was.

Before we got our mines running, we would have to dig deep holes to put telephone poles into the ground. We had to build a top house to bring the coal out to dump the coal in. We had to run our own power lines about one mile before Alabama Power would hook them up to their transformers. Walter Finley came by one day as three of my brothers and I were helping my daddy with the poles and running the power lines. He said he had never seen a family work together like we did for no pay. I lost thirty pounds the first month I was out of the air force from working so hard in those coal mines.

Walker Finley

House in Piper, Alabama

Walker was the paymaster in Piper when it was a booming community back in the thirties and forties. Piper and Coleanor together had between 565 and 700 houses at one time years ago. All the houses were eventually torn down, except for the one that we lived in and one other house beside us. The one beside us was the one where the so-called big wheels lived when Piper was booming. The railroad was right in front of our house, but the trains weren't using them anymore since the mines had shut down. The railroad people had one of those three-wheeled carts in front of our house on a sidetrack. It was lightweight, so we could move it to the railroad tracks by hand. It had a little handle on it, so you could pump it back and forth to make it go up and down the tracks. When we finished playing with it, we would put it back on the side ramp. They finally came and got it before they started taking the railroad tracks up.

We lived right below where our schoolhouse had been torn down years ago. The foundation of the school is still there. We had no running water where we lived, and we had to go about three miles to draw water out of a well on the back porch of an empty house in Hawkinsville. The house belonged to a schoolteacher named Hershel Day, and he didn't mind us doing that. We had to boil our water before we could drink it to be safe. We had a fifty-five-gallon barrel raised up outside of the back of our house to catch rainwater. A hose ran from the barrel to the bath for when we got out of the coal mines from working all day. When we took our baths in the wintertime, it would be cold standing naked under that cold water outside. In the summertime, I would just go over to Big Cahaba River and jump in there to take my bath. Those two houses are still in Piper, and people live in them both. The people living there now had wells put in and updated the houses. We had outside toilets and used Sears, Roebuck catalogs or newspaper for toilet paper. We didn't know what store-bought toilet paper was. When Tutwiler bought Piper from Calvin Jones and started selling off the houses, the people that bought them would have to tear the house down as part of the deal so that Tutwiler could strip the land for coal. Most people bought two or three houses, tear them down, and then build their own house. The two-story house where Franklin was born sold for $500, and our big high school sold for $500 too. We helped Glover Lovejoy tear down his three houses and then helped him build a new one in Wilton, Alabama, which is close to Montevallo.

Sears, Roebuck catalog

I was at Holiness church on Smith Hill one night after my breakup with Tommie Ruth Mowery. I was standing outside of the church with some boys looking through the church windows, which were open due to not having air-conditioning. I saw this beautiful girl inside the church who, to me, looked a lot like the actress Elizabeth Taylor. Edward Earl Moore was standing beside me, and I asked him if he knew who that girl was. He said, "That is my sister." Then I remembered that I had seen her before when she was a little chubby girl back when I used to go to Sherry Moore's house on Smith Hill for wiener roasts. I said, "That little chubby sister of Sherry Moore has grown up to be a beautiful woman." I waited until church was finished to talk to her. I was going to take my brother Franklin back to the University of Alabama, where he was attending college at the time, and I asked if she would or could go with me. She said she had to ask her daddy, Mr. Edgar Moore. He was a very good Christian man and very strict, but he let her go with me. I didn't know at that time that she was dating my best friend, Alfred Seagle, who I grew up with.

Edgar Moore

Alfred and I were both crazy about Nettie Jo. She liked both of us, and whoever got to her house first was the one she would go out with. Alfred was always a nice boy, and Nettie Jo was going out with him first, before I got out of the air force. I would finish up for the day in the coal mine, get cleaned up as fast as I could, and go ninety miles per hour on the dirt roads in my daddy's old 1958 Buick to try to beat Alfred over to her house. I would go around the curves so fast that the gravel hitting underneath my fenders sounded like machine gunfire. One day, I got a call from some woman telling me to slow down because they were passing me going the opposite direction. They were getting off work at the garment factory in West Blocton. I was a smart aleck, and I told her to stay on her side of the road and I would stay on mine. I was stupid because I was endangering my life and theirs.

One day, I was in a hurry and almost to Nettie Jo's house on Smith Hill when I saw my friend Bo Seagle on the ground, drunk, with a knife in his hand. Bo was noted as a knife fighter, and there was someone standing over him, trying to take the knife away. Bo wouldn't give it to him, so I asked Bo to give me the knife. He said, "Okay, Whatley, I'll give it to you." Then I helped him get up off the ground. He was just a hundred feet from his house, so he went on home. On another occasion, my brother Franklin and Bo were at a nightclub called the Green Lantern, which was a pretty rough nightclub, when a man pulled out a knife and threatened my brother. Bo said, "Stand back, Whatley! I'll take care of him!" Then the man said, "Oh no, Bo, I'm not going to fight you." That man knew Bo's reputation with a knife, so that was the end of the squabble.

One of my cousins worked for a Chevrolet dealer over in Montevallo and came over to our mines one day, trying to sell me a car. I could get a brand-new 1958 Chevrolet convertible any way that I wanted it and in any color with mud flaps and mirrors for $3,000. I asked my daddy if he would loan me $1,000 to make the down payment, but he said he couldn't afford to. I was drawing my pennies while I was working for my daddy, so I bought my first car which was a 1931 Model A that cost me $100. I was twenty-three years old, and that was my first car. It was in perfect condition. I bought it from a man named Mr. Sewell in Lowery Town who had it for nineteen years. I took him the money on Sunday. He was a good Christian man, and he wouldn't take the money on a Sunday. So he told me to come back on Monday, and he would take it. When the battery ran down in that car, I would have to use a hand crank on the front of the motor, and I would have to be careful because the hand crank could kick back, and it could hurt you. I put a hand paint job on that Model A and wrote the words "Batmobile" on it. Nettie Jo and I went to Bessemer in my Model A one night with another couple, double-dating. The motor got so hot coming back home that it was red. The boy that we were with didn't have a lighter to light his cigarette, so he got out and lit it by touching it to the engine manifold. I had a thermostat out in front of the hood so that I could tell when it was getting too hot. I would have to get out and add water to the radiator. One time, my lights quit working, and we had to go through West Blocton with Nettie Jo holding a flashlight out of the door window. After I let Nettie Jo out at her house and had no one to hold the flashlight, Mr. Herman "Horse Collar" Cliner, the sheriff in West Blocton, told me, "Boy! You'd better get those headlights fixed!" I would drive forty to fifty miles per hour with no lights in the dark on the dirt roads. Sometimes the moonlight would glare off the dirt roads and make it easier to see, but I eventually got my headlights fixed and just in time.

Nettie Jo and I on our Model A

Herman "Horse Collar" Cliner

I was going from West Blocton to Piper one night, and just as I started up this hill, there was a log truck, loaded with logs, broken down. The truck and the trailer had no reflectors on it, and there was no one in the truck. If I hadn't gotten my headlights fixed, I would have hit the back of that trailer because there is no way I would have seen it with no headlights, and I wouldn't have had time to swerve to dodge it. The Lord was with me again.

My brother Franklin had a Harley Davidson, and sometimes I would take Nettie Jo out on dates driving that. Nettie Jo would put on her leopard-skin outfit, and I would wear a black jacket like Marlon Brando. We didn't have to wear helmets back then, which is pretty stupid. I remember when I was about fourteen years old, there was a man from out of town going to the Number 2 Coal Mines in Piper, and there was this big water pipe in the road. The dirt had washed out, and the pipe was on top going across the road. The motorcycle hit the pipe, and it threw the man and the motorcycle into a tree beside the road and killed him. The man had no helmet on.

Sometimes Nettie Jo and I would break up because of Alfred. Then I would have dates with different girls, lined up two weeks in advance. I felt like if I didn't have a girl in my car every night, that night was a total loss. I never cared for any of those girls like I did for Nettie Jo. She was so beautiful to me.

We had a 1958 Buick that five different drivers in the family drove. As soon as one person was finished with it and drove up into the yard, someone else would take it out. One night, I had a date with a young lady, and we pulled up in the yard. My intentions were to take her home in the Buick, but Franklin told me that he had to go back to the University in Tuscaloosa. Bennie Ray took Franklin back to Tuscaloosa, and the only other thing that we had at the house was a dirty old dump truck that we used to haul coal. I had to take my date back home in the dump truck, and that was pretty embarrassing. That was fifty-four years ago, and I met that lady again, by coincidence, at the Wild West Weekend. I was talking to this lady that I didn't know, and she told me she dated a Whatley boy when she was young and that he had to take her home in a dump truck. I told her it was me. We had changed little in fifty-four years. She still looked pretty, but I had gotten ugly and bald-headed.

One day, I had a bunch of boys riding down the road with me, and I told them that I was going to stop at a house where I knew this girl to see if I could get a date. I asked her if she was going to the dance at West Blocton High School that night, and she said yes. I asked if I could drive her home after the dance, and she agreed. I went to the dance, but I did not take her home like I had promised. The girl's so-called friend came up to me and asked me to take her home. I always felt bad about that and stupid for breaking our date for this other girl. I mistreated some girls and told them lies just to get what I wanted, but we don't realize when we are young how we hurt people's feelings. As we get older, we appreciate people and don't want to mistreat anyone or break their hearts.

Every now and then, a bunch of boys would ask me to take them to the Green Lantern in Bucksville to get drunk. They knew that I was not going to drink and that I would get them home safely. I would order a cheeseburger and a glass of milk while they were getting drunk. I would see men and women fighting sometimes. I never drank because of what I saw alcohol did to my father, and it just made me want nothing to do with it. Boys in the air force would offer me $5 just to take one sip of alcohol. Five dollars in the fifties would be like $50 today. I was thirty-three years old before I tried a beer, and I didn't like it.

My brother Bennie Ray was always pulling pranks on people. He and a buddy would walk along the sidewalks in Blocton, and if they saw a couple of old ladies looking their way, he would punch the palm of his hand real loud, and his friend would fall down like Bennie Ray had just hit him. The older women would think that they were really fighting. As you leave West Blockton on the main road, there was a little hump that took you to a second road. Bennie Ray would get three or four boys in the car and start down the hill. He would pretend that his steering wheel had broken, and he would sail over that little hump to hit the second road. The boys would be scared to death, thinking that they were going to wreck. Another joke that Bennie Ray and his friend would play is telling men that they knew where a woman was that they could have a good time with, and they would tell the men to just come with them. They would have a man in an empty house with a shotgun, and as they walked with the man onto the front porch of the house, the man inside the house would step out and start shooting the shotgun, yelling, "Leave my daughter alone!" It would scare the men to death, and they would run through the woods, getting all scratched up. They thought the man was really shooting at them in the dark. Bennie Ray and three of his buddies were drinking one night, and Bennie Ray had a pistol. They went to a nightclub, and he started shooting the pistol in the air, and his buddies would fall on the ground like they were dead. They did that at two other places, and then the police caught them. The police said people were calling in saying that Bennie Ray had already shot two people and was still shooting. The police arrested all of them and put them in jail. All of them were bailed out, except for one. His mother let him stay in jail for three days to teach him a lesson before she got him out. The police kept Bennie Ray's pistol, and he never got it back because it wasn't registered.

We had a scrub baseball team in West Blocton. We would play against teams in Green Pond, Abernant, or Montevallo. Joe Namath was going to school at Alabama at that time. He would come up and spend every weekend with the Hicks family, my mother's next-door neighbor. Bear Bryant didn't know Joe was playing with us, or he would have chewed him out. Joe played center field for us, and I pitched. Occasionally, Joe was my relief pitcher. He was offered $100,000 to play baseball, but he got $430,000 to play football. Football was the highest-paying sport back then in the early sixties. I was watching *The Johnny Carson Show* one night, and the guest was the chairman of the National Football League. The chairman told Johnny that Joe Namath didn't have the experience to beat them. Back then the Superbowl was played between the top National Football League (NFL) and American Football League (AFL) teams. Joe played for the New York Jets in the AFL. He was on Johnny Carson a week later, and he told Johnny Carson that he was going to win. He did. Joe Namath and the New York Jets beat the Baltimore Colts sixteen to seven and won Superbowl number 3.

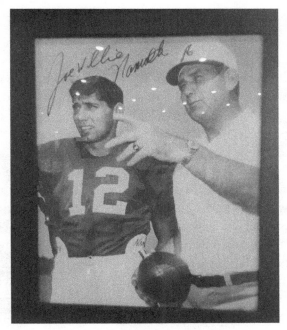

Joe Namath and Paul "Bear" Bryant

One night, I was in West Blocton getting gasoline for our motor that we used to bring the coal out of our mine. I filled two five-gallon cans up with gasoline and put them in the trunk of our 1958 Buick. I started home and got behind a car with two Black men in it. I think the men thought that I was the police. They started driving real fast on those dirt roads, and I was driving fast to keep up with them. I guess they were relieved when I turned onto the road to my house. After I got home, I remembered the two five-gallon cans of gasoline that I had put in the trunk. I opened the trunk, and both cans had turned over, and there was gasoline everywhere. I guess the Lord was watching out for me because the car could have caught fire or blown up.

After we had our mines up and working for a few months, we were selling all our good coal, but we had accumulated a big pile of coal slack that we could sell to anyone. My daddy got permission from someone at Montevallo College who said they would take all the coal slack that we had at a certain price to burn in their furnace. The coal slack didn't look too good, so Franklin and I loaded fifteen to twenty loads on our dump truck with hand shovels as fast as we could. We were hoping that the college wouldn't change their mind when they saw how bad it looked. It was a hard, backbreaking work throwing all that coal slack high up into the dump truck by hand. Franklin flew down those old crooked dirt roads for about five miles before we got to the paved roads. Then it was about fifteen more miles to Montevallo. We were very lucky that we didn't have a wreck. Franklin was going to college at Montevallo at this time, and sometimes he would bring some boys from the college over to our mines. They would come down in the mines and have to stop and rest on the way down. I would laugh at them because I could run in and out without stopping. We worked all day bent over.

This mining inspector came over to our mine one day to inspect our mine for a safety inspection. He saw how I was hustling around and working hard. He told me to go over to Montevallo where Alabama Power had mines and to tell them that he sent me. He said I would have a good-paying job. I discussed it with my girlfriend at the time, Nettie Jo, and she said that she didn't want me working in the coal mines. She said her daddy had and still was working in the coal mines at that time, and he was all banged up and crippled. I heard later on that the mining inspector was down inspecting someone else's mine, when a coal car got loose somehow, came down the mine, and killed the man.

Smith Hill church

Nettie Jo and I decided that we were going to get married as soon as she finished high school. She finished in May, and we got married on June 17, 1959. We were the first couple to get married in the First Baptist Church on Smith Hill. Nettie Jo was nineteen, and I was twenty-three. The preacher was so nervous that he turned Nettie Jo and I toward the audience after he married us and asked Nettie Jo to say the prayer. Then the preacher asked me where we were going from there. I guess he meant if we were going somewhere to have a reception, but I said, "We are going to a motel in Bessemer." And that is what we did. That was our reception. I didn't have any money, so my brother Franklin gave the preacher $5 for marrying us. We started out living with Nettie Jo's parents for a while until we got on our feet. We saw right away that it wasn't going to work living with her parents. Two families just can't live in the same house. Most females just don't seem to get along with other females.

After we were married, my daddy loaned me $200 to put down on a 1956 Chevrolet. The car turned out to be a dud. It had a new paint job, but it started giving me trouble right away. I bought it from a car dealer in Bessemer, and he didn't want to repair anything, even though I bought the car less than thirty days before it gave me problems. I told him that I thought the car had been wrecked and that I was going to let him have the car back. Then he told me he would fix the car, but I said no. He said he would fix the car and make the first payment, so I let him do that.

CHAPTER 4

THE STEEL INDUSTRY

I was at the unemployment office one day when they told me that O'Neal Steel was hiring. A friend of mine that worked in my daddy's coal mine told me that O'Neal Steel was hiring a few days before that, but I hadn't given it another thought. His name was W. F. Horton. He was a very hard worker in the coal mines, and when they all shut down, he worked hard at the steel plant. I worked with him at the steel plant for a time. He passed away in January of 2011 at the age of ninety-eight. I went by Smith Hill to get my cousin, Willie C. Romager, to go to O'Neal Steel with me to try and get a job, but he said he was sleepy and didn't want to go. He was an experienced painter and would have gotten the job if he would have gone with me because they ended up hiring me to work in the paint yard, and I knew nothing about painting.

Willie was the son of Rip and Ruth Romager and had a brother named Jimmy and a sister named Nancy. O'Neal Steel hired six of us new employees that day. The personnel manager that interviewed me asked me if I cursed, and I said no. He asked if I smoked; again I said no. He asked if I was Christian, and I told him yes, but I had been backsliding a bit lately. He hired me anyway. Out of the six people that O'Neal Steel hired that day, I was the only one to keep the job after the thirty-day trial period. The other workers started complaining about one thing or another, but to me that work was like an ice cream factory compared to the coal mines.

The manager gave me some small pieces of steel to paint. He only had a five-gallon bucket of paint to do the job. He gave me some gloves to dip the short pieces of steel into the vat, but I pulled the gloves off and did a good job fast. The boss took a liking to me because I did good work and I was fast. He let me work overtime the first Sunday I was there, painting a room in the main office. The union didn't like it, but since it was office work, they had no say. After working in the fabrication paint shop, they transferred me to the steel warehouse to work. The manager told the superintendent, who happened to be his brother-in-law named Paul, that he was bringing a man down there that didn't take time to s——t through the day. Here again, not learning in school came back to hurt me. I didn't even know how to read a ruler. I didn't know what one-eighth of an inch was on a ruler, what a gauge was, what one-thousandth of an inch was, or how to read a micrometer. I had four thousand gauges and sizes of steel that I had to learn in thirty days. I asked the other men, "How do you know what a decimal or gauge is?" And they told me, "You will learn." I was embarrassed and afraid of losing my job, but later the men told me that I learned it faster than anyone they ever had there before.

Nettie Jo and I decided to move to Birmingham. She had a sister named Dorothy who lived in some apartments right down below the Vulcan Iron Man statue. We moved from my parents' house to those same apartments. Nettie Jo and I would get up early every Saturday morning in the wintertime and take the 1956 Chevrolet, with no heater, to West Blocton to work for my daddy in his coal mine. I just did it to help him out. My daddy didn't pay me or pay for our gasoline to come down, and we could barely pay for it ourselves. Nettie Jo never complained about how cold it was in the car because she got to see her parents.

The apartments that we moved into were on a steep hillside, and we had to climb thirty-two steps from the road to our front door. Nettie Jo was pregnant with our first child at that time, but she ended up losing the baby. Maybe it was because she had to walk up and down those steps all the time; I just don't know. We buried our baby girl in West Blocton in 1959. Nettie Jo and I had gone to her doctor eleven hours before the birth, and his nurse said that she did not hear the baby's heartbeat. But she had to write down that she did, or the doctor would chew her out. The baby was born dead eleven hours later with the navel cord wrapped around her neck. Doctors didn't catch things back then like they do now. We named her Kathy Jean, after my middle name Gene. Our baby was three weeks premature, so we were responsible for burying her. We bought four burial plots at Hillcrest Cemetery, right across from Mount Carmel cemetery, for $10 each.

Kathy Jean Whatley headstone

Nettie Jo's aunt Myrtle told us that we had better have another baby in a hurry, or else we may not ever have any children. Eleven months later, we had another little girl, and we named her Carol Bethlyn Whatley. She was the first girl born into the Whatley family in sixty-five years. My daddy said that if she was born on his birthday, he would buy her everything for the first year. She was born in the hospital in Alabaster, Alabama, at about 10:30 p.m. on November 30, 1960, on my daddy's birthday.

Left to right: Kareen, Lula Mae, Benjamin, and Carol Whatley

We had moved from Aldrich, Alabama, to a Black Diamond Coal Company house in West Blocton. The house was where the bank is now, and it cost $15.00 a month for rent. Our power bill back then was about $12.00 a month, and the water bill was about $4.00 a month. I was only making $67.00 a week at O'Neal Steel Company, so it was hard to make those payments back then. The minimum wage was $1.25 per hour in 1960, so $67.00 a week ($1.68 per hour) was good money at the time. The company house was old, and we could see the ground through the cracks in the floor. We had a big potbellied stove in the living room. When we put coal or wood into it and opened the door in the top, smoke would just pour out of the stove into the living room. In the wintertime, I would put as much coal in the stove as I could, hoping it would stay warm enough for Carol in her baby bed. Sometimes the fire would go out without us realizing it, and poor little Carol's eyes would be matted together the next morning. My parents lived across the road from us, and my daddy would ride Carol around town in his truck. He was crazy about Carol since she was the first girl born into the family in sixty-five years and was born on his birthday.

I was thinking of going to Montevallo College to be a school-teacher on my GI Bill, so I moved from West Blocton to Aldrich. Aldrich is a little town right outside of Montevallo, where my brother Franklin and his wife Beaulah had finished college. My cousin, Nora Whatley, owned four houses along a railroad track, and she rented one of them out to us. Nettie Jo and I would go down to Aldrich and double-date with Nora's son, Jack Whatley, and his girlfriend before we got married. All of Nora's houses had outside toilets, so I made a little extra money digging toilet holes for $15 each whenever she needed one dug out. Nora owned a little grocery store in Aldrich and had a hotel over in Montevallo. Her husband had died, and Nora was a good, smart woman. I took the test at Montevallo and passed it, but at the same time, O'Neal Steel offered me a foreman job. I decided to stay within the steel warehouse.

Franklin had a 1949 Coupe Chrysler and a big Harley Davidson motorcycle. He would let me borrow the Harley Davidson when I lived in Aldrich to drive back and forth to my job at O'Neal Steel in Birmingham, which was about one hundred miles each day. That saved me a lot of money. Later on, Franklin was helping me move from Aldrich to West Blocton, and my brother-in-law, Edward Earl, was riding in the back of the truck. Franklin was in a hurry to get home and watch the football game, and we didn't have the furniture tied down too well. Franklin was driving too fast, and we hit a dip in the road which caused a mattress and a dresser to fall off the dump truck. It nearly knocked Edward Earl off the truck and tore our dresser all to pieces.

My daddy worked in the coal mines from about thirty-five to forty years altogether. He worked in coal mines in Piper, Marvel, Blue Creek, and finally had his own mines in Piper and another on the Chase property up near Birmingham, next to the Big Cahaba River. After working inside the mines, he dug strip pit coal where Mr. Tutwiler had stripped before and left a lot of coal in the banks. Anyone could dig the coal out of the banks and sell it, like I did for $5 a ton while I was working at the steel plant. When we were young, he worked in the Number 2 Coal Mines in Piper, which was very dangerous. A lot of people got killed or had their legs cut off.

Sometimes a fire would start in the mines. I remember my daddy telling us that he was fighting one fire, trying to put it out, and hoping that the fire didn't get behind him because he would have had no way of getting out. Mr. Hershel McBurnette got electrocuted by fooling with electricity out in some water. A Black man had warned him not to mess with it. Mr. Earnest Sanders and Mr. Harry Fulman got their legs cut off. Mr. Frederick got killed, but I don't remember how many more. That is all I can remember since I was a young kid back then. My daddy was a hard worker. I remember his knuckles would bleed in the wintertime from eczema, and his nose would drip from sinus issues. This young Chase College boy popped off at my daddy one day, saying that if my daddy couldn't get more coal out of the mine, he would find somebody else that could.

My daddy was paying him royalties for each ton that he was pulling out. That little spoiled college boy didn't know how close he was to getting his butt whipped, but I had to hold back from saying or doing anything because I knew it would have just caused my daddy more trouble. I had just gotten out of the air force at the time and hadn't been married long. That little college boy had no idea how hard my daddy was working and probably didn't realize how close he was to a butt whipping. I never mentioned what I was thinking to my daddy. My daddy was very smart and very hardworking. I know he had a hard time supporting eight people when we were children, but I never heard him complain at all. He just did the best he could.

My daddy would pick up some of his workers in Helena, Alabama, to work in his mines on the Chase property. One Black man got killed in those mines one day. My daddy was on the outside of the mine, and he thought something was wrong because there hadn't been any coal coming out of the mine for some time. He went down into the mine and found three of his workers had passed out due to black damp. "Black damp" is when there is very little oxygen in the air, so he woke them up to save their lives. Once they got out of the mine for more oxygen, they would go back in once they felt it was safe to work again.

My father-in-law, Edgar Moore, had his own little wagon mines also. And just like my daddy, he struggled just to survive. Sometimes

I would go to his mines on Sundays to pump water out so the miners could work the next day. We had the same problems in my daddy's mine. We would work on Saturday and skip Sunday, and we knew when we got back to work on Monday, we would have rock piles to clear and water to pump out. If the pump didn't work, we would put the water in tubs and haul it out in the coal cars. The community where Mr. Moore lived, Smith Hill, was two miles from West Blocton. They never had running water in their house, and everyone got their water from two community wells. Mr. Edgar and Minnie Moore never had running water or automobiles in their lifetime. Two of his sons-in-law, Larry Baum and Bobby Jo Franks, and two of his sons, Edward Earl and Arlet, and I decided to dig Mr. Moore a well to get running water to his house. Larry Baum and Bobby Jo Franks were going to the University of Alabama at the time. Larry was married to Nettie Jo's beautiful sister, Dorothy Moore, and they had two children named Susan and Steve. Edward Earl married Patsy Seagle, and they had four children named Eddie, Jeff, Pam, and Amy. Arlet married Linda Jo Lucas when he was seventeen years old, and they had three children named Lynn, Rocky, and Crystal. I went to my close friend, Harry Fulman, who was a road commissioner, and explained the situation to him. Harry let me borrow his jackhammer and my daddy gave me some dynamite from his coal mine so we could begin digging Mr. Moore's well. After we dug the well to the point where we hit water, we put a pump in the well and ran pipes to Mr. Moore's house so that he had running water. We never put bathrooms in his house, so he continued going to his outside toilet.

Top: Edgar Moore, Nettie Jo, Minnie Moore
Bottom: Carol

Dorothy Moore Baum

Harry Fulman was not only the road commissioner; he was also a great humanitarian. He was the road commissioner for twenty years, and he helped a lot of people back then that were struggling. He had compassion and would help anyone if and when he could. If a man was out of work, he would put the man on the road commission payroll and give them work until they could find work somewhere else. When someone died, he would send a crew out to dig the grave and didn't charge anything for it. Mr. Fulman lost one or both of his legs in a coal mining accident. Someone was kidding with him one day, saying, "Why don't you run for road commissioner?" And he said, "I think I will." He ran against Mr. McGraw who was a very good man that had the position for a long time before Mr. Fulman. I don't think anyone thought Harry had a chance to beat Mr. McGraw in the election, but he won. Harry had two daughters that lived on his land near him. Gaynell was the oldest daughter. She married Earl Sims, who later became a preacher. Faye was his younger daughter, and she married Joe Goggins, who was also a very good man. Earl and Joe are both deceased now. Mr. Harry lost his job as road commissioner after twenty years and just spent the rest of his life on his land, tending to his cattle.

After I moved to Mobile, I would always try to go by and see Mr. Harry whenever I came to visit my parents. Even into his eighties, he was still putting hay in his old pickup truck and taking it to feed his cattle. I went by to see him one day, and his daughter Faye told me he probably wouldn't recognize me because his mind was getting bad. She was right; he didn't recognize me. I think he lived to be ninety-two years old. He had hundreds of acres of land on both sides of the Little Cahaba River. One day, he told me he paid $6 and $10 an acre for all his land years ago. I am sure he was worth over a million dollars when he passed away, but he was content with his little shotgun house that he built out of the old Piper coal company houses that Mr. Tutwiler sold to him for $50 per room years before. I think Mr. Harry bought the big old building where the hay was kept to feed the mules when the mines were open.

When I got the job at O'Neal Steel, we lived in West Blocton. The only recreation that we had in West Blocton was the pool hall behind Bully Harris's barbershop. I worked second shift, so I would get up and go to the pool hall until Nettie Jo had dinner ready. She knew I liked devil's food cake, so she would cook me one when I asked her to. I would eat half of the cake at one time. Occasionally, I would beat my brother Franklin when we played pool. He would always say that I was just lucky, and my daddy would say, "Well, Bob, you did luck out playing pool today. Just kidding, Franklin."

Our house in West Blocton

We had a family that lived down below us by the name of Pickett. They had one son named Jackie that was younger than Nettie Jo, but he liked her a lot before we got married. Dana was their oldest daughter. She never married, but she would come by to visit us after Nettie Jo and I were married. Linda, Dorothy, and Mary Lou were all younger than us; but they also liked coming by to talk with us. Years later, my brother Bennie Ray married Linda.

Sometimes Carol would get sick in the wintertime, and we would take her down the street to a retired lady, Dr. Montgomery, who was married to Dr. Crowder. They were married but went by two different last names, probably for tax purposes. Dr. Crowder had passed away, but people would still go see Dr. Montgomery even though she was retired. She would check Carol out, give us some medicine, and then ask us if $1 was too much. That is all she would charge anyone. She was a wonderful old lady, probably in her eighties. She and her husband had a son named John Crowder, who I went to school with at West Blocton High School. John passed away in 2010. I think he was a couple of years behind me in school.

We were having a hard time paying the bills when we lived in that old company house in West Blocton. Even though rent was $15 a month, I remember a time when we were three months behind on the rent. Sometimes I would go to work at O'Neal Steel in Birmingham with no money in my pockets. My daddy would say, "I wouldn't go that far with no money." I told him that he would if he didn't have a choice. Bobby "Nootchie" Miller had an Amoco service station in West Blocton, and he would let me have a credit of up to $300 to buy gas. We were always friends, and he knew that he could trust me not to rip him off. He was the same person that I would always beat playing marbles back in the third grade.

I would usually get home from O'Neal Steel at midnight. I would get up early the next morning, go to Piper, dig coal in the strip pits, and sell it for $5 a ton to help pay our bills. That would pay our water bill. We later moved from the company house to a better one on Main Street in West Blocton. We had our second child, Teresa, while we lived in that house.

Nettie Jo decided that she wanted to work at the garment factory in West Blocton, just to have something to do close to home. We hired a babysitter named Ms. Emma to stay with the children. I don't remember her last name. Nettie Jo would clear about $45 each week, and we paid Ms. Emma $25 each week. That left us just enough money to pay the electric and water bill out of her check. One winter, we had a frozen pipe under the house that had been leaking. My side was about to kill me; it was hurting so bad, but I kept working to fix the water leak. As soon as Nettie Jo came home from work, I told her how bad I was hurting. She said that we had better go to the hospital in Alabaster to see what's wrong. As soon as we got to the hospital, they told me that my appendix had to come out. They called a doctor out of Birmingham to perform the operation. The other doctors told me that he did a very good job. I was in the hospital for a week, but I have never had any problems since. Dr. Stinson was my regular doctor at the time. He delivered all my mother's children and my two oldest daughters. He also told me that the surgeon who operated on me did a terrific job.

We moved again from the house on Main Street to a house next door to Mr. Gilbert, but we didn't live there for long before we moved to another house across the street from the water tank. Then I heard about a house that Sue and David Pickett had for sale on Iris Lane. They sold it to us for $2,000. Nothing down and $25 a month. My second wife, Midge, lived on that street all her life. She was married to Gordon Reach before we were married many years later. Gordon was a good man, and they had four children. My son Michael was born at Druid City Hospital in Tuscaloosa while we lived in that house. I always wanted a boy so that I could build him a tree house whenever he was old enough, but we never seemed to have enough extra money to build it. I always regretted not having enough money to build one. It would have been nice for him and the girls to play in. Once Michael got to where he could walk pretty good, he would drag a little blanket around with him until he was about three years old. He wore the end of that blanket jagged. Sometimes he would be naked as a jaybird, dragging it around. The backyard was full of kudzu vines when we moved in. I got out in the backyard and dug every vine up by the root. Some of the kudzu roots were 1 to 1½ foot deep. After I dug them up, I planted us a garden in my whole backyard. That was the richest, most productive garden that I have ever planted. I had a lot of good and big Irish potatoes.

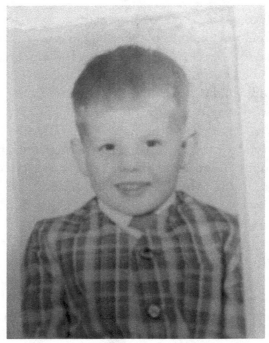

Michael Whatley

I didn't know at that time that Midge Gentry, who Nettie Jo and I had double-dated with, lived just four houses above us on the same street, on the opposite side of the road. Gordon lived in Lowery Town, just outside of West Blocton. Gordon and Midge got married just two years after Nettie Jo and I got married. Nettie Jo and I were married for forty-eight years before she passed, and Gordon passed forty-two years after he and Midge were married.

When Nettie Jo and I lived in the house across from the water tank, I pulled a dirty deal on a car dealer in Tuscaloosa, but I shouldn't have. I had an old car that had a blown motor, and this car dealer was halfway down the hill. I got someone to pull that torn-up car from West Blocton to the top of that hill in Tuscaloosa. We unhooked the chain, and I coasted down the hill, right up into the dealer's lot. I told him that I wanted to trade my car in. They sold me a brand-new Demonstrator Renault for $1,500. They went out to crank my car, but it wouldn't start. I knew it wouldn't, and I said, "Doggone!

It was running when I brought it in here!" They said they would try it again later, and I left with my new Renault. It was a little car, but the most comfortable car that I ever had. I hated to do the car dealer that way, but it is usually the other way around where the dealer takes advantage of the customer. I brought the Renault home, parked it on a hill, and put it in park. I came out later and saw that it was gone. I thought Bennie Ray was playing a trick on me, but I looked down the hill, and the car was across the ditch, but not turned over. I didn't know that park didn't hold like the other cars. I was supposed to pull the emergency break up, which is something that I normally didn't do in my other cars. Nettie Jo, the children, and I were in the Renault in Birmingham one day, and this truck in front of us had stopped. I pulled up behind him pretty close, not knowing that he was trying to back up into his place of business. He didn't see that little Renault behind him, so he backed up and crunched my hood with the flatbed of his truck. Later on, the Renault wouldn't change gears from second to third, so I drove it back and forth to work in Birmingham doing seventy miles per hour in second gear until I finally blew the motor up. I only had ninety thousand miles on the car, but I did good until one time that I didn't put enough oil in the motor. I went ahead and bought me another car after I blew the engine in the Renault. I learned a good lesson to always keep the oil and water checked.

When Nettie Jo and I lived across from my parents in West Blocton, my mother was still taking care of her daddy. At that time, he was ninety-one years old and frail. I would go by their house every day before I went to work and ask how he was doing. On June 24, 1960, the superintendent at O'Neal Steel called me in to work early. I was in such a hurry that I didn't have time to go to my parents' house and check on my granddaddy. After I was at work for about three hours, Nettie Jo called and told me that my grandfather had passed away. I left work and went home right away. He lived with us for seventeen years and was a very smart and talented old man. Before he got sick, he would go out every night and look at the stars. He would tell us that he was more accurate at predicting the weather than those people with their million dollars' worth of equipment, and he was pretty well right as long as it wasn't cloudy that night.

We would always go out at night to find the Big Dipper and Little Dipper in the sky.

I got tired of traveling from West Blocton to Birmingham, so we decided to buy us a house in Birmingham. We bought our first house there in 1962 for $10,000 from a nurse. We paid $63 a month for the house. The nurse had the whole backyard planted with rows of rose bushes. Every time I would mow the yard, I would run over a rose bush until I finally had a yard with just grass. Nettie Jo didn't mind me cutting the rose bushes down because she didn't care for flowers that much. I should have dug them up and sold them. I didn't want rose bushes keeping the children, Nettie Jo, and I from being able to play. The main reason that I wanted to move to Birmingham was because I was falling asleep on the road every morning when I drove back home from work. I was trying to work two jobs, play pool, and play ball games at night. I missed hitting a bridge by about one foot one morning. I would drift off the road going sixty or seventy miles per hour. That would wake me up, and I would jerk the car back onto the road. We had our fifth baby, Cheryl, while we lived in that house. When the first Jack's Hamburgers opened in Birmingham, we would go there quite often. They sold hamburgers for $0.10 each, and we had to feed so many children with little money.

After Nettie Jo had our fifth child, the doctor told her that she had to have a hysterectomy. She was twenty-nine years old, and the doctors didn't like doing it because she was still young, but they went ahead and did it. She had the hysterectomy at the University of Alabama at Birmingham (UAB). The doctor operated on Nettie Jo and later brought her to her room. She told me that she didn't feel too good, and right away, she fell asleep. I stayed in the room all day. Different candy stripers, as they called them, kept coming in the room to try and get her pulse rate. Something didn't seem right, so I went to the front desk and told them that they needed to call Nettie Jo's doctor at home. This was early in the morning, but her doctor didn't come in to check on her until about 3:00 p.m. He pressed down on Nettie Jo's stomach and then took off running, calling for help. They rushed her to the elevator to take her downstairs to the emergency room. One doctor pronounced her dead, but another doctor said that she had a heartbeat. The elevator was full, so her doctor and I had to go down the stairs. She had bled six pints of blood inside of her body. I told the doctor that I asked his nurse to call him, but she said he wasn't home. He got very upset and said that he had been home all day and no one had called. The doctor told me that was the third time that something like this had happened on that floor and that he was going to have Nettie Jo moved to a different floor. He told me that if I had any more problems, please call him.

While we lived in that first house in Birmingham, we had some neighbors behind us that were always making a lot of noise with their cars, revving the motor up, late at night. We went over to their house to see what was going on, and Nettie Jo found out that our neighbor behind us was her cousin, Jessie Faye Jackson. She was married to a man named Jimmy that raced cars. Nettie Jo hadn't seen her cousin in years and didn't even know that she lived in Birmingham. Jessie Faye's mother had fourteen children, and she was the oldest child. Jimmy worked on and painted houses, so he had plenty of time to work on race cars. Jimmy had a neighbor that was a tractor trailer driver that we called Red because he had red hair. Jimmy, Red, and I went bowling one night. We bowled three games, and that was the best bowling night that I ever had in my life. They both thought that I could really bowl. It didn't seem to matter how I hit the pins; they would fall. I averaged a 235 over three games, and my lowest score was a 175. Red's wife thought he was stepping out on her, so she decided that she was going to catch him. Red had a place in the trunk of the car where he hauled his dog around with him. His wife got into the dog contraption, and Red got into the car and started it up. She must have thought, "Oh, boy, I am going to catch him now!" But all he did was circle the block and parked his car. He went up and sat on the front porch and heard someone calling him. She had gotten into that dog pen and couldn't get out. Red had to go and get her out of that dog pen. She explained what she had done, and we all got a kick out of that and kidded with her about it from then on.

My brother James had a Volkswagen that he loaned us so we could go on vacation somewhere in Georgia. I don't remember what town it was, but we were going to see my sister-in-law, Sherry, and her husband, Bobby Jo Franks. On the way to their house, I saw a Black policeman. And I asked a man at this store when we stopped, "When did they let Black people be policemen in Georgia?" He said he had never known about it, and that was a surprise to him. At that time, there were no Black policemen in Alabama. We didn't know how to get to Sherry's house, and I nearly wrecked going around this curve too fast in the foggy night. We got lost, going the wrong direction, so I crossed over illegally to the highway going the opposite direction. We finally found their house, and we stayed there with them for a week. Bobby Jo was coaching football at a high school, and while we were there, his team had a game. They put me out there moving the yardstick with another person on the other end of the chain.

When James loaned us the Volkswagen, I don't know how he got to work. He loaned it to us to save on gasoline. Undoubtedly, he had another car. I remember one time he was about to lose his car to repossession because he was behind on the payments. He jacked the car up and took the wheels off, thinking they couldn't get it. Wrong! They brought some more wheels out, put them on the car while he was at work, and then charged James $300 for the tires and repossessed his car. The first time I saw a Mustang was when my children were small. Sometimes we went to my brother-in-law Arlet's house, and there would be a man named Travis Daily there visiting with them. Our children were scared to death of Travis Daily. If he just looked at them a certain way, they would start crying. We all got a laugh out of it. I was going two or three days without going to bed. I was like a walking zombie. My father-in-law would ask me how many days it had been since I had been in bed.

Arlet Moore

Once I got the rose bushes out of the way at our house in Birmingham, I wanted a table tennis set up, but I didn't have the money to buy one. I built one out of a scrap one-foot-by-four-foot wood. It was very lopsided, but we had a good time with it. The ball would hit a crack and go a different direction. One day, my neighbor across the street asked if I wanted his three-bedroom brick home, and all I had to do was take up the payments. I told the neighbor that I wanted it, so we went to the real estate man to tell them what we were going to do. The real estate man asked who was going to pay the closing costs. My neighbor told the real estate man that he would, to keep his credit from going bad. The real estate man looked at him like he was crazy. I moved into the three-bedroom house and rented my other house to my brother James and charged him just enough to make the payment. The neighbor that let me take over his payments came back a year and a half later and wanted to know if I would let him have his house back. I was so stupid and said, "Yes, give me $140, and you can have it back." About that same time, I had seen a nice big house that I wanted for $7,500. I bought that house. It had a front porch, side porch, and a basement. I didn't have to put any money down. I just made monthly payments.

One of the lady's ex-son-in-laws came by one day and told me that the lady we bought the house from had been married three times. They thought she had killed her husband in that house and gotten away with it. He also told me that she would get that house back one way or another because that was how she made her living. She would sell a house, and after someone made the payments on it for so long, she would figure out a way to get it back. It did eventually happen.

We had great neighbors there by the name of Johnny and Mary Warren, which are both deceased now. They had five children that were all the same ages as our children. Johnny was a painter and always had trouble with a slipped disc in his body. They had a daughter named Lova. My second daughter, Teresa, said that if she had a daughter, she was going to name her Lova. After Teresa married Timothy Davis, they had a son named Timothy Paul who we all call TJ, and then they had a daughter. Naturally, they named her Lova.

When I first started working at O'Neal Steel, I had to learn how to hook and unhook tractors and trailers. The first time that I backed one up, it was as crooked as a snake, but after I practiced a few times, I could back them up as fast as I could go forward. Our boss would give us a handful of bills to load on the trailer. The driver had maybe fifteen stops to get the steel off, so we had to load the trailer in order for the truck driver to be able to off-load at each stop without having to move everything around. After we loaded a trailer, we had to drop it and then pull in the next empty trailer and so on. We would have as many as thirty-eight short trucks and trailers to load on second and third shifts. We really had to work hard and fast in order to get the trucks loaded in time for the drivers that would come in at all hours of the night. We would call them to let them know when we had their trailers loaded. O'Neal Steel was making bombs for World War II. When the war was over, they made a steel warehouse and fabrication shop to continue staying in business.

We had only one barrel in the wintertime where we would burn wood to heat our hands. We would get so cold that I would have to wait until I got the truck loaded before I could go into the office to warm my hands before I could sign the paperwork. We always worked hard and fast because they gave us a bonus at the end of the month based on how many lifts of steel we put on all the trucks. Later on, they cut our bonuses out. That is when my union representative and I went round and round for about two hours at the union hall meeting. I told him that he had lied to me. He said, "That's the first time I have been caught in a lie." He had told me earlier that the insurance that we had would cover my wife's pregnancy. After my wife had our first child, who was stillborn, we had to cover all the bills. He was only getting us a $0.05 to $0.08 raise each year, which wasn't very much. We asked him about that since O'Neal Steel put in the paper how much money they had cleared that year. He said, "You never ask what to get." And I said, "Okay, let's go for twenty-five cents this contract." He said, "Oh, you want to go after it all at once?" And I told him, "You said we didn't ask. Now we are asking." The men voted me in that night as one of their negotiators.

We union leaders started having meetings to see what we were going to ask for. Every time we had a meeting, I would go out into the plant and explain to the men what we had discussed. The union leader told me not to go out into the plant and tell the men what we discussed. I said, "Hey! I am representing those men, and they will know what we discuss." He wasn't trying to do anything for the men at all. All the negotiators were old men before they elected me. I told the union leader that if he got less than $0.15 when he met with the company officials, he shouldn't talk to me. We met with the company officials, and the first thing they said was "We can't afford anything right now." The union leader reminded the company that they put how much money they cleared in the Birmingham news the past year. Then the union leader asked for a $0.25 raise each year for the next three years. The company said they could do $0.01. Then the union leader said $0.23. The company said $0.02. The union leader said $0.21. Every time, the company would go up $0.01, and the union leader would come down $0.02. Finally, the union leader had gotten below $0.15, and the company was up to $0.08. He asked me what I thought. And I said, "Man, I already told you don't speak to me." Then he brought in a union man from Florida to try and get me to change my mind. He told me to tell the men that I did all that I could for them, and I replied, "Oh yes! I am going to tell them that." The company asked all the older men if they accepted. They all dropped their heads and said yes. They got around to me, and I said no. The other men didn't vote to strike.

Right after the negotiations, they made me foreman. I thought maybe they were making me foreman so they could fire me, but they didn't. I had made foreman faster than anyone had before me. I gained thirty pounds in two or three months after that and started losing my hair. The union people got peeved about my promotion. They said that every time they found someone who would fight for them, the company would move them up some way to make them a company man. I told my daddy that I was about to be promoted to foreman after working for O'Neal Steel for four years. He knew I was pretty easygoing, so he told me I had to be hard as a foreman. He was a boss in the coal mines for twenty years and always produced more coal on his shift than any of the other bosses on the other shifts. I told him that all I had to do was to treat people how I wanted to be treated. I would go to work after I married Nettie Jo, and I could hardly wait to go back home to my beautiful wife. I loved her so much. After a couple of years as foreman, I had a Black man working for me that was a very hard worker. I talked O'Neal Steel into making him the first Black foreman at the company because he was such a dedicated worker and a good person. Any time they needed someone to work, they would ask us people from the coal mines if we knew anyone that needed a job because they knew that we knew what hard work was all about.

Kenny Phillips got a job at O'Neal Steel because Lewis Goggin, from Pea Ridge, recommended him. Pea Ridge is right out of Montevallo. Kenny worked for me while I was foreman and was the hardest worker that I ever had. He later was made foreman and then went on to be an assistant superintendent. One day, one of the headmen named Jack Blackwell came around and said something to Kenny. Kenny got nervous, and I laughed at him. He said, "G. D. Whatley, you laugh at everything." I told him, "The headmen put their pants on the same way that you do. There is no reason to get nervous if you are doing your job, and you do that."

Before they made me foreman, I was running a complete bay all by myself. The overhead crane was radio controlled, and I had a little box with three levers on it hanging down around my neck. I could make the crane go up and down the tracks with one lever, make the chains go up and down with another lever, and make the trolly go back and forth with the third lever. I could load and unload trucks by myself without a crane operator or any other help. The crane had a cab on it in case we needed someone to run it from above. My picture, running the crane, was put in fifteen different magazines in June of 1964. I still have one of the magazines.

"Femco Radio Controlled Crane and Operator make Truck Unloading a One Man Job."

Me operating a remote-controlled overhead crane

One day, the top engineering person who was in charge of O'Neal Steel was up on top of one of our cranes with the maintenance man, working on the crane. The engineer told the crane operator to go one way with the crane, and the operator went the other way. It threw the engineer off the crane, and he fell about thirty feet and hit his head on the cement floor below. He died before they could contact his wife. He was an Auburn graduate and very smart. He was only thirty-three years old. His brother-in-law was the superintendent of the warehouse where I was working, but he got fired later for stealing from the company. I hated that he got fired because he was a good boss to work for even though he had a drinking problem. We could smell it on him every day. I guess he thought that they would not fire him because his brother-in-law was the head engineer for O'Neal Steel.

Me pictured in *Plant Engineering*, June 1964 (top)

O'Neal Steel hired another superintendent who was a thirty-three-year-old Auburn graduate. He was very smart when it came to paperwork, but he didn't have the know-how to run a warehouse or handle men. I told him that he was fortunate to be a superintendent at thirty-three years old. I wish I could have been a superintendent at such an early age.

We had a stacker system at O'Neal where the day crew would work up material for the second shift to load on trucks and trailers. If the second-shift worker couldn't find the material that he was looking for, he would go and pull the same material that we were working every Saturday that had to be put up twice. We salaried people weren't getting paid for working Saturdays, but the workers were making time and a half. I went home one morning so disgusted with working on Saturdays because the extra work was uncalled for. I called the owner, Emmett O'Neal, and told him that I could save him one hundred thousand dollars a year. He told me to come to his office, and I explained to him how to save the money. They did things my way, and we quit having to pay the men overtime because we weren't working on Saturdays anymore. I told Mr. O'Neal that I didn't want anyone to know that I came to talk to him, but about that same time, the union men went on strike. All the salaried men had to do the work to keep the company running, including Jack Blackwell and the office personnel.

Jack Blackwell was the top man next to Mr. O'Neal. He came up to me and said, "I heard you went to Emmett." That sort of embarrassed me, but he didn't mind. We salaried people got paid a lot extra for keeping the plant running. The men were on strike for a couple of months. And new employees, called scabs by the union, came in and filled the emptied positions. Finally, the union men came back to work for less than they went on strike for. Then the company let all the scabs go even though they had promised them a permanent job. O'Neal immediately removed the superintendent from his position and put him somewhere else in the company. They had another steel plant in Florida. I had worked for a different superintendent when I first got there who was transferred to the Florida plant. When they took the Auburn graduate superintendent off the job, they called my old boss in Florida to be the acting superintendent over us again.

We had one truck driver at O'Neal Steel that had one bad eye and one good eye. The left eye was his bad one. He would joke about it and say that he was the only driver that could see straight ahead with one eye and watch women on the sidewalk with his other eye. We had a tractor trailer driver that drove for us for years, but we had to take him off driving because he kept thinking he saw people jumping out in front of his truck as he was driving down the road. He ended up having to go to the hospital because of his nerves. We let him work in the plant for a year, but he wanted to start driving again, so we let him drive. The same thing happened again. He thought people were still jumping in front of his truck, so he had to come back and work in the warehouse from then on until he retired. Another incident that happened, concerning one of our truck drivers, is someone called our office one day saying that one of our Black drivers needed to quit looking off the road or he was going to wreck. We checked the driver and found out that he had his hat on with the bill pointing sideways instead of pointing forward like it was supposed to be.

The personnel manager who hired me resigned, and the company hired a new one. The United Fund people came around, wanting all the employees to donate to their fund each month, so O'Neal Steel would donate the money by taking it out of our checks. We were to write down where we wanted our money to go, even though we had no way of knowing where it actually went. I told them that I wanted my money to go to the crippled children because they took care of my brother Billy until he was sixteen years old. We didn't have to buy crutches, braces, a wheelchair, or anything. One day, a man came by my house when I was living next door to Johnny Warren, and he told me that he had to pay $200 for his child's braces. I asked him if the crippled children's fund would pay for them, but he said no. He had to pay for them. That sort of made me mad, so I went to the new personnel manager, told him what happened, and told him not to cut the donation money out of my check anymore and that I would personally give my contribution directly to the person that needed it. I told him that donation money was probably paying someone to oversee the money instead of going to where it was supposed to help. He said, "Oh no! I am on that board." And I said, "That's exactly what I mean." That really made him mad because I insinuated that he must be getting paid to be on that board, which he probably was. I guess I shouldn't have said that, but that was how I felt after hearing that man had to pay for his child's braces. The personnel manager and union president were out to get me fired after that escapade.

I was foreman on the midnight shift, and I had a run-in with the union because I let a new employee go because he couldn't learn how to do the job. He had been there for twenty-nine days, but according to the union contract, we only had to keep an employee on if they completed the thirty-day probation period. I hated to let the employee go, but if the job isn't done fast and right, it looks bad on the foreman. He wanted to talk to everyone instead of learning his job. I had a good man named Johnny who was my crane operator. He went home at the end of his shift one day and left his gloves on the steps. He called and asked me to put them up for him, and he would get them the next day when he came in. He didn't make it back. After he called me, he had a heart attack and died.

I was working eight hours each night, and as soon as I got off work, I would go to a trade school for six hours using my GI Bill. The government was paying me $168 a month to go to school and learn how to be a cabinetmaker. There was another veteran that was going to the trade school with me, but the rest of the students were from high school. I think we built one set of cabinets in two years. The students would build a piece of furniture or really nice, heavy-built rocking chairs. I would get scrap lumber from O'Neal Steel and make gun racks or porch swings. I would cut out all the parts for the swings, then put them together on the weekend, and sell them for $5. This man had a flea market business in Woodlawn, right on the edge of Birmingham, and he gave me $5 for all the swings that I could build. I sold the gun racks for $5 as well. It was all profit because the wood was free. All it cost me were a few nails, bolts, and screws. Sometimes, I would go three days and nights without sleep. I would work all night, go to the trade school, then play softball four or five nights a week.

One time, I was going from Birmingham to West Blocton by myself, and I fell asleep going seventy miles per hour. I woke up going sideways down the edge of the highway near the West Blocton exit. I ended up back on the pavement, still going sideways, and ended up stopping, facing oncoming traffic with a Greyhound bus behind me. I had mud on my motor and left a pile of mud on the highway. I guess the bus driver probably thought I was drunk. My good Lord must have been watching out for me and kept me from flipping the car. When I had my children in the car with me, they would watch me from the back seat in the rearview mirror. They would remind me to stay awake if I looked sleepy. I had so much going on that I didn't have time for sleep. I was a hazard on the road and very stupid for not getting rest. I was endangering other people's lives and my own.

Nettie Jo was working at the hospital on night shift when I was playing softball, so I would open a can of beef stew or spaghetti to feed the children, and then we were off to the ball game. I concentrated on playing ball so much that I never knew what the children were doing or where they were. When the children were grown, they told me what they would do during my ball games and how the police had picked them up somewhere one time and brought them back to the ball field. I broke my ankle one night as I was sliding into second base. I thought that I had only sprained it, so I went into work. It got to where it hurt so bad that I ended up going to the hospital, and they told me it was broken. They put a cast on my leg and gave me a set of crutches. Since I was a foreman and didn't have to do any manual labor, I went back to work. I had only missed two hours of work.

After my ankle was better, I was in the restroom at work with the door locked. The restroom was only built for one person. The union president went and told the superintendent that I was in there asleep. The superintendent took the union president's word for it, called me into his office, and told me to either resign or he would have to do something else. I told him that I would resign if that was the way he felt. I went up to Emmett O'Neal's office and told him what had happened. He told his secretary to type out a letter of resignation that I could use to find another job. I could tell that he didn't like what had happened because I had been there for eleven years, but he didn't want to go against the superintendent's decision.

We had a sandblasting machine at O'Neal Steel that we used to knock the rust off the sixty-foot steel beams so they could be painted smooth. My brother James had a good friend named Jack Wade who lived in West Blocton and worked at O'Neal Steel as a maintenance man. During a shift change, he told the foreman to watch for him as he went down into the sandblasting pit where the steel beams were to check on something. He told the foreman not to let anyone throw the switch while he was down there. While he was down in the pit, the foreman walked off and left the switch unattended. Someone came along, not knowing that Jack was in the pit, and threw the switch. I had already resigned, but from what I was told, the sandblaster tore Jack apart and left nothing but his bones.

I was about to go to West Virginia to work in the coal mines with my brother Bennie Ray. The day after I had resigned, Jack Blackwell who was the headman at O'Neal Steel called me and told me that he had a good friend in Knoxville, Tennessee, that needed a plant superintendent. I told him that I wasn't interested and that I was going back into the coal mines. Bennie Ray was making $500 a week, which was a lot of money in the early seventies. Jack told me to call Harold Hale in Knoxville and to let him know that Jack had talked to me, but I didn't call him. Harold Hale actually called me and asked me to come to Knoxville to talk to him. He said to bring my whole family and spend a week in a motel, and his company would pay the expenses. I told him okay and that I would come up there and talk to him. I took Nettie Jo and the children with me to stay in the motel like he had suggested. Mr. Hale took Nettie Jo and I to downtown Knoxville, and we talked and discussed different subjects. He told Nettie Jo that she had a smart husband. We went back to his big, three-story house, and he fixed me some sort of Russian alcoholic drink. I sneaked over to the end of the porch and poured it out. I didn't drink, but I didn't tell him that. I told him that I would take the job, and he said that I would be over two steel plants. The other one was in Johnson City, Tennessee, about a hundred miles away. I would have to go up there every three weeks to make sure everything was running smoothly. After I accepted the job, he moved our furniture from Birmingham to Knoxville at no charge to us. I had put a lot of years' worth of hard work, and it finally paid off. I became a superintendent at the age of thirty-three, just like the Auburn graduate, and I had no college education. What I did have was a lot of dedicated work experience.

After I took the job in Knoxville, I rented out my big house next to Johnny Warren to a friend of mine. He told me that he would take care of my house and have the payments sent to me on time. I had explained to him the situation that I had with the lady that I bought the house from and how she would probably try to get the house back. We really enjoyed living in that big house. It had a big attic fan that would pull the air throughout the house in the summertime, so we didn't have to turn the air conditioner on. Nettie Jo decided that she wanted to have her picture taken while we lived in that house in Woodlawn because they were running a special on pictures.

Nettie Jo Moore Whatley

The photographer took a really good picture of her, so we got a twenty-inch-by-twenty-four-inch print. She was so pretty in the picture that the photographer asked if he could put it up in his showcase window for a month so other people could see what good work he did. We agreed to let him do it. We had a pool table in the basement of that big house, and if we went to West Blocton or anywhere, we would just let the neighborhood kids come and play as they pleased in our basement. Sometimes when it rained, we would get a foot of water in the basement. I had an electrical pump that I used to pump the water out. It was a miracle that I never got electrocuted. The pump was down under the water in the sump, and I walked around in the water barefooted. If the pump had shorted out, I would have been in big trouble, but I wasn't thinking about that.

We had two cocker spaniel dogs outside of our house. We had gone to West Blocton for the weekend to see our parents and left the basement door open for the neighborhood kids to shoot pool while we were gone. When we got back home, we found out that someone had stolen our two dogs. I told the kids that were in the basement that there would be no more playing pool in our basement until the dogs came back. I don't know who took our dogs, and I never asked, but they showed back up the next day. So I let the neighborhood kids keep shooting pool in the basement until we moved to Knoxville and I rented that house out.

I sent the lady a payment thinking that my renter would send me his payment on time, but he didn't. That caused my check to bounce, and the lady that I bought the house from didn't inform me that my check had bounced until I got a letter from her lawyer saying that she had repossessed the house. I went to Birmingham from Knoxville to talk to a lawyer, and I asked him if I could get my house back. He said it would cost me $1,000, and he couldn't guarantee that he could get it back for me, so I told him to forget it. I didn't have the money to pay the lawyer, and the lady got the house back just like her ex-son-in-law said. Later on, a chain motel bought every house on that block, so she probably made a lot of money on that house. She probably knew in advance that the motel was coming there.

We moved to Merchant's Drive in Knoxville. We lived right on the main road. We moved in and cleaned the house really good and told the landlord that if he bought the paint, we would paint his house at no charge. He bought the paint, and we painted the rooms the colors that we wanted. After we lived in that house for a few months, I got scared one night. It was raining, and Nettie Jo and the children had gone to the store. They came back to the house and were all shaken up and crying. I thought something had happened to one of the children, but they told me that one of our cocker spaniels had been killed. Another incident that happened while we lived there occurred when Nettie Jo and Cheryl were going somewhere in our car. A girl in another car didn't stop at a stop sign and hit our car. Cheryl was only four years old and was standing up in the front seat. Back then, we didn't have seat belt or car seat laws. Nettie Jo had just told her to turn around when the cars collided. Cheryl was in the hospital for two weeks, and Nettie Jo was in for four days. The girl that hit them never went to see them or called to see how they were doing. The girl had no insurance, so we sued and got $20,000 because I had an uninsured motorist policy. In a way, it was a miracle. Cheryl had internal bleeding while she was in the hospital. The doctor found out that she only had one kidney. They said if they hadn't found out about that, she would probably have needed a kidney transplant when she was grown. They repaired her kidney by putting some sort of tube in it.

Cheryl Whatley

We had a nice older couple that lived next door to us. They liked our children. They had both been married twice and were retired. John would come over to visit with us sometimes, and he would throw change on the floor to watch the kids scramble to pick it up. His wife's name was Shirley. When I started working for Tucker Steel as superintendent, my manager Harold Hale told me that there was a man out there in the shop working who was planning on retiring the next year, and Harold had orders to get rid of him. I had no reason to fire the old guy. About six months later, Harold came up to me and said, "It's you or him!" So I had to go out into the warehouse and tell the old man that he was fired. It was for no reason at all. It was very hard for me to do that back in 1973, and I know that it was hard for Harold too because I knew he was a compassionate man, but we had our orders. We had a steel warehouse, which I was over, and the company had a fabrication shop above us. I fired him from the warehouse, and they hired him as a new employee in the fabrication shop the next day. They did it to keep him from getting his retirement. Forty years later, in 2013, that practice was still going on. Companies hire people as temporary employees to keep from having to pay them benefits.

Harold Hale told me that he wanted to get his steel plant looking like O'Neal Steel. The man that owned both Tucker Steel plants had a third-grade education. He started out with a welding rig on a pickup truck and said he surrounded himself with smart people. He must have been pretty smart himself to go from a welder to a millionaire. Harold was the smartest manager that I had ever worked for in all my thirty-three years of working in the steel industry. All the managers that I worked with were smart, but he was the best. Mr. Tucker, the owner of the plants, was a good man. He didn't think he was above anyone. He had an eighteen-year-old girlfriend, even though he was fifty-three and married. His wife and his grown children knew about the girlfriend, but they didn't seem to care. He kept her in a new car and paid for her motel rent. Sometimes, he would eat in the same restaurant with his girlfriend while his wife and children were there. He was just an old country guy that didn't look like he had anything. I was traveling around Tennessee and Georgia in my car, looking for a big saw to cut steel. Mr. Tucker came up to me and told me that if I needed to go anywhere else and I wanted him to, he would fly me in his plane. I said, "No, thank you. I will just stay on the ground." I had heard that once he got in the air, he would turn the controls over to you. Tucker Steel had a company car that was serviced and always filled with gas, but the company sold it for $50 just to get it off their books.

One of the traits that I liked about Harold Hale is that he showed no partiality to anyone. He would take up for the janitor as much as he would take up for the president of the company. He would come out to the plant on any given day of the week and say, "Let's go to Johnson City for three days." Our company rented a house on a lake near the Johnson City plant so that we had a place to stay when we went up there. The company only paid $100 a month for rent. We ended up closing down the plant in Johnson City before I left Knoxville. It just wasn't making enough money to keep it open. When Harold told me that he wanted his plant to look like O'Neal Steel, I immediately had racks built to store the steel. When I first started working there, you could hardly see the floor because they had so much steel lying around all over the place. A month or two after I was there, people across town would come in and say that I had the place looking good. I had to terminate two of my foremen because they would not do the things that I told them to do. They did not seem to like change. I felt bad about firing them, but they just wouldn't change their old ways. They wouldn't load the trucks and get them out the way that I wanted. I promoted two other men to foreman, and they did a better job than the previous two, and they did things the way that I wanted them done.

One day, Mr. Hale came to me and asked if my family and I wanted to stay in his three-story house for a few weeks while he was on vacation. He said we could just pretend it was our house and make ourselves at home and do whatever we wanted. I told him that we would be glad to stay there because we were just renting our place. Mr. Hale's house had five bedrooms, five bathrooms, and a TV in every room. The top floor was just one big room, and that is where Nettie Jo and I slept. We really enjoyed spending those three weeks in that big house. Shortly after Harold got back from his vacation, my daddy had gotten deathly ill down in West Blocton. I told Harold that I had to go home to be with my daddy. He told me to go home and take all the time that I needed, so I went home for three weeks. Harold didn't object at all. He was a very compassionate person. Harold Hale always let us know that he appreciated how hard we worked for the company. One night, he paid two men to cook half a hog all night so that we could have a good dinner the next day. He didn't care what it would cost the company.

My daddy had cancer of the lung, liver, and stomach. We boys would ride him around Piper to get catawba worms off the catawba trees, pretending that we were going to take him fishing. The doctors said that he only had about thirty days to live, but he lasted ninety days. He was just about out of his mind and slobbering at the mouth when he was riding around with us. It was a sad time, but I felt lucky that I got to hold his hand as he took his last breath. I told him that I would be with him in heaven later. After my daddy died, my mother bought a house on Main Street, across from Nanny and Johnny Rice. Every year, the entire Whatley family would meet there for Thanksgiving to eat dinner and socialize. There was usually about fifty-three people, all having a good time. My mother would always cook puddings, pies, and cakes. Everyone else would bring a dish or two. We did that every year, except for the last year that my mother was alive because by then she was sick and in bed most of the time. Frank and I let Bennie Ray's son, Keith, and his wife, Allison, keep her for the last year that she was alive. We paid Keith and Allison $1,400 a month to take care of her and paid Bennie Ray's daughter, Crystal, $300 a month to help take care of things, like my mother's hair. My mother was a terrific woman and mother. She lived to be eighty-nine years old.

My family always enjoyed going to Cape Cove at Gatlinburg to watch all the deer running around. The deer were so tame that they would come up and eat bread out of our hands, although they had signs up saying not to feed them. Our family would go to Gatlinburg every few weeks. It was just forty miles from Knoxville, and it was a fun place to go. My children always enjoyed going over there, and I still like to go up there occasionally. It is a terrific place to take a vacation.

Once we finally got the warehouse in an organized shape, I didn't really need all the employees to do all the work, so I had to let two men go. I let the two go that had the least seniority to cut costs, and boy, here came the union again saying that I was cutting their membership down and they didn't like it. Their top union representative told me one day that one of his members was lazy, and he would not have the guy working for him. I told him, "If I let him go, you would file a grievance to reimburse him for lost wages." He told me that it was his job to protect his members, and I told him that was the trouble with unions. They have to protect even the sorry workers that didn't try to make money for the company. The owner has to make money in order to be able to afford raises. The less money that he makes, the less money that he can give to you. I told him that he should tell the employee (a union member) to get off his ass and work hard like everyone else or he won't protect him. The other employees shouldn't be forced to take up his slack.

We had a pretty good ball team in Knoxville, and one weekend, we were supposed to go to Birmingham for a ball tournament. My manager, Mr. Hale, decided that we had to have an inventory that weekend, so my ball team went to the church tournament without me. I told them that I would come down as soon as we got through with the inventory. I got into my car and went down to Birmingham, and when I got there, my team had just been knocked out of the tournament because they had lost two games. A coach of another team was about to play, and he said he didn't have a pitcher for the game. I don't remember what happened, but maybe their pitcher had to leave for some reason. My ball manager told him that I was a pitcher, so he put me in the game and listed my name as someone else. That wasn't being too good of a Christian. We won that game. I didn't know it was for the championship, but they gave me the game ball and told me that if I ever came back to Birmingham, let them know. They wanted me to pitch for their team, but I never moved back. I also played flag football until I was forty-seven years old.

While we were living in Knoxville, we had gone to West Blocton one weekend, and on the way back home, we stopped in Chattanooga. We rode the incline up the mountain to a park where there was a battlefield from the civil war. We went inside of a cave, and in that cave, there was a lake. We got in a boat with a glass bottom, and we could see fish swimming in the water underneath us. The park had guns and other things that were used in the civil war and plaques explaining different events that had happened in the war.

I helped negotiate the contract between Tucker Steel and the union, but this time I was negotiating for the company instead of the union. So I have negotiated for both sides, and I tried to be fair on both sides. I have learned over the years, because I have negotiated for unions that like Democrats and companies that like Republicans, that they don't seem to want to come to a happy medium. If there is no union, the company sometimes takes advantage of the employees, but if there is a union, they tend to take advantage of the company. One example is the union protecting an employee that is not doing his job and causing other workers to cover the extra responsibility of the work he isn't doing.

When I was working for Tucker Steel, one company that owed Tucker Steel a lot of money went bankrupt. Our manager, Mr. Hale, was smart enough to get a lien on all their assets, just in case they couldn't pay for all the steel that they got from our company. Because of the lien, we had to go to the bankrupt company's site and label everything that they had for a cheap price so that we could get the money that was owed to Tucker Steel. They had some material that was brand-new. We got an auctioneer to auction off everything at a bid. Everything that we couldn't auction off, we just practically sold at a giveaway price. We bought a forklift for $600. We finally got enough money for what they owed to Tucker Steel, so I guess the other people that were owed money only got part of their money or none at all.

Shortly after we negotiated the contract, Mr. Tucker decided that he wanted to sell his steel plant to a couple of millionaires. When they took over, they told our very good and very smart manager, Mr. Hale, what he had to do differently. He had more knowledge of how to run a steel plant in his little finger than they did in their big, dumb heads. Harold finally got so disgusted that he asked me if I wanted to go up to their office with him to resign. I tried to talk him out of it, but I couldn't. The new company brought in an interim manager who didn't know what he was doing. Right away, he let our secretary go. My family had gone on vacation, and when I got back, the new manager said they didn't need me anymore. After I left, I heard my foreman, Ted Mullins, took over my job. He couldn't handle it, so then the union president took the job. They thought they had heard the last of me, but it all came back to haunt them when they saw me again. The union president had been one of my tractor trailer drivers that I had caught multiple times on the road between Knoxville and Johnson City asleep. He had shot some bull to the interim manager about me, which wasn't true, to try to get me fired. They were still unhappy because I had let the two union employees go. I had told Harold earlier that we should fire the union president after I caught him asleep on the road, but Harold said to just let it go because he didn't want to fight the union.

The union president had a brother named Jim that also drove a tractor trailer, but I never had any problems out of him. Jim was on the road one day on his way back to the plant after delivering some steel. It was drizzling rain, and he had a very bad wreck. I was in my office when I got the call that one of my drivers had a wreck, and I thought he had killed two people. I got in my car and went to the scene of the accident. It was bad. Five young boys, all seventeen years old or younger, were supposed to be across town shooting basketball, but they were instead on this stretch of road drag racing. They were going really fast when their car went off the edge of the road. The driver lost control of the car and shot across the road right in front of Jim's tractor trailer. Jim hit the car broadside with his front wheels, and it made the driver's side of the car look like a convertible. He had killed four of the young boys. The fifth boy survived, but he lost both of his legs because the truck had to be pulled across his legs to get him out. When the truck hit the car, it threw the driver of the car about seventy-five feet down the road and punctured a hole in his skull that was the size of a baseball and scattered his brain up and down the pavement. It was still raining, so blood and brains were everywhere. Jim didn't have the nerve to ever drive a truck again. We just put him to work in the steel plant from then on. After I left Tucker Steel, an elderly couple pulled out in front of another one of our trucks, and it killed both of them.

We had good friends in Knoxville that we played ball and cards with, and we hated to leave. We had two couples that we played cards with. We would start playing cards at night and would stay up playing and eating until the next morning while our children were sleeping. Their names were Jimmy and Sue Honeycutt, and the other couple was Tommy and Nancy. Jimmy and Sue had five children, but Tommy and Nancy were younger and had no children. Sue was the preacher's daughter where we went to church. We learned later on that both couples had gotten divorced.

I had a friend that worked for Tennessee Steel in Nashville, and I asked him if they needed anyone to work. He called back saying they needed a night foreman and to come on down to talk to them. I went down, and they hired me right away. I traveled from Knoxville to Nashville for a while until we found us a place to live. We had a really pretty two-door Chrysler. I was leaving Nashville, headed back to Knoxville, at about 2:00 a.m., and as I was turning off the interstate, my gas line broke on top of the motor. The motor was so hot that it caught on fire and burned the car up. We then bought a Ford station wagon with the insurance money from losing the Chrysler.

Nettie Jo and I had four pretty little children that were all well disciplined, but people didn't like renting to people with children. I guess they thought that the children would tear their house up. I can only remember one incident of doing any damage to any of the houses that we rented. Mike shot a BB gun in Goodlettsville, right outside of Nashville, and damaged one little eight-inch square window, but I repaired it. Tucker Steel moved our furniture from Knoxville to Goodlettsville at no charge. We cleaned that house up before we moved in like we did to the house in Knoxville. We told the landlord to buy the paint and we would paint the house. When we moved out, we cleaned the house up really good again.

Carol and Teresa playing in the snow

The children loved Goodlettsville. It snowed quite a bit, and we all liked playing in the snow. I would play in the snow barefooted with no shirt on, and it didn't bother me when I was young. The people across the street had a house trailer. It caught fire during one big snow, and it burned to the ground because the fire department couldn't get there to put the fire out. There was too much snow. A really pretty, shapely woman lived there with her husband. Before the trailer burned, she would get out in the front yard and lie on a pallet in her bikini. When a car would come down the road, she would get up and prance around. I couldn't look because Nettie Jo was at the window watching me. I wasn't even allowed to speak to the girl. I guess the girl thought that I was stuck-up. She had a husband, but I guess he was working.

Our children had a lot of good friends in Goodlettsville. They liked their school, and we lived close to three country music stars. Kitty Wells and Lynn Anderson lived not far from our house. Both of them had country music hits. Boots Randolph was famous for playing some instrument, and I have some of his records. We would pass Lynn Anderson's house, and sometimes, she would be outside riding her horse. She loved horses. The stars just lived in older country homes instead of the big fancy houses that they could have if they wanted to. They were content living out in the country.

In 1972, Nettie Jo, the children, and I had been somewhere in our station wagon. And on the way home, a young girl was coming the opposite direction on a country road. The girl dodged a cat that had run across the road and hit our station wagon head-on. We were both lucky because each car was going about forty miles per hour. I think it hurt one girl in her car. My car was leaking gasoline down the road, and I was hoping that it wouldn't catch on fire because I couldn't get my door open. My chest bent the steering wheel. Nettie Jo was wedged under the dashboard. And all the children were originally in the back of the station wagon, but now they were all against the back of our seats. No one had a seat belt on. We all went to the hospital to be checked out, and luckily, everyone was okay. Our station wagon was totaled. That was about two weeks before we moved to Mobile, Alabama. The girl's insurance furnished a car for me to drive for about a week until I got us another car. Our station wagon was only worth $575, according to the book value, so I called the girl's insurance company to see what they were going to do to settle. They said, "We paid the hospital bill, so about another $250 should be okay." I told them that my lawyer said they should pay $1,000, and they said that was close enough and to come on down and get the money. I didn't even talk to a lawyer; I just told the insurance company that I did. One thousand dollars was a lot of money to us back then. It seemed like every time that we started to move in Tennessee, we had a car wreck.

People in Tennessee warned me to make sure that I had insurance because it would snow ten to twelve times a year and the overpasses would ice over really bad. One day, we went to West Blocton for the weekend, but we didn't go prepared for cold weather. It was fifty-eight degrees Fahrenheit in Blocton that day. I was sitting in my car, and I had left the radio set to a Nashville station. I couldn't believe my ears; the radio announced that there was a blizzard that was hitting as far down as Nashville. I didn't even have a coat. None of us did. I didn't even know if we would be able to get back to our house because we lived way up a long hill in Goodlettsville. We got back home, and it was so pretty because it looked like a Christmas card. Ice and snow were everywhere. All the tree limbs were hanging down, covered with snow and ice. They were beautiful.

I was the night shift foreman at Tennessee Steel. I worked with another foreman named Jim. Our superintendent was a Yankee named Ray, and the foreman that worked with him on day shift was Tom Ferguson, a big old fat guy. Ray was a typical Yankee, a big talker that would tell you all that he could do and how good he was. The men went on strike at the company, trying to organize a union. That was when we found out that Ray, the superintendent, didn't know how to do anything. We salaried employees had to start loading the steel into the trucks and delivering it ourselves. Sometimes, the union men would climb over the fence and let the air out of the tires or disconnect the fifth wheel, which connects the tractor to the trailer. They were hoping that we didn't notice and that we would get in the tractor to drive off, pull it out from under the trailer, and let the trailer hit the ground. But that didn't happen. We would check everything before we got into the truck. Ray didn't even know how to hook a tractor trailer up or how to drop them on the yard after we had them loaded. The men stayed on the picket lines for about two months before they decided to come back to work with no union. They were about to starve.

I had a good friend of mine named Hershel Morris who worked for me and would invite my family over to his house to eat and throw horseshoes. I always associated with the men that worked for me rather than the company people. They respected me for that. I never tried to think that I was better than them just because I was a supervisor. Jim, the other foreman, and I would help the men get their work done if they needed us to. My good friend, Jimmy McGriff, offered me some Chiclets one day. I thought he was chewing them too, but he tricked me and had given me Chiclets that made my bowels move. After a little while working, they would ask me something concerning the work, but I would have to say, "I'll be right back. I have to go to the bathroom." Eventually, they started laughing and told me what they had done. They knew that I would eat anything that they offered to me if it was free.

Railroad cars would come into the warehouse at night for us to unload. If we didn't get the railroad car unloaded within two days, the railroad would charge the company so much for each day that it was there. Jim and I would always try to get them unloaded to save the company money. Ray told us not to unload so many because the more that we unloaded, the more the people in the office would expect us to do. We told the salesman inside what Ray told us, and one night, we had gotten caught up with nothing left to do, so we unloaded another railroad car. The next morning, Ray and the fat slob foreman Tom called me into the office and commenced to chewing me out. I just started looking out the window. Fat Tom spoke up and said, "Look at him, Ray, looking out of the damn window and not paying any effing attention to what you are saying!" I wanted to pop him in his big, fat mouth, but I had a family to feed, so I maintained my composure. When Ray was through, I just said okay and walked out into the warehouse. A couple of months later, Tennessee Steel sold out to Ingalls in Birmingham. Ray told all the supervisors not to tell the new owners any more than we have to. Jim and I were working on night shift when one of the important men from the new company came around and started asking us questions. Jim said sarcastically, "Bobby, we are not supposed to answer any questions because we were told not to." I said, "That's right, Jim." The man from Ingalls said we could answer anything that he asked, and then he asked who told us not to answer. We both said Ray, the superintendent. Oh, boy, here we go again!

Nettie Jo didn't like Goodlettsville too much. I took the children to a church outing one Sunday, but Nettie Jo didn't want to go. When the children and I got back home, my neighbor told me that my wife was in the hospital. I asked him what happened, but he said he didn't know except that the ambulance came and got her. I went to the hospital and talked to the doctor. He told me it was her nerves, and I replied, "That's what you say about everything," being a smart aleck. I could tell he didn't like what I said, and I couldn't blame him.

I called my sister-in-law, Linda Moore, and asked her if she could come up and babysit for a week until Nettie Jo got out of the hospital because I still needed to work every day, so she agreed.

The vice president of Ingalls, Bill Kearney Jr., talked to me one day, and I told him that I was quitting as soon as school was out and that we were moving back to Alabama. He asked me if I wanted to go to one of the Ingalls locations in Mobile, Alabama, to be the super-intendent. I told him, "Sure, I do!" He told me to go down and look over Jones and Armstrong Steel. Nettie Jo and I had been to Panama City Beach, Florida, or Gulf Shores, Alabama, the year before that. And we had taken the wrong road on the way back and ended up in downtown Mobile. We went down Government Street and saw these big oak trees on both sides of the street, extending out over the road. They were really pretty. I told Nettie Jo that I would like to live in a town like this, so when Bill Kearney Jr. said that, I was ready to go. Nettie Jo and I went down to Mobile to look for a house to rent, and we found one in the paper. I didn't know anything about Mobile, so my new boss, Ron Biggs, took me over to the house and got a speed-ing ticket on the way. I felt bad, but he told me not to worry about it. Ron was a good manager and knew how to sell steel. We knew that when he left the office to visit some of his customers, we were going to be really busy the next day. Ron and I were the same age. His wife was a schoolteacher, but she passed away in her fifties.

When Hershel Morris heard that we were moving to Mobile, he and his wife cooked a big supper for my family before we moved. They were very nice people. They lived out in the country where he and his boys raised fighting roosters, which was against the law. They had hogs, chickens, cows, dogs, and cats. That brought along with it a bunch of flies. Hershel's wife made a big banana pudding, and a fly landed right in the middle of it. The fly didn't eat too much of it before we got it out and finished eating the rest of the pudding. It was really good. Hershel had some horseshoes. So he, his boys, and I threw horseshoes all afternoon after we had eaten.

Ingalls moved our furniture from Goodlettsville to Mobile free of charge. We moved into a rental house that Pickett and Adam's Real Estate had advertised and that Ron had taken me to. About three months later, we found a good bargain to buy a house on Rochelle Street, which was named after a woman that lived two houses down from us on our side of the road. The woman's daddy owned all the land where the road was built and named it after his daughter, Rochelle Huebach. She was married to a man named Ronnie. They had five children, but she was still pretty and shapely. I got orders from Nettie Jo not to look down that way.

We had an empty lot next to our house between us and Charlie and Barbara Knall. Their children, our children, and Rochelle's children were all about the same age, and for years, the neighborhood kids would get together to play ball and other games. Our house was Grand Central Station. We bought that house for a bargain because the couple that sold it had separated or divorced. The wife was about thirty-five years old and was living there with a boy that was eighteen years old. She told her husband that if he moved her into a two-story home, she would come back to him. He sold it to us for $3,000 or $4,000 cheaper than what its value was, and he was nice enough to paint the house before we moved in, after we had already bought the house. He didn't have to do that for us, but it was nice of him that he did. My payments for the house were $200 a month for a three-bedroom brick home. We heard later on that his wife had gotten pregnant by the eighteen-year-old boy, but the husband didn't know it when he took her back. I heard they got a divorce later on.

Not long after we moved into the house on Rochelle Street, our neighbors up the road, Carl and Joyce Doyle, sent us some king mackerel. It was already cooked, and we didn't know what king mackerel even was at the time. We weren't used to saltwater fish because we had always fished in freshwater rivers and creeks. We became good friends with the Doyle family. Carl had a big boat, and they would invite me to go fishing with them sometimes. They said they went to Dauphin Island or Gulf Shores when the water got warm, so I told him that I would love to go.

Carl and Joyce both worked at International Paper until they retired. I was superintendent of Jones and Armstrong Steel, which belonged to Ingalls out of Birmingham. We started doing things together. They had five acres of land in Tillman's Corner and a house that they rented out on the land. There was another lot next to their land that was five acres with a brick house that was for sale for $35,000 in 1973. Nettie Jo didn't want us to buy it, but it was a very good bargain. Two years later, the land came up for sale again for $50,000. We decided to buy it this time, and now there were two house trailers with families living in them on the land. The families were paying the landowner rent for the trailer lots. After we bought the land, the owners of the trailer homes sold me the trailers after they moved away. One was $2,500, and the other was $2,800. Nettie Jo and I never lived on the land, so we put everything up for rent. Three of my children and their families lived in the three-bedroom house during the years that we owned it. Mr. and Mrs. Doyle planted a big garden on their land, and we planted a big garden on ours.

Later on in the years, an organization called ALM started up. It was a worm-growing organization who raised and sold red worms by the pound. ALM stood for Alabama, Louisiana, and Mississippi. They would start us out by making six three-foot-by-eight-foot beds and supplying five thousand worms in each bed for $2,000. It would be up to us how many beds we had after we got started. Red worms lay a lot of eggs, and each bed would produce thirty pounds per month. After I took my first pound of worms, ALM called a meeting with all the people that they started up and said the government said that we couldn't transfer worms across state lines, so the company folded. I switched from selling red worms to selling wiggler worms to bait shops. I had one acre on my land that I used to grow wiggler worms that I had gotten out of Florida from a worm grower. After I would run out of worms on my land, I would order ten thousand worms from Jimmy Carter's (our president at the time) brother in Georgia to supply my customers. He would send them to me in a day or two. We had worm machines that would separate the worm eggs, dirt, and worms. The eggs and dirt would fall through the screens, and the worms would come out of the end into a bucket. We were told there was a process of drying the worms out and using them in dog food, lipstick, and eye shadow. I ate a piece of worm cake one time. Worms are 73 percent protein.

Later on, I tried raising crickets after some of my worm customers said they would like to buy crickets with the worms. To raise crickets, I had to have a building that stayed about seventy degrees Fahrenheit day and night. I had a building on the land, but I had no way to control the heat. So I just bought crickets from a Black man that was raising them in this big empty house and resold them at a higher price. I met this old gentleman, Bob, who was about eighty years old in Theodore, Alabama, right outside of Mobile. He was raising rabbits to dress and sell five hundred pounds at a time to the ship captains that came in to the Mobile docks. He told me that if I wanted to get into the rabbit business, he would sell me some rabbits to get started. He would take all that I could raise once they got to about six weeks old. They usually weigh about three pounds when they are six weeks old, and he paid by the pound. So I started raising rabbits on Mr. and Mrs. Doyle's land next to mine. They had a shed, so I got me some rabbit cages. Not long after I started raising rabbits, I had more than five hundred of them. The shed kept the sun off the rabbits, and I put a fence around them to keep dogs from getting to them. Tame rabbits are all white meat, like chicken, and wild rabbits are dark meat. Tame rabbit is the highest nutritional meat that we can eat. It has no fat or cholesterol. A female rabbit can have two to thirteen babies every sixty days. If one rabbit had two babies at the same time that another rabbit had thirteen babies, I could take six of the thirteen, and the rabbit that only had two babies would nurse the six from the other litter as if they were her own.

One day, two federal men came into Bob's place and told him that he wasn't sanitary enough. Bob figured that his competition in Mississippi had put the feds on him. Bob was sanitary and could clean a rabbit in two minutes. He got mad and told the two feds that he was eighty years old and didn't have long to live, so if they walk in that door again to harass him, he would kill them both. They did not come back. A couple of years later, Bob did pass away, and that was the end of me raising rabbits. I had no other outlet to sell them to. A rabbit has to be cleaned by the time they are six weeks old and tender. After six weeks, the meat gets tough. The rabbits can get up to fifteen pounds, but after six weeks, the meat is not good to eat.

Williamson High School, in Mobile, was an all-Black-people school that was just across the road from the Jones and Armstrong Steel plant. One of the Black teachers was talking to me one day out in front of the school. I was telling him about the hard times that we had coming through the Great Depression and World War II with no government programs to help us. We had to struggle just to have something to eat. Eventually, the government came out with a commodity program that allowed a man without a job to get a little cheese, beans, and rice. I was telling him that I didn't try hard to learn anything in school and that it came back to haunt me once I got out into the real world. I told him that I had worked two jobs in all my years after I got out of school and that I had worked really hard to become the superintendent of a steel plant. After he listened to my story, he told me that he had some problem children that either couldn't or didn't want to learn, and he asked if I would be willing to come and tell them the same stories that I had just told him. I told him that I would be glad to. I went over the next day and talked to them. The children seemed to enjoy me talking to them, and I really hope that my story inspired them. One of the boys came up to me and said, "Man, you are cool." Then I went on back to work, hoping that I had made a good impression on them.

A few months later, I was talking to Mr. Phoebe in the same place that I had talked to the teacher. He was the principal of the school and a very large man. He told me that he did not argue with students or parents and that he kept a pistol in his pocket for protection. He said that if a student gave him trouble, he would just call the police to come and take the student downtown. Then he would call the child's parents and tell them that if they wanted their child, they could go downtown to pick them up. I remember seeing police cars over at the high school pretty regularly. He told me that he was going to retire the next year and that they could have it. That was on a Friday. When I came back to work the next day, which was a Saturday, I found out that he had committed suicide. I had no idea that he had that on his mind. I heard that he had prostate cancer and owed the government $63,000, so he decided to commit suicide to get out of it all.

One time, Bill Kearney, the vice president of Ingalls, wanted me to come up to Decatur on a Monday morning. I left Mobile on a Sunday and stayed with my brother Bennie Ray so that I could get up early on Monday morning to drive the remaining seventy-five miles to Decatur. It was drizzling rain that morning as I was going through Hueytown. I was the first car to start out at the red light after it turned green, and there was a line of traffic on the opposite side of the road waiting to turn. I got about fifty yards up the road when a young boy, about eight years old, was between two parked cars on the opposite side of the road and waiting on the traffic to cross the street. He jumped right out in front of my car, and it knocked him about thirty feet into the air. He came down on his head, which knocked a hole in it, threw one of his shoes off, tore up his coat, broke his leg, and knocked him unconscious. Around his eyes were really dark, and I thought that I had killed him. My son was also eight years old at that time, and that just flashed through my mind. The boy came to by the time the ambulance got there to take him to the hospital. The neighbor told me that it wasn't my fault. The boy's father told me that he had told some people that if they didn't stop jaywalking across that street, someone was going to get killed. I went on to Decatur to work that day, but I called to check on the boy and was told that he was doing okay. On my way back to Mobile that Friday, I went by the hospital to check on him. I brought some comic books with me, and I gave them to him along with some money.

A couple of months after I had gotten back home to Mobile, I found out I was being sued for $200,000 by some jackknife lawyer who was trying to get money out of the situation. I had insurance with State Farm, so they gave me a good lawyer to go to court a year later. I was scared to death because I only had $20,000 worth of insurance coverage. They had me a witness that said it wasn't my fault. She was a Black lady that drove the school bus and had seen what happened. When the neighbor that had told me that it wasn't my fault was on the stand, the lawyer asked her what happened. Well, she changed her story. That neighbor was waiting on one side of the street for the boy to cross and get into her car. My lawyer asked how fast I was going, which I had just started out fifty yards before from a red light, and she said, "About sixty miles per hour." My law-yer asked her how she knew that, and she said that she was looking in her rearview mirror. Then he asked why she didn't roll her window down to yell at the boy not to cross the road. She told him that she couldn't get her window down. He knew she was lying and then got the boy's mother on the stand. He asked her one question, and after she answered, he said, "Wait a minute! You told me something else a year ago. Were you lying then, or are you lying now?" She said, "I was lying a year ago." Then the judge spoke up and said, "All right, that's it. You all come back in my chambers." And that was the end of the trial. Their lawyer got really upset and said that he lost $15,000 on that case. The little boy was all right, but his broken leg was half an inch shorter than his other leg.

After we moved to Mobile, Nettie Jo got a job working at a fast-food restaurant called Colonel Dixie. Two men were partners and owned eleven locations in Mobile. She worked for them for nine years and became assistant manager. I talked to one of the partners one day, and he was a real nice person. His wife was spending money faster than he could make it, so he decided to hire a hit man for $10,000 to kill his wife before she financially broke him. He told the hit man to go ahead and take the big diamond rings off her fingers, and he could have them. The Federal Bureau of Investigation (FBI) started an investigation and ended up catching the hit man. The hit man told the FBI that the husband had hired him to kill her for $10,000, and they both got sent to prison. Then her husband sold his part of the business to the other partner. Eventually, the remaining partner sold out all but one of the locations, which stayed open for many years later. The dead woman's husband became trusted while in prison. He happened to be at the warden's house doing work for him when another prisoner escaped and killed both him and the warden.

Nettie Jo then started working in the hospital as a unit secretary. She worked there for fifteen years until she found out that she needed a liver transplant. She always wanted to work in a hospital to give the patients better care than she had gotten in the past, but when she put forth a little extra effort to help the patients, some nurses would tell her not to. She really did a good job, and everyone bragged about her and what a good job she did. She said that she wished she had gone on to become a nurse because a lot of the time, she would have to tell the nurses what to do.

In 1999, Nettie Jo found out about her liver. The hospital in Birmingham called us sometime in 2000 and said they had a liver for her, so we got ready, and I drove ninety miles per hour most of the way to Birmingham, hoping that a patrolman would see us and stop us for speeding. If we were stopped, I was going to ask the patrolman for an escort to the hospital, but I never got stopped. We got to UAB in Birmingham and found out that the liver had gone bad. We were upset over the bad news, but the hospital told us that they would call as soon as they found another liver. We went back home, and the very next morning, they called and said that they had another liver. A nineteen-year-old boy had a car wreck and had died. We rushed back up there, going ninety miles per hour again, but we still were never stopped by a patrolman. We got to the hospital, and they admitted her right away to start the operation.

The doctors at UAB were terrific. They came out to our family in the waiting room and explained everything that they were going to do and asked if we had any questions. Five or six doctors worked as a group, and during Nettie Jo's operation, the doctors would call the waiting room and let us know what they were doing as they operated. After the operation was finished, they all came to the waiting room to let us know how she was doing and to see if we had any questions. Nettie Jo stayed unconscious for three weeks in the emergency room. The doctors and nursing staff really matched with how well they took care of her. No one knew if she was going to make it or not. Nettie Jo was crazy about Elvis Presley, and we had talked about going to Graceland in Memphis. As I watched her lying there, unconscious and not knowing if she was going to live or die, I prayed to God and told him that if he spared her life and brought her back to us, I was going to take her to Graceland. She finally came to, and the doctors put her in another building next to the hospital. She stayed there for a month to get her strength back. God spared her life, but she had to quit work and get on disability. She also had a bad case of diabetes which prevented her from working anymore.

187

Elvis was forty-two years old when he passed away. He was on *The Ed Sullivan Show* on TV when he started out singing. He was famous for his swiveling hips when he sang, but Ed Sullivan wouldn't allow him to be seen from the waist down. He would let other artists do whatever they wanted to on his program, so that was the end of me watching *The Ed Sullivan Show*. I didn't like him after that. I was taking inventory for Ingalls Iron Works in Decatur when Elvis passed away. I would have to travel to different locations from Mobile to take inventory for one to three weeks at a time when I was superintendent. I would travel mainly to Decatur or Birmingham, but one time, I went to Knoxville while the children were still in school. I know that put a hardship on Nettie Jo, trying to work and keep the children in school. My boss Ron Biggs didn't like me leaving the Mobile locations, but the vice president of Ingalls would tell him that they needed me to help take inventory at the other locations. Bill Kearny Jr. was the vice president of Ingalls, and his father, Bill Kearney Sr., was the president.

One morning, I got a call from a friend of mine that worked for one of Ingalls companies in Florida. He asked me to come meet with him in Knoxville and not to tell anyone anything. I was supposed to tell my manager Ron when I was going out of town, but I didn't tell him. I met my friend in Knoxville, and he introduced me to two lawyers. I had been the superintendent of Tucker Steel in Knoxville, and Ingalls had bought them out. The lawyers told me that Bill Kearny Jr., the vice president of Ingalls and a good friend of mine, had been stealing money from the company along with some other people. The lawyers gave me an address to go check out and see where they were storing the steel that had been stolen. I asked the top inside salesperson, who had been with the company for seventeen years, to tell me what was going on, or he was going to lose his job. He told me nothing. So I told him to get into the car with me, and we went to the location that the lawyers told me to go to, but I didn't see anything. The salesperson told me that was the first time he had been over there in a long time. I got word that someone had called Ron Biggs in Mobile, wanting to know what I was doing up there. Ron told him that he had no idea and that I did not tell him anything. I got back to the motel and couldn't shake the feeling that something wasn't right. I decided to go back over there the next day. One of my truck driver friends that worked there said that something was going on, but he did not know exactly what it was. After I got back to the address that the lawyers gave me, I went a little farther up on a hill and found the steel that they had been storing. When I told the lawyers that I found it, they had discovered that Bill Kearney Jr., the manager, the top inside salesperson, the new superintendent, and a foreman were all involved. They were all fired that Thanksgiving week. I missed being home with my family that Thanksgiving, and I don't know how the Knoxville plant ran after all those people were fired, but I assume that Ingalls replaced everyone temporarily. Later on, I found out that my brother in Birmingham was Bill Kearney Jr.'s probation officer, and he told me that Bill had said that he had no hard feelings toward me. I had to testify in court against him, but I was just doing my job.

A man by the name of Mr. Presley worked at Ingalls shipbuilding in Pascagoula, Mississippi. He decided to buy some land beside the Mississippi River on the Alabama-Mississippi state line and told some of the men that he worked with that he was going to make a million dollars. He and his sons started clearing out the land that he bought and named it Presley's Landing. He developed it into a vacation and recreational site. He had everything that anyone would want to do, such as horseshoes, basketball, pool tables, a café, and restaurant. There were tables and seats placed both outside and inside the restaurant. There were volleyball courts both in the water and out of it, and there were between fifty to seventy-five campers there that belonged to individuals who paid so much rent each month.

Nettie Jo always said that she would love to have a place down there. I went down there one day and bought a camper trailer that had a porch with two overhead fans. I told my oldest daughter, Carol, what I had done and said we would take Nettie Jo down there to pretend we were looking at the trailer. We went into the trailer, and Nettie Jo said, "I wish I had a place down here." So I reached into my pocket and told her, "Here are the keys. It's yours." We really surprised her, and she liked it for a while, but she didn't like the

Mississippi water. After going down there a few times, she was tired of the camper trailer, so we sold it to my daughter and her husband, Carol and Roger McKeown. Later on, they sold it to someone else. Mr. Presley had canoes for people to rent, and people could ski and fish on the river. He turned it into a terrific vacation spot, and he made his million dollars just like he had set out to do after working hard for many years.

We had some good friends in Nashville named Andy and Janelle Matovich that we played cards with. Andy worked for me at the steel plant when I was a foreman. He was retired from the army after serving for twenty years. When they found out that we were moving to Mobile, his wife talked him into selling their two-story home to follow us down there later on. They came down to see if they were going to rent a house or buy one. Nettie Jo and I showed them around town, and they liked Mobile. They found a house to rent and later bought them a house and moved in. The day that they came down, we all went out and played carpet golf.

Andy was retired, and Janelle was on disability. Andy and I started doing a little reel and rod fishing across the Mobile Bay near the *USS Alabama* battleship. I didn't know that there were alligator gars and alligators in the water. I would wade out as far as I could to cast my line. The bottom was so murky that I could hardly walk. I would pull one foot out of the mud; then the other foot would go down in it. Andy stayed on the bank, and I was very lucky because later on, we would hear about alligators being killed in that spot and people catching alligator gars, which were very big. Someone killed one seven-foot-long alligator on the causeway where we would cross the pavement.

While I was superintendent of Jones and Armstrong Steel, I did all the purchasing of materials for the warehouse and trucks. One day, a tire salesman came by, trying to sell tires for the trucks and trailers in my steel plant. He told me about all the fish he was catching and how he had to fix different lures for the different kinds of fish in salt or brackish water. He caught redfish, Spanish mackerel, and bluefish. He used spoons and dragged them at about five miles per hour behind his boat. He asked me if I wanted to go fishing that Saturday so he could show me how to catch saltwater fish, so naturally I said yes. To catch king mackerel, he had to put a cigar minnow on a special hook and drag the line about five miles per hour. If the lure went too fast or slow behind the boat or if the water was really slick where the fish could see the hook, they wouldn't bite. To catch the larger king mackerel, we would go out to the oil rigs and bottom fish. One time, we caught a big king mackerel. When we pulled it up, I found that the fish had a rod and reel attached to it from where someone had tried to catch it before. So we got a large king mackerel and a bonus rod and reel.

I loved saltwater fishing. We would put out three lines from the back of the boat and one on each side, all in rod holders, then let about fifty to seventy-five feet of slack into the line. We would sit down while we were trolling and waiting for the fish to bite. To catch the Spanish mackerel and bluefish, we had three hooks on each line. Most of the time when we went through a school of fish, we could catch two or three at a time. When we saw birds diving into the water or fish jumping out of the water, we knew that they were feeding on the schools of fish, so we would go through that spot. We would keep circling to drag our hooks through the bait fish as long as they would bite. When the fish stopped biting, we would find a new spot where the fish were biting. My friend and I would go almost every Saturday if the weather and the water were right. Whenever the water was slick or there were more than two-foot waves or white caps, it is no good for fishing. Fishing is best with no white caps and waves one to two feet. If we wanted to catch redfish, with scales as big as a silver dollar, we would use six-to-eight-inch silver spoons with no bait on them. Big redfish have worms in them sometimes, and the smaller ones are better to eat. We would stop the boat and bait the hook with shrimp to catch two-to-three-pound redfish.

I had another friend named Huey Walker who lived in Wilton, Alabama, which is two miles from Montevallo. He would come to Mobile to visit his daughter, and he had a boat that he kept at her house all the time. Huey was married to Betty Langston, the daughter of Bill Langston who worked with me at O'Neal Steel in the sixties and seventies. I didn't know it until later, but my cousin Jimmy Lovejoy married Bill Langston's other daughter, Wanda. My brother

Bennie Ray and my mother came down to Mobile one weekend to go fishing. Huey, Bennie Ray, and I were fishing in the ship channel on Saturday with big silver spoons. We caught sixteen big reds that were between ten to sixteen pounds each. Bennie Ray said that he wanted to take them home to show my mother and that he would help clean them. We got home, and he showed them to my mother and then went to bed. I wasn't going to clean them all myself, so I gave all of them to my next-door neighbor, Barbara Knall. They cleaned and ate all of them.

Red Fish

Five redfish with my brother Bennie Ray in the back and I, Bobby Whatley, in front

While my mother was down visiting us, all my children and I decided to take her over to the gambling boats in Biloxi, Mississippi. The casino that we took her to had simulated rides that were pretty rough and would jerk you around. My mother was eighty-four years old at the time, and she would ask, "Is the next ride this rough?" And I would say, "No, Mamma," knowing that it was. Bennie Ray kept hollering, "Yes, it is, Mamma!" She rode all of them and really enjoyed herself. One of the hurricanes destroyed that casino, and they never replaced it. I didn't care about going to the casinos that didn't have the simulated rides.

I went fishing with another friend of mine the weekend after my mother and Bennie Ray came down. We were in the ship channel in Dauphin Island and caught nine huge redfish that were between sixteen and twenty-six pounds each. I also gave those to my neighbors, the Knalls. Another Saturday, my friend, my son Mike, and I were fishing in Dauphin Island. We stopped to eat breakfast, and my friend and I ordered eggs. Mike said that he didn't want eggs, but after they brought ours out, he said they looked pretty good. Mike was about eight or nine at the time, and we told him they were seagull eggs. He really wanted those eggs, and after he ate them, he said seagull eggs were better than chicken eggs. We didn't tell him any different, and he really thought that they were seagull eggs. Mike caught a big fish called a crevalle jack which is not good to eat and is hard to bring in. They come in sideways and will really get your hands tired, but Mike kept on reeling it until he finally got it in. I got it on camera and put it on a DVD. I had an eight-millimeter movie camera that I used to film him catch it. The fish was about thirty-five pounds and three feet long.

After people found out that I liked to fish, I had about three different people with boats that I would go with just about every Saturday or Sunday: the tire salesman that I met at my warehouse, my neighbors Carl and Joyce Doyle up the street, and Huey Walker out of Wilton, Alabama. I bought me a seventeen-foot inboard and outboard so I could fish any time that I wanted. I didn't have life preservers, a depth finder, a compass, or any safety equipment, like flares or radio. I tried not to go too far out to where I couldn't see land.

I would fish in the bay, near the *USS Alabama*, and the tide would drop so low that it would cause me to run aground because I didn't have a depth finder. I couldn't tell if I was in six inches or ten feet of water, so I would have to back up and try to go again. Back then, we had no rules to go by. Now your boat has to be fully equipped or the water patrol will give you a ticket, just the same as if you were on the land in a vehicle and broke the law. We would sometimes catch ten or twenty fish when we went out on our boat, but my best two days' fishing was when I took three or four of the children out and we caught 103 Spanish mackerel. We were close to Petit Bois Island, about two miles from Dauphin Island.

One day, Huey Walker came down from Wilton, and we decided to go fishing in my boat. We went to Dauphin Island and put the boat in the water. We started fishing, and a storm came up on us. My boat had a place where you could get out of the rain, but it was a tight fit getting in and out. After the storm passed, Huey decided to come out, but I kept hitting big waves on purpose, and it would knock him back down. I finally let him out with his skinned-up elbows. Nettie Jo got in the boat with me one time, and she said she wouldn't get back in it again. I would get my son Mike and his friends in the boat and hit seven-foot waves head-on. One time, my three Black friends that worked with me at the steel plant decided to go to Dauphin Island with me. Alfonse Hill, his brother-in-law Charlie Carter, and Johnny Wilkes got in Alfonse's boat, and my son and his friend were in my boat. Me and Alfonse got our boats going around and around with water coming into the boat, just having fun, and Alfonse's brother-in-law Charlie got scared and said he wouldn't get back in the boats with us fools.

My uncle Eddie went fishing for redfish with my son, Bennie Ray, and me close to the big bridge going to Dauphin Island. Uncle Eddie laid my rod and reel down in the boat, and a fish got on the line and pulled the rod and reel out of the boat. We lost that rod and reel, and he told me he would replace it because he shouldn't have laid it down. He did replace it later on.

I asked this friend of mine if he wanted to go fishing with me in my boat, and he said yes. We put the boat in the water at Dauphin

Island, but the water was getting a little rough, so we decided to go to Petit Bois Island. After we passed Dauphin Island, I looked at the back of the boat and saw oil bubbling. I didn't know what was happening, so I got closer to the shore and put my anchor down to stop the boat. The anchor didn't stop us because the rough waves kept pushing us closer toward the shore. Finally, the waves sunk my boat close to the shore. We got all my fishing equipment out of the boat before it sunk all the way. We put everything way up on the beach, and my friend was so mad that he hitchhiked back to Mobile. He said that was the first and last time that he went fishing. We were both soaking wet. I got back to my car, about two miles back after catching a ride, but my friend had already gone. I tried for a week before I finally got my boat out of the water. It had washed next to the beach. I got my Black friends to go with me every afternoon to try and get it out. The same day that I sunk my boat, I borrowed my Black friend's boat to try to pull my boat back into the water since we couldn't get it out by land. I sunk his boat while I was trying to get mine out, so I sunk two boats in the same day. I got paid for my boat with the insurance, and then my Black friend informed me that he had borrowed his boat from another friend, and it didn't have insurance. A boy with a jeep finally got my boat out on the beach, but we never got the other boat out. They didn't make me pay for it.

I found out that the reason my boat had an oil leak was because my son and son-in-law, Michael and Timmy, had worked on the boat but forgot to put the oil plug back in tight. They forgot to tell me and didn't know that I was going fishing. I think that was the worst week of my life. On top of everything, I thought that I had put my fishing equipment far enough up on the beach, but when I got back there the next day, the tide had gone up and washed half of my stuff into the ocean, and I never got it back. I never got another boat after that. I just went fishing with our neighbors, the Doyles, from then on.

Nettie Jo and I had been around salt water a couple of times earlier in our lives. We went on vacation one year with our children and rented a place on a canal as you are going into Gulf Shores. The canal went from Gulf Shores to Florida. The water is brackish, which is a freshwater and saltwater mix, and we fished in the canal. We mostly caught hardtail catfish which are saltwater catfish, but occasionally we would catch a freshwater catfish. The hardtail catfish have fins that are poisonous, and if you get stung by their fins, it causes bad soreness. My brother Franklin stepped on one, and the fin nearly came out of the top of his foot. It put him in the hospital for three weeks. Another time that we had an experience with the gulf waters was when Nettie Joe and I and two other couples chartered a fishing boat in Panama City, Florida, for a two-day fishing trip. We went out about fifty miles to where the water was six hundred feet deep. We started catching big red snapper, about two feet long, and grouper. We caught one grouper that was forty pounds, and we nearly had all the coolers full on the first day. Nettie Jo and the other two couples got seasick and went to bed. We had electric reels, so I decided that I would do some shark fishing after dark. I put a one-foot grouper on my hook and gave the line a lot of slack. I caught about five sharks, but the last one that I caught was huge. I would pull it in a little with the electric reel, and then the shark would pull the line back the other way. It felt like I was pulling on a truck, and he had my fishing rod bent over. I finally got it up to the boat. The captain said he would shoot it, but he had left his pistol at home. It took me two hours to get him up, and the captain said it looked like it weighed 1,100 pounds. The next morning, everyone got up feeling bad after throwing up all night. We started fishing again, catching red snapper and grouper. We caught so many that we filled our coolers up and had to go back in early. We had 1,100 pounds of grouper and 565 pounds of red snapper. We would be pulling a red snapper up sometimes, and a shark would come up and bite it in half before we could get it into the boat. We went on back to the pier and sold all our fish for more money than it cost us for the trip. We had a good time and made some extra money. My group said they wouldn't go on a two-day trip again after getting seasick. They said that was one bad sickness.

Another time, Nettie Jo and I decided to go to Panama City with a twelve-foot camper that we had bought. The camper would sleep six people and had a stove, refrigerator, air conditioner, and a sink. We didn't have a ball joint on our station wagon to hook the camper to. Carl Doyle told me he could weld me a brace with a trailer hitch to the station wagon. As soon as he got finished with the hitch and ball joint, we hooked our camper up and went to Panama City the next day with our children and one of Cheryl's friends. Cheryl wanted to know if she and her friend could ride in the camper, and stupid me told them that they could as long as they stayed hidden where no one could see them. After a while of going down the interstate, we noticed that everyone who was passing us were staring. Shortly after that, a highway patrolman pulled us over and wanted to know where we were going. We told him that we were going to Panama City on vacation, and he said to get the children out of the camper and put them in the station wagon. Come to find out, Cheryl and her friend were waving at everyone after they told me that they would stay hidden. The highway patrolman took me back to his car and showed me a picture of a camper that had gotten disconnected from a car while it was on the interstate. The camper had gone off the road and was just torn to pieces. He said, "This is what could have happened to your children." And stupid me should have thought that maybe Carl didn't weld the brace to the station wagon too good and it could have done just like the patrolman said. I wasn't thinking and just let the children have their way, not knowing the danger. The highway patrolman didn't give me a ticket and told us to go on and enjoy our vacation. Our four children and Cheryl's friend wanted to sleep in their tents when we got to the camp ground rather than sleep in the camper. After we finished our vacation and were about to go home, our station wagon broke down. A bad storm was coming, but we managed to get the station wagon fixed and got back on the road before it hit and went back on home. We all had a good time on our vacation. Nettie Jo and I slept in the camper all by ourselves very comfortably.

We lived in Mobile when Hurricane Frederick hit in 1979. It was all wind and very little rain. The wind blew so hard that we could feel a suction in our house. My son Michael and I walked across the street to the neighbor's house, not realizing that the hurricane was as bad as it was until the next day. All the power lines were down, and there were trees on the road. Mike, the neighbor, and I would shine a flashlight on the pine trees as they fell in the neighbor's yard. A tornado must have hit his side of the street because I had ten pine trees in my yard, and none of them was damaged or fell. Nettie Jo and the children were scared and said they did not want to stay at home if another hurricane hit. The storm had knocked all the power out in Mobile and did a lot of damage. We went to West Blocton for the weekend for about three days. We got some ice for our coolers while we were in West Blocton to take back home to Mobile, thinking that the electricity would be off for a long time. We were surprised to see that the electricity was back on when we got home. The neighborhood behind us didn't have electricity until about three weeks later. I went to Jones and Armstrong to check on the steel plant, and the electricity was out, and there were so many trees across the road that I could just barely get to the plant.

After the electricity came back on at the steel plant, I bought me a saw. I asked Alfonse Hill and Charlie Carter if they wanted to help me cut trees out of people's yard and split the money, and they said they would. We would cut trees and pile them out by the road for the trucks to come pick them up. We made some pretty good money for a while until Mobile had the city all cleaned up. We would cut trees after we got off work and on the weekends. My cousin Freddie Lovejoy came down to help from Aldrich, Alabama, near Montevallo to help clean up. He brought his tractor trailer and camper to live in. He made a lot of money until it was all cleaned up and said he was going to go wherever a tornado hit because he had made so much money in a short time.

Shortly after the storm, Ingalls sold Jones and Armstrong Steel to Trinity Industries out of Texas. They sent all foremen and superintendents from the plants that they bought in Mobile, Atlanta, and a couple in Pittsburg, Pennsylvania, to their main plant to explain how they were going to run the organization. My round-trip plane tickets were $550. I kept a bunch of keys in my pocket to open all the locks and doors at our steel plant. Well, I decided that I wouldn't need them on my trip to Pittsburg, so I left them at home. On the flight back home, the captain got on the radio and said whoever had the most keys in their pockets would win five thousand free miles in the air. The man that won it had twenty-eight keys. I got home and counted mine, and I had thirty-three keys that I kept in my pocket every day. I sure wished that I had brought them with me. I could have gone to Hawaii for free. I don't know why they sent us to Pittsburg because the next month, they terminated the people that went, and shortly after that, they closed our plant down.

CHAPTER 5

LAWN CARE BUSINESS

I had a friend named Carlton Yarborough from Decatur that was
Sheetrocking the condominiums in Gulf Shores. He lived next
door to my brother-in-law Bobby Jo Franks and his wife Sherry
Moore. I called to see if I could work for him, and he hired me. He
used me as an inspector to make sure his other workers were doing
the job right. Right away, I know that kind of work wasn't for me.
I helped build four or five condominiums down in Gulf Shores. I
would leave Mobile to ride with a friend down there. After work,
everyone, except me, would drink beer and sit around to talk. And
we wouldn't get home until after dark. We had to go around and pick
up some of the workers that didn't have transportation, but yet they
had the money to get up drinking beer for breakfast. They would
get drunk at night and fight one another and then work with one
another the next day. Four or five of them would rent a place to
stay in and split the costs because they knew it was a temporary job.
Carlton had a big fishing boat that he bought for $20,000, and he
would just quit working in the middle of the day and say, "Let's go
fishing!" We started out one day at about 1:00 p.m., and we ran into
a bit of fog after we got a few miles out. We had to turn around and
come back in because we couldn't see ten feet in front of us. We were
afraid that we might run into another boat.

I had a friend, Jim, who was the manager of a fast-food place
called What-A-Burger, but he had to quit. He got into the lawn care
business and told me that he knew a fireman that had gotten into

lawn care on the side and was making $165,000 a year from working both jobs. I asked if I could work for him because I did not want to build condominiums anymore, and he hired me. After I worked for him about three months, he said he would help me start my own lawn business because he knew I wanted my own. He loaned me an old trailer that had big Ford Model A tires on it, a riding lawn mower, and a push mower. He also loaned me an edger and a weed eater and gave me fifteen of his customers that he really didn't want. I was glad to have them. Ray Whatley was staying with us at the time, so I paid him $3 an hour until I could get some more customers. I advertised in the paper, but I only got two new customers that way. The way that I got the most customers and built my business up was through word of mouth. I would do a good job for my customers, and they would recommend me to their friends and family members. When the fireman was quitting his lawn care business, he told me that he would give me his customers if I paid him one payment of what he was getting to cut each yard. If he was getting $25 to cut the yard, I had to give him $25 the first time that I cut it. If he was getting $50 for a particular yard, I had to give him $50 the first time and so on. After paying him for the first cut, the customers were mine from then on.

I got my customer base built up, and I bought me some good equipment to use from then on, and I gave back the equipment that Jim loaned me, which was still in good condition. I had to hire two more boys to help me because I had too much work for Ray and myself to do. I had that business for twenty years until I sold out and moved away from Mobile. At the end, I had 182 customers, two crews going in the summer, and one crew in the winter. My daughter Cheryl ran one crew for two years and did a really good job. My son Mike worked with me sometimes when he wasn't working his regular job. I had three grandchildren—Robby Reed (Carol's son), Justin Whatley (Mike's son), and Kevin Nguyen (Cheryl's son)—that worked with me sometimes, and they were very good workers. They cut up all the time, but they enjoyed working and making the extra money. I had different people working for me over the years, but just before I left Mobile, I had two brothers working for me that we called Alky and Dopey. One drank beer every day, and the other smoked marijuana every day. They were very hard workers, and that is what I needed. Neither one had a car, so I would have to pick them up every morning and take them home every day after work.

I had two good customers that were special to us. One was Mrs. Doris Turner, and the other was Mrs. Walker in Saraland. We cut Mrs. Turner's yard for $25, but she always had a box or package of cookies when we finished her yard. Mrs. Walker would give me $140 to cut her yard, which took about two hours to cut. If we did a little extra work, she would give me $250. She was ninety-one years young, had plenty of money, and was a very sweet lady that could talk your head off. She had blueberry bushes, and she would give us all that we wanted as long as we picked them ourselves. Her blueberry bushes were always loaded. Some of my customers that had plenty of money wanted their yard cleaned every week, which wasn't needed most of the time, but they didn't want to see a leaf or any pine straw in the yard. We would get a load of pine straw out of one yard and then sell it to another customer for $50 to put around their bushes. I had three McDonalds that only took about ten minutes to tend to. In the winter, it was mostly just blowing the pavement clean. I got $60 each week for taking care of them.

We worked seven days a week in the summer and in the winter. We did churches on Saturdays, businesses on Sundays, and regular customers during the week. I would take the trash to the city dump, where we could take it for no charge. Sometimes, trucks would dump furniture and mattresses out there, and I would load some of it up to take to my rental properties on my land. The city employees at the dump weren't supposed to let anyone haul anything away, but they never stopped me because we were friends. If a company couldn't sell certain items, they would take it to the dump. The city finally closed the free dump down, and another man opened another dump, but we had to pay when we went to use that one to unload our trash.

Cheryl and her family lived in Mississippi for a few years. She lost her youngest son to crib infant death syndrome at eight months old, and we buried him at Trinity Gardens in Mobile. His name was Huy. After I had my lawn care business going pretty well, I bought her a house trailer in Mobile. After she lived there for a few months, the trailer burned to the ground, and she lost everything that she had. Nettie Jo and I had bought a big four-bedroom, three-and-a-half-bathroom house a week before the trailer burned down. We just moved her and her children into the house with us. I am glad that we had room for them when they needed us the most. The children grew up and did very well for themselves. I am proud of them and all my grandchildren and great-grandchildren. Nettie Jo passed away a few years later, and she is buried next to Huy, and I will be buried on the other side of her. My headstone is there already for when I pass away. Cheryl will be buried on the other side of Huy. He was a pretty little bald-headed baby.

Nettie Jo's headstone

My elbow has gotten flabby since I got old. When we are together at an outing, Mike's daughter, Kayla, and Cheryl's daughter, Vi, like to fold up my flab or loose skin on my elbow. And they play with it and laugh. Now Cheryl's grandchildren, Taylor and Kayson, like to play with my flabby elbows.

In 2000, some of our family decided to go to Gatlinburg during the New Year's week to watch the ball come down on New Year's Eve. It was really cold that night, and I just had a little coat on and didn't have any pockets. My hands nearly froze. I had taken a big coat that hung down to my knees and had pockets, but I forgot that I had it with me until I got back to the motel. That made me feel stupid and mad. A bunch of us went and had a good time. Nettie Jo and I were there with Bennie Ray, Linda, Ray, Keith, and Allison. Mikala and Emily were there, and so was Brian and Crystal Chesser and their son, Colton. Linda got really sick, and Bennie Ray and their children thought that she had taken her medicine twice, but she told them she didn't. I don't think they believed her. After everyone went back home, she went to the doctor and found out she had bone cancer. So that was why she had gotten sick. We all thought that it was taking twice her medication because my mother had done the same thing years before, and she had the same symptoms. Linda took chemo treatments for a while, and it made her hair fall out, but then it came back as pretty as it was to begin with. Later on, the cancer came back, and she passed away at fifty-nine years young.

I played baseball and softball for fifty-three years straight without missing a year. I started in Tripoli, Libya, in 1955 and finished the last thirty-five years in Mobile, Alabama, in 2008. I started out practicing throwing a ball behind my back and catching behind my back. I became very accurate and could pitch around seventy-five miles per hour. One day, someone asked me if I wanted to pitch in a fast-pitch game, and I told them I would. I was so accurate that a man could hold his glove in four different spots, and I could hit his glove without him moving it. I didn't learn how to pitch in front of me until later because in some leagues it was illegal to pitch behind the back. Some teams didn't care which way I pitched the ball. The rule is to throw within six inches of your body, and the ball cannot be out of the view of the batter at any time. When I throw the ball behind me, it is out of the view of the batter for a split second while it is going behind me. That rule should be changed. It's like telling a baseball player that he can't throw a curve ball. When I throw it behind my back, I am still throwing it within six inches of my body. I was chosen for an all-stars softball team while I was in Libya. Once I left there, I continued playing ball in Tampa, Florida, and then in my hometown of West Blocton. I pitched sidearm very fast and could hit the corner of the plate good. I was pitching in Abernant, right outside of West Blocton on time, and I had just started practicing to warm up. It was February and still cold. We had a coach that didn't know much about baseball, and he decided that he wanted me to throw overhand curves instead of sidearm. As a result, I threw my arm out and could not throw sidearm or overhand very hard anymore. That is when I started pitching softball again. I could still throw about seventy-five miles per hour behind my back without hurting my arm.

For a couple of years, we played against a five-man team out of Bessemer who played against "the king and his court," which was a team of only three players. I remember one night we played on our high school football field and I hadn't struck out all year until I played against them. I struck out the first three times that I was at bat because their pitcher was so fast. The next time up, I got a triple. We beat them one game to two. The pitcher that played against us was "the king," and he and his court would travel all over to different states. He was so good he could pitch 115 miles per hour. That is faster than any baseball player can pitch. In softball, you pitch from thirty feet closer to the batter than you do in baseball. That was why it was so fast. He could strike batters out, pitching from second base, and could pitch blindfolded. If I wasn't pitching for my team, some other manager would put me in their team to either pitch for them or as a cleanup batter. I couldn't hit home runs, but I would get on base more than anyone else on the team. If it was by a hit or a walk, I would get on base. I remember once I got on base thirteen straight times.

When we moved from Birmingham to Knoxville, I got on a ball team there. Then when we moved from Knoxville to Nashville, I got on a ball team there too. Through my ball playing years, I played open league, church league, and industrial league for three days a week. And I was in a softball tournament nearly every Saturday. Later on, I started playing on coed teams, and one year, we won first place. The team that won also had my second daughter, Teresa, my son Mike, my granddaughter, Kerry Whatley, and my two son-in-laws, Timmy Davis and Roger McKeown. I had half of the coed team in my family. I was put on the front page of *The Mobile Press Register* on June 19, 2000, with the Tiger Woods, the golf professional, and Shaquille

O'Neal, the basketball star. Then Randy Patrick ran a news story about me pitching, and I gave all my children a copy of the DVD.

Our men's team would go to different ball fields in Mobile, Montgomery, and Jackson, Mississippi. We went to state and national championships for age thirty-five and older. We should have won state easily. We had five home run hitters, but they had a bad day. Only one of them hit a home run. We won a lot of first—and second-place trophies over the years. Our manager was from a business called Smith Services. He called me one day and wanted to know if I would start pitching on his ball team. We had never seen each other before, so I said, "Do you know how old I am?" He replied, "Yes, I heard you were fifty-nine years old, but I also heard you were the best in Mobile." I thought that was a good compliment since we had never seen each other. I pitched for him for a few years, and we won a lot of trophies.

News article from *The Mobile Press Register*, June 19, 2000

Excerpt from the article

I was playing for another team when this man from the next street over from our house came over on his bicycle. After talking to him for a while, I realized that he was mentally impaired. I told him that I played softball, and he wanted to know if he could go with me and watch us play. He told me his name was Tommy, and he lived on the next street over with his aunt. I told him what time I would pick him up, and he was next to the street waiting on me. From then on, I took him to all my games. He was fifty-two years old and said he had never been to a ball game. The ball players would carry on with him, and he enjoyed going to the games every week. He would always come by my house and ask what time he needed to be ready. Then every time I went to pick him up, he would be out next to the street waiting on me. Whenever one of the players would hit a home run over the fence, he would always run out there to get the ball and bring it back to us. We won first place one year, and we all agreed to give him the big trophy for getting the home run balls and helping us out. He was so proud to get that trophy. It was a nice, big trophy. When I took him home that night, his aunt said she wanted to put the trophy on their table, but he told her no, it was going in his room. His aunt thanked me for spending time with him, and he always did look forward to going with me to the games every week. He would pass my house every morning while he was going down to the service station, just to sit around most of the day and pass the time. He would stop by and talk to us as we were getting ready to leave in the mornings to go tend to lawns.

We had a real good church team, and one of the deacons was our manager. His name was John, and he knew how to run a ball team. Any team that played against us knew they were going to have a tough time beating us. We won a lot of games by one run, and we won a lot of first—and second-place trophies. I could catch just about any ball that came back toward the pitcher's mound. My catcher would tell the batters that they couldn't get one back through the pitcher. I was also a spot hitter since I couldn't hit home runs. One person told me one day that they didn't know how to play me. They would start moving around in the field. I batted right-handed, but my favorite spot to hit was right over the first baseman's head. One Saturday, we went to Jackson, Mississippi, to play in a tournament with twenty-one teams. If we lost two games, we would be out of the tournament. We lost the first game at 8:00 a.m. I pitched seven ball games that day in ninety-five degrees Fahrenheit heat. We finished playing at one o'clock the next morning, and out of the twenty-one teams, we finished in second place. Our deacon manager said he expected to see all of us in church later that morning. We came back from Jackson to Mobile and were all in church a few hours later.

I asked Nettie Jo several times after she had to quit work if she still wanted to go to Graceland, but she always said no. She still had diabetes really bad and had to take insulin shots twice a day. She wasn't really doing all the things that the doctor was telling her to do to manage it. She couldn't stay away from Coca-Cola. She had to take a blood shot every month, and the doctor told me it really made her suffer. She was in bad shape the last year of her life. She couldn't turn over in the bed and had lost the control of her bowels. I changed her diaper five times one morning in fifteen minutes. We had a nurse coming by the house three times a week, and she could have given her the blood shot at home, but the nurse told me that Hillary Clinton passed a law that made it a requirement to go to the doctor for it. We would have to lift her out of bed, put her in a wheel-chair, take her out to the car, and lift her back out of the wheelchair to put her in the car. And when we got to the doctor's office, we had to go through the same procedure. It put her through a lot of pain. Her skin was so red and thin that if she touched anything, her skin would peel and start bleeding. That tells me that politicians can pass any law that they want to and we won't even know it until we get into a situation like that.

When I lived in West Blocton fifty years ago, we didn't have anything going on, except for the poolroom. In present day, we have a few things to look forward to. The town has upgraded the Coke ovens and have a trade day once a month for people to buy and sell at a bargain. They have a Wild West Weekend the last weekend of June every year. We have a fish fry on Friday night where they serve fish, fries, hush puppies, and a drink. After everyone eats, we have dancing in the street. They give away ten to fifteen free prizes by calling out ticket numbers. The tickets are raffled for $1 each before everyone eats. Then we have a butter bean dinner on Saturday from 11:00 a.m. to 2:00 p.m. and the old-timer's ball tournament later that night. You have to be fifty years old or older to play in the old-timer's game, and I pitched in it every year. After the ball game, there is a tremendous fireworks show. We have a lily festival in May, before the Wild West Weekend, and people come from everywhere to see the lilies blooming in the middle of the Big Cahaba River. We have a turnip green dinner the night before the football homecoming game. It has a good variety of foods to eat. We have a Smith Hill reunion, a Piper reunion, a Lovejoy reunion, and a Marvel reunion. We get to meet up with people once a year that used to live in the community. So things have changed a little over the last fifty years to keep us more occupied. There is also a dollar store and a new ball field.

CHAPTER 6

THE LOVEJOY FAMILY

There were a lot of Lovejoys in Piper, and the ones that seemed to be around the most was Uncle Morgan, Aunt Myrtle, and their children. They were a model family that all other families should follow as an example. Uncle Morgan was a great inspiration to a lot of us young children. He was the number 1 man in my life and the lives of many other children. He molded so many young lives in the right direction when we were young. I have met thousands of men in my lifetime, but I put Uncle Morgan in a class above preachers since he had such an impact on so many young children. Some of those children came back to thank him after they were grown. He spent a lot of time with young people and taught us a lot of simple things in life, but it meant a lot to us. I tried to pattern my life after him, but I didn't come close. All their children did really well in life because of their upbringing. They were raised the way that all children should be raised. There was always a lot of love in their family, and it showed. One thing that they used to do which seems to have been lost on most modern families was to give thanks to our Lord at mealtimes. It seems that we have become a generation that is getting further away from God.

Morgan and Myrtle Lovejoy

We had to be tough around Uncle Morgan, but we enjoyed him being rough on us. If we walked close to him, he would kick us in the shins, so we would kick him in his shins. He would ask if we knew how a horse ate corn, and he would get us up on the tender part of the leg and pinch until tears came out of our eyes. When we went swimming, he would put us on the bottom of the river and hold his foot on us until we started bubbling. Then he would reach down and pull us up while we were strangling and gasping for air. If we went fishing at night, we couldn't go to sleep by the fire because he would put a match between our toes, light it, and let it burn all the way down to our toes. If anyone does something like that now to a child to make them tough, the parents would get mad and sue for child abuse. If we waved at Uncle Morgan while he was on the back of a pickup truck, he would wave back at us with his feet. Sometimes, some of us boys would go up to his house while he was milking his cow. He would tell us to look and see how much milk he had in his bucket. If we got within five feet of the cow, he would turn the cow's tit up, squeeze it, and hit us in the face with the milk. He could squirt the milk at least ten feet. If the cow swatted him in the face with her tail while he was milking her or kicked over the milk bucket, he would haul off and hit the cow in her side so she learned not to do it again. Uncle Morgan and Aunt Myrtle practically raised my daddy, and we were always closer to the Lovejoy family than we were to the Whatley families. My daddy only had two brothers, Uncle Curry and Uncle Eddie, and we were never close to them.

Uncle Morgan and Aunt Myrtle had a friend named AJ Wells. Out of the blue one day, he brought me a little play rake, shovel, hoe, and a bucket to put dirt into. I probably wasn't more than four or five years old, but he didn't realize how much that meant to me. I felt like a million-dollar kid. That was during the Great Depression and right before World War II. Everyone was poor, and we didn't have any toys. When my brothers and I got a little older, we would go up to Uncle Morgan and Aunt Myrtle's house to play games. We would play Monopoly all night until the next morning. I would fry french fries while we were playing, and the more Uncle Morgan bragged on my fries, the more I cooked. He would fill balloons up with helium and let them loose, and we would watch them go out of sight. We would write notes and put them in the balloons to see if we could hear from whoever found the balloon far away, but we never did. We had no TVs back then. I remember Aunt Myrtle always listened to Brother Thomas on the radio, and it always put a smile on her face. She always cooked my birthday cake every year. I would get away from home on my birthday to avoid getting a birthday paddling from everyone. I remember one day, Uncle Morgan told me there would be a plane that just lifts off the ground and goes upward. Years later, they came out with a helicopter, and now they have jet planes that rise off the ground before takeoff.

Uncle Morgan served in World War I. I remembered Jack Lovejoy coming home from the marines in World War II with a handlebar mustache. Bill (Corky) Lovejoy was always a daredevil and became a paratrooper in World War II. Bob Lovejoy was a colonel in the National Guard during peacetime. Now, all their names are engraved in the veterans' memorial monument wall in West Blocton, along with me and three of my brothers: James, Franklin, and Bennie Ray who were in the army. I had a top-secret clearance as an international Morse code operator. When I was a young man, Uncle Morgan told me that when I was grown and married, I should let my wife know that I was the boss within the first six months. That didn't work with Nettie Jo, and she let me know that she was the boss for the rest of our married life. Bob Lovejoy married Gail Price, and Jack Lovejoy married Nell Brantley. After Nell passed away later on in life, Jack married Francis Hardman. She was and still is crazy about Jack, even though he passed away. She said he was a great man and that she still misses him. Bill Lovejoy married a beautiful lady by the name of Margie Adams. Betty Lovejoy had been double promoted in grammar school because she was so smart. She was about to be double promoted again later in her school days, but she decided to drop out and married Harold Campbell. That was like a match made in heaven. She could not have found a better man, and he could not have found a better woman. Their love for each other is as strong now as it was when they first got married. When we were between the ages of eight to ten years old, my brother Frank dared Betty to shoot me with a BB gun. Betty didn't take dares, but she shot me in the calf of my leg. It didn't hurt too bad even though it was close range. I don't think we ever told anyone about it before.

West Blocton veterans monument

Betty Lovejoy

Betty was thirteen years old, and Harold was seventeen years old when they got married. Mott Lovejoy knew that Betty and Harold were going to Mississippi to get married. And Uncle Morgan got a little irritated with Mott for not telling him, but he could have never found a better son-in-law. And later in life, he realized that. I remember Uncle Morgan wrestling out in the yard with Harold after he and Betty were married. They would throw each other all over the ground. I thought at the time that Uncle Morgan was too old to be wrestling a youngster, but I realized later that he wasn't much older than Harold. Betty and Harold had a hard time when they first got married because it was hard to find work to make a living back then. They did okay after a few years. Everyone was having a hard time back then.

When we got a little older, Uncle Morgan would take us on long hikes in the woods and wade across certain parts of the Little Cahaba River. If the water was low on the shoals, we would get flat rocks and make them skip across the water. We would go to sink cave and saltpeter cave back in the woods. Saltpeter cave had a creek running underneath it. We would go inside the cave and see beavers sliding off into the creek when they saw our flashlights and carbide lamps. We would go in saltpeter cave and catch bats. There would be clusters of bats in that big cave, and they would come flying out, hitting us in our heads. We would hold our heads down so they didn't hit us in the face. We would catch a bunch of bats, put them in our pockets, and take them to our house. By the time we got back home, half of the bats would have already gotten out of our pockets. We would let the remaining bats loose in our bedroom. They seemed to want to go up in the ceiling around the lights. We would write our names in the caves using the carbide lamps.

They got saltpeter out of the caves during the civil war. We closed a fox in the cave while we were on the way to saltpeter cave one day. We went back two weeks later to see if the fox had died, but when we unblocked the caves, the fox shot out. So he didn't die after all, and we never saw the fox again. Uncle Morgan would raise tame rabbits to eat. He had beehives for honey, and we would go with him into the woods to hunt for bees. He would put a little honey on the

215

ground, and when a bee found the honey, we would watch to see what it would do. Uncle Morgan would get dressed in his bee suit so the bees couldn't sting him. He would saw the tree down to where he could get to the honey and the queen bee. We would get way up on the hill while he was sawing the tree, thinking we were far enough away, but occasionally a bee would find us and sting us.

When Uncle Morgan and his family moved from Piper, he found a job close to Wilton for $100 a month and free rent, working for a retired serviceman. He was tending to the black angus cattle, repairing fences, or whatever the man asked him to do. The man had one black angus bull that weighed two thousand pounds. When we would sit on him, our legs would stick out both ways because he was so wide. I was over at Uncle Morgan's one day and helped him load hay onto his truck to haul to the cattle. I didn't have a long-sleeve shirt on, and the hay stuck little pinholes all over my arms. We still have the Lovejoy reunion every year in Six Mile, Alabama. Usually, Lyman Lovejoy and JoAnn Hayes are the masters of ceremonies. All the Hayes and Rodenberrys are at the reunion, and everyone brings food and has a good time. Betty Lovejoy always took charge of making sure everything ran smoothly. She would let everyone know where the reunion would be and what time it would start, but she passed right after the reunion in 2013. We all really miss her. She was a real Christian and has gone on to be with our Lord and her husband Harold in heaven. The Lovejoy family had a very big impact on the Whatleys when we were young. We would have never had the great childhood that we did if it hadn't been for the Lovejoys. We were kinfolk and were around each other every day, one way or another.

Uncle Joe and Aunt Fannie Lovejoy had some older children than us, but some were our age. In total, they had fourteen children. Uncle Crawford and Aunt Lid also had older children, but we were always around Uncle Crawford and Aunt Lid. Their son, Glover, had children that were our age. He was married to Emma Lee Mitchell, who wanted me to be one of her pallbearers when she passed, but I was in Knoxville taking inventory at the steel plant and I couldn't get away. I always hated that I couldn't be there. Every time a black cloud came up when we were kids, everyone would go to the storm pits at their house because the old wooden company homes weren't very safe to stay in. Some of the families had their own storm pits and would let the neighbors come in when the storms came. I dug a second storm pit for Uncle Crawford and Aunt Lid with little dirt seats for $15.00 when I was small. Aunt Lid had diabetes pretty bad, but she would drink Pepsi-Cola every day. She would give us $0.50 just to go to the store and get her a Pepsi-Cola every day. I remember one time, it looked like a couple of her toes were rotting off. I don't know what she did to heal them, but I do know that Pepsi-Cola didn't help the situation.

Uncle Crawford and Aunt Lid had a daughter named Annie who married Junior Lumpkin. Junior had a sister named Helen, who I used to joke about being my girlfriend all the time. She was in my grade in grammar school and would help me get my lessons. We were very lucky to come up in an era where families in the coal mining communities were very close. My aunt Fannie and uncle Joe, who had fourteen children, had a daughter named Billie Jo (Fry) Lovejoy who had eighteen children. All the houses in the community were two—and three-bedroom houses. I don't know where all those children slept. I guess, like us, five boys in two beds in one room. Billie Jo's brother told me that she rolled over on one of her babies in the bed by mistake, and the baby died. Aunt Fannie knew how to read music, and she sure could play the piano and sing. Most of her children learned to play different musical instruments and could sing and dance. Their son Charles, who everyone called Sully and is now deceased, got a guitar and learned to play it. He would hook the guitar up to loudspeakers and play it at night. We could hear him playing from just about anywhere in Piper; it was so loud. He played in a lot of nightclubs with different bands once he was grown, and he was working a regular job. Fannie and Joe had another son named J. Winifred "Mott" Lovejoy. Mott's picture is in the issue number 9 *Tributaries* from 2006, written by Jim Brown out of Montgomery, which talks about the redhorse fish. They also have an article in that book about Uncle Morgan. Mott was a good baseball catcher, and the Birmingham Barons called him up to play for them professionally. I heard he got $3,000 a year to start with in the forties, which was a lot of money at the time. I was making $4,000 a year for O'Neal Steel when I first got out of the air force in 1959, and that was still a lot of money then. He turned them down. The Barons were a minor league team. Mott is now deceased.

I wasn't around too many of Fannie and Joe's children because they were older than I was. Doris was one of the oldest, and she loved to dance and play the guitar. She had four or five children, but the only ones that we knew were Alton and Patsy because they were our age. Doris and her husband, Bill Fritz, lived in Plant City, Florida, in 1958 while I was stationed at MacDill Air Force Base in Tampa. I would go visit to let Doris teach me how to dance. She could really dance, but I never caught on to anything, except slow dancing. I gave up on dancing fast. Janie was about two years older than me, and Lucie was about two years younger than me. Sim Lovejoy was a few years older than me and was a great marksman with a slingshot. He was in the Birmingham news several times telling what all he had killed with a slingshot. He and his wife had two sons named Lyman and David.

Judge Lovejoy was one of Fannie and Joe's oldest sons and was married to Virginia Seagle. Judge was working out of state somewhere, and he sent his parents an Emerson TV. As far as I can remember, that was the only TV in Piper at the time. We only had three channels on TV back then, and they all went off the air at midnight. Aunt Fannie and Uncle Joe already had a house full of kids, but they didn't mind how many other people would come over to their house. We would be in the chairs, all over the furniture lying down, and out on the porch in the summertime looking through the doors and windows. Everyone left their doors and windows open at night anyway because no one had air conditioners.

Everyone loved watching wrestling every week from New York City. We didn't realize it was mostly fake. I remember a wrestler named Argentina Rocker. He was small compared to most of the other wrestlers, but he was very acrobatic. If the other wrestler started to grab him, he could jump over their head. One night, two wrestlers were slamming each other down in one corner of the ring over and over again until they knocked part of the flooring out of the corner of the ring. They cancelled wrestling that night for a week, I guess so they could repair the ring. Another show that we liked back then was *Dragnet*, the detective series.

Aunt Fannie and Uncle Joe had another son named Bobby Lee, who we called Boggy, who was the same age as me. Johnny Hriber, Boggy, and I always ran around together. Boggy is deceased now, but he was still selling slingshots to a hardware store in Brent, Alabama, until he passed on.

Billie Jo was really pretty, and no one ever knew why she married this man named France Fry. He was a big liar, and I guess she fell for it. He would be down at the store where the men congregated every day. I remember him telling a lie that he and his Paw were going down the road and this big "bar" (bear) stopped them. He jumped out of the car, and the "bar" picked the car up with Paw still inside of it and threw it up into a pine tree, and the car just stayed there with Paw in it. Another lie I remember is when he said four men jumped him. He pulled out his knife and started stabbing them. When he stabbed the last one, he looked down and just had the knife handle in his hand. The blade had come off inside of one of the men. I don't know how many of Billie Jo's eighteen children belonged to France Fry. I understand that she remarried four more times after him. If France didn't do anything else in life, he left his mark on people with his made-up stories. We need to be alert of what impression we leave on people as we go out of this world. Hopefully, it is a good one.

CHAPTER 7

THE MISTREATMENT OF BLACK PEOPLE

I can truly say that some of the best friends that I have had in my lifetime were Black people. We were friends and still are, even if we were taught to think otherwise while we were growing up. I had two Black friends while I was in the air force stationed in Libya that I always felt would fight to protect me more than any White people if we had been in battle. We were about to go to war over the Suez Canal back in 1955. I still have two Black friends in Mobile who used to work for me when I was superintendent of the steel plant. They did and still would help me any time I called them. If I broke down in my car, I could call Alfonse Hill, and he would come out to help me get the car started and never charged me anything. His brother-in-law Charlie Carter was the same way, but he passed on some time back. It was my two Black friends in Libya that taught me how to play golf, even though I was never any good at it.

The last time I played golf was with my two brothers, Franklin and James. We were in Birmingham on the golf course when a bad electrical storm came through. We just kept on playing while the lightning was getting bad. All the other golfers had gotten off the course, except for us, and we were soaking wet. I put my golf ball on the tee and swung. Both the ball and my club went into a pond. So we decided to quit playing and just wade in all the ponds to get all the balls that golfers had lost in the water. A golf ball looks as big as a softball when it is in the water. We filled our pockets with golf balls and went home. That was fifty years ago, and I haven't been on a golf course since that day. We were lucky that we weren't struck by lightning, as bad as it was, but I guess the Lord looks out for fools.

I remember when I was fifteen or sixteen years old, we heard about a bad train collision in Woodstock, Alabama, about six miles from West Blocton. We lived in Piper at the time, so we went up there to see how bad it was. It was really bad. The two trains hit head-on, and the two engineers were mashed in all that steel in a standing position. Seventeen Black people were killed, and I don't remember how many people were hurt. I saw a little Black girl's head cut completely off. She couldn't have been more than six years old, and I didn't see her body anywhere. The Black people were complaining that they had to ride in the front of the of the passenger cars, but they were made to ride in the back seat on the buses. My uncle Morgan was in Birmingham that day and almost got on that train. For whatever reason, he changed his mind and decided to ride the bus. He was glad he made that decision because he would have been in that collision. I don't remember if any White people were killed or hurt at all. I don't think that they did because they were all in the back passenger cars.

Woodstock train accident

When I was fourteen years old, I had a paper route in Piper. A man would bring the papers to my house, and I would deliver them all over Piper because I knew everyone and I knew where they lived. I delivered to both White and Black neighborhoods. Sometimes, I would ride with my girlfriend, Eleanor Ann Lemley, on the handlebars. I would have the newspapers in a basket in front of the handlebars and in another basket behind my seat. There was a good old Black man who was the principal of the Black school in Piper. He had children who were schoolteachers. Not many people finished college back then, especially poor Black people. Both Black and White people were struggling just to make a living. People did well to finish high school and find a job because times were really hard. My daddy finished tenth grade, thanks to Uncle Morgan and Aunt Myrtle taking care of him, but he was probably smarter than most people that finished college. Every day on my paper route, I would ask the Black principal how he was doing. He would always say, "Just fine," even though he wasn't in good health at all. He appreciated me checking on him every day while I was on my paper route. He started putting a chicken in his coupe and fattening it up every year around Christmas and would tell me to come get it after a couple of weeks. I always thought that was really nice of him, and I always appreciated him thinking of me at Christmastime, even though I didn't expect him to be so nice to me. He was a real gentleman and a very smart man.

My mother would tell me not to be shooting marbles with the Black kids while I was on my newspaper route, but I did it anyways. She also told me not to say, "Yes, sir" or "No, sir" to the older Black men, but to always say it to the older White men. I said, "Yes, sir" and "No, sir" to both. I just didn't feel right by not saying, "Yes, sir" and "No, sir" to the older Black men. As we age in life, we look at things with a different perspective. I can look back and see where the Black people were mistreated. I can also look back now and see how we mistreated our animals. Back when I was a boy, there were no animal cruelty laws. If there had been, we would have been in real trouble for how we treated our animals. The Black people were mistreated back then on the same level as animals. That was wrong. If a Black person came to a White person's house, they had to go in through the back door. They were not allowed to come in the front door. If they went to a municipal building, there were separate water fountains for White and Black people. Black people weren't allowed to rent or buy a house in a White neighborhood, which means our government was as racist as some of the White people. Black people weren't allowed to be policemen until the sixties.

I witnessed a few things when I was young and did little mischievous things that I shouldn't have, but it was because of our upbringing. From what I heard as a young boy, my father nearly killed a Black man with a sledgehammer in the coal mine. We were taking a Black man somewhere once, and my father and the Black man were drinking. The Black man decided that he was going to drive our truck against our wishes, and my father and the man got in an argument. My father got a tire iron from behind the seat and was going to hit him, but then they both settled down, so he did not hit him. Another time, there were some White men and Black men beside our house, drinking and arguing. My daddy got an axe and went over the fence to help the White men, but again they settled the dispute without a fight. My father would loan Black people $5.00 until payday with the understanding that they would pay him $7.50 once they were paid. A Black man came to the back porch one day, and my daddy asked him what he wanted. The man was drunk and kept telling my daddy, "I want you!" Every time my daddy asked him, "What do you want?" he would reply, "I want you!" My daddy reached up over his head and grabbed a hatchet off the rafter. He was coming down with the sharp end but flipped it over and hit the Black man right above his eye with the blunt side. It knocked him down about fifteen stairs and knocked his hat off. The man was bleeding pretty bad, but he got up and ran off. My uncle Crawford came out on his porch, which was right next to our house, with his shotgun and said if that man came back, he was going to kill him. The man never came back though.

There was a Jewish man that would come out of Birmingham and loan Black people money until payday also. He was always around on Fridays when they got paid to make sure he got his money back. When World War II ended, my daddy bought a canvas-topped army truck, and the Black people would pay my daddy to take them to ball games, parties, or dances. There was an incident when my father took a crowd of Black people to a party that was about twenty miles away. This one Black man didn't go, but his wife did. He was drunk and went to another Black man and asked if he could borrow his horse to go check on his wife. His friend wouldn't let him borrow the horse, so he stole it. My brother James had gone with my daddy to take the Black people to the party. My mother got a little worried, so she got the next-door neighbor, Mrs. Gaddy, to go with her to get my brother at about 2:00 a.m. They passed the Black man that had stolen the horse in the middle of the highway and just barely missed hitting them with the car. My mother got my brother and brought him back home. In the meantime, my father was on his way back home with all the people who had paid for a ride and ended up hitting the man on the horse. It killed the horse and broke both of the man's legs. My daddy was always drinking too when he would take them to parties or ball games. He went to see the Black man in the hospital and took him two cartons of cigarettes. I guess that was the end of it. I never heard anything else about that escapade. Another situation was when my mother got sick and my father paid a Black lady to come over and cook for us. When the Black lady sat down to eat with us, my mother threw the silverware and plate away instead of just washing them.

When I was young, a Black man couldn't look at a White woman unless he tilted his hat and said, "Ma'am." Just about all men wore hats back then, whether they were Black or White. One Black man named Mickey went to Chicago, Illinois. He would walk around prissy-like, and one day, my mother told my daddy that Mickey looked at her. My daddy said, "Well, I'd better go talk to Mickey." I don't know if he ever talked to Mickey about it or not.

Now back to my mischievousness. Me and another kid would hide behind the trees on opposite sides of the road with a thin wire that was hard to see. If a man was walking up the road, we would knock his hat off with the thin wire stretched across the road. Sometimes, we would get in the ditch and put a billfold in the road, hooked to a thin wire that was hard to see. People would bend over to pick it up, and we would jerk it away just as they bent over. One man saw us in the ditch one day and outsmarted us. He managed to get the billfold and pretended that he wasn't going to give it back to us. Another thing us young boys would do is get some car tires up on a hill, and if a person was walking down the road, not really paying attention, we would roll the tire at them and try to hit them. We would also get behind our closed-in back porch and shoot marbles at people with our slingshots while they were walking down the road. We would try to hit them in the back and then duck down, so they couldn't see who was shooting at them. I shot a marble and hit a Black man in the heel one day. He was looking around, trying to find out where the marble came from. I was just a kid, but I still should have gotten my butt torn up for that. If my mother had known I was doing these mischievous things, she would have torn my butt up.

If we were walking down the street and met some Black boys, we wouldn't move over, and neither would they. We would get about forty yards past each other, and both sides would start slinging rocks at each other. Luckily, no one ever got hurt. We had a small branch of water behind our house that was about two feet wide, but it got wider on down behind the Black neighborhood. The part near the Black neighborhood was about the size of an ambulance, and that is where we learned to swim. But every time we went swimming there, the Black boys would throw rocks at us and hide. We would always have to leave before one of us got hit in the head.

We would always see snakes swimming in that same pond, but we didn't have enough sense to be afraid of them while they were on top of the water. My daddy had always told us that snakes wouldn't bite underwater, but we learned later that they would. We had heard about a kid that went swimming somewhere nearby, and he yelled back to the rest of the boys not to come over there because something was biting him. Someone said they got out over sixty snakes in the pond where the boy was swimming. One day, we finished swimming in that pond and started back home. The wind was blowing a little, and I decided to strike a match to some high weeds that were dry. When I lit the weeds, the wind started blowing the fire, and we couldn't put it out. We took off running to our house. Later on that day, our cousin Freddie Lovejoy asked us where we had been. We told him, and he said we nearly set some Black people's houses on fire.

We always told my mother that we ducked our heads in the water right behind our house to cool off. Later on in the years, we could swim like ducks, and we told our mother that we had learned to swim in the water behind the Black neighborhood. She tore Frank's butt up right then, but she didn't whip the rest of us. I don't know why she didn't whip James or me. I guess she just whipped Frank because he was the oldest.

I can only remember two or three Black people in our community of over seven hundred houses that had cars. Most either had a horse or nothing at all. One real nice Black couple that had a car was Dan and Sadie. Another Black man had a car in Piper, and he had a bunch of little bobbing animals and trinkets all attached to his hood in some way where they wouldn't fall off. Hoods back in those days raised up on both sides of the motor. Some cars and trucks had the spare tire mounted to the side of the automobile. Some doors would open frontward instead of backward. The back part of the army truck that my dad bought after the war had a wooden bed with a window cut out so the people in the back could talk to the people in the front. The cover over the cab and the bed were all canvas.

My daddy, my uncle Eddie, and I went over to a Black man's house who was a good friend of ours. His name was Bo Hell. Bo always had some chewing gum in a suitcase, and he would give me every time I went to his house. My daddy and uncle Eddie were drinking, and they talked Bo into getting into the army truck with them. Bo and I were in the back, and my daddy and uncle Eddie were in the front. The truck had a lot of slack in the steering wheel and no power steering at all. We drove out the big road, later named Crows Feet Road because there were three roads leading off it at the end. One road went to Marvel; the middle road went to Montevallo, and the last road went to Bulldog Bend. We got up to where the road forked, and we turned around. My daddy started going really fast, and when we got to the other end of the road, leading into Piper, he hit the brakes and turned sideways. Dust was flying everywhere because it was a dirt road. Bo got thrown through the window going from the bed to the cab. We could have flipped over, but I guess since they were drinking, they didn't think about how dangerous it was.

Later, my daddy bought a 1940 Chevrolet and decided to provide a taxi service, mainly going the six miles from Piper to West Blocton. He would charge fifty cents. Every time Bo Hell got drunk, he would want to go to West Blocton to get some hominy to eat. I drove Bo in the Chevrolet one day. He was in the back seat, drunk, and I drove really fast over the dirt road. When the gravel hit the fenders, it sounded like machine gunfire. Bo got scared when we started going over the rolling hills, just before we got into Blocton, and he got down on his knees right behind my seat because he thought I was going to wreck. When I got ready to go back to Piper, I asked Bo if he was ready to go, and he said, "No, sir! I will find another way back!" I was sixteen years old at the time, and he would never get in the car with me driving after that day. Earnest and Orean Sanders had a taxi at the time, so I guess he rode with them after that.

I remember when Bull Conners was the chief of police in Birmingham. He turned fire hoses and let dogs loose on Black people when they were peacefully marching and protesting the way they were being mistreated. I remember when George Wallace was playing politics, pretending he was going to keep Black people from attending college at the University of Alabama. Years after he was shot, he had some close Black friends. He knew there weren't many Black people who were registered to vote, so he was trying to get all the White votes. I remember when Nat King Cole came to the Birmingham auditorium to sing and people in the audience started throwing things at him. He had to be escorted out of the back of the building to keep from being hurt or killed. Nat King Cole was a very famous singer and a very humble man. If White people had been Black for a year back then, they would understand what the Black people had to go through and how much they suffered. Martin Luther King Jr. and Fred Shuttlesworth were heroes. Martin Luther King Jr. sacrificed his life at an early age for what he believed in. One of his quotes was "The ultimate measure of a man is not where he stands in moments of comfort and convenience, but where he stands at times of challenge and controversy."

CHAPTER 8

THE CORRUPTED JUSTICE SYSTEM

I discovered at an early age that some of our police officers are not honest people. I know we have to have law and order, but one bad apple makes the whole basket look bad. In between working at different coal mines, my daddy would sell bootleg whiskey whenever the mines were shut down or the workers went on strike. We would go to Tuscaloosa and get three or four five-gallon jugs of bootleg whiskey in our Chevrolet, take it back home, and put it in pint bottles to sell. He would go out into the road and hand it through the car windows to whoever wanted to buy it, in broad daylight. All my life, I hated him selling whiskey, but as I got older, I realized that was all he knew other than coal mining and that he had eight people to feed. He got caught by the sheriff one day, but he told my mother he would be right back because he knew all the policemen. He did come right back and was not even fined. The policeman allegedly said he could go and gave my daddy a .38-caliber pistol and instructed him to "take care" of any Black people that started any trouble. My daddy said the policemen would take whiskey from one Black man and sell it to another Black man as he was getting out of jail.

I had a bad experience in Mobile in the mideighties. Huey Walker from Montevallo would come down to visit his daughter and go fishing in Dauphin Island while he was in Mobile. One weekend, we were in front of my house about to leave to go fishing, and we heard a loud noise that sounded like a car wreck. There was a nightclub about two or three miles up the road, so I figured it may have been a drunk driver. I walked down the hill to see if it was, in fact, a wreck. This drunk man had hit a telephone pole and cut the pole in half, and a guide wire was hanging over the road where part of the pole had landed. After hitting the pole, the man's car went over into a creek. The creek wasn't that deep, so the driver was able to crawl out and was lying on the ground shaken, but unhurt. Another one of his drunk buddies came along and stopped his car halfway on the dirt with the other half in the road. The drunk that had wrecked got off the ground and lay on the hood of his buddies' car. I told his buddy that he needed to get his car all the way off the road into the dirt, or there was going to be another wreck. He agreed and moved it. My neighbor's daughter and her boyfriend turned into their driveway to see what was going on. My neighbor's daughter was about to marry her boyfriend, and he was turning nineteen in a couple of days. Her boyfriend got out of the car and walked down to the creek where the first drunk wrecked. He was standing beside the car that had just been moved off the road, but the guide wire from the telephone pole was still across the road and hanging in the air where it was still connected to the pole. I heard another car coming, so I started waving at him to slow down. Instead of slowing down, he just switched lanes and hit the guide wire that the young man was standing next to. The guide wire caught the boy and twisted and slammed him against the pavement. He was instantly killed. Blood was gushing out of his mouth like a dog that had been hit by a car. I ran up to my neighbor's house and told them to call the police and tell them that someone had just been killed. The driver of the car that hit the guide wire was also drunk. He could see me six hundred feet from where I was waving, and he went another three hundred feet before he stopped after killing the boy. He came walking back over to me, and I told him, "You just killed this boy!" He didn't say anything.

I went to my house to get a pen and some paper to write down everything that had happened. I was so nervous that I could hardly write. I was the only witness, except for the other two drunks, but I don't think they were paying attention or would be reliable witnesses. I measured how far away I was from the scene of the accident when I was waving at the car to slow down and how far before he stopped.

Two policemen came to the scene, and I explained what had happened. They didn't seem too interested, and I found out later that one of the policemen knew the brother of the drunk that killed the boy. I wrote down six pages of what had happened and what was said. I called the policeman later after we got back from fishing and asked if he took the drunk driver to have a sobriety test. He said, "Yes, he was drunk and tested positive." I asked if the policeman arrested the guy, and he said no. I asked the policeman if he wrote the guy a ticket, and he said no. I asked, "Why not?" And the policeman said, "Well, I just didn't." I found out later from my neighbor's daughter that the nineteen-year-old boy had lived with his grandfather. I got the boy's father's phone number from the neighbor and called him in Monroeville, and he said to just throw his son in the ditch as far as he was concerned. I gave him a few choice words, and then I called the boy's mother in California. She told me that she didn't have the money to come to her son's funeral, so I just hung up on her.

I went to the boy's wake two days later, and his father was there. I was ready to pop him if he said anything to make me angry, but he just said, "Mr. Whatley, you are a good man." I found out later that the boy had bought his dad a car, and the dad was drunk and wrecked it the day before his son was killed. There was a trial about six years after the boy's death, and his grandfather had hired a little jackknife lawyer. The grandfather came to court with his overalls on. I told his lawyer that I had everything that happened and what was said written down, and he said the judge probably wouldn't accept it as evidence. I asked him, "Why not? I was the only witness." We got into where the judge was, and I could hear the drunk talking about the nightclub that he was going to go to that night. They started picking jury members, and the grandfather's lawyer left a policeman on the jury. I also knew the foreman that was left on the jury, and we didn't like each other. I asked the lawyer why he left them on the jury, and he told me he couldn't just mark everyone off the jury. Then his secretary spoke up and said she was thinking the same thing that I said. I saw her later on after the trial, and she said she had left that law firm.

I got on the stand to testify and explain what had happened that day. I started to pull the six sheets of paper that I had written everything down on out of my pocket, and the judge told me I couldn't do that. It seemed like everyone already had their minds made up before we even got to court. Now if that drunk would have killed my son like he did that boy, I would have killed him for sure. I probably would have been sent to prison for life, but they let that drunk off free. The drunk killed a boy. No arrest, no ticket. Now, doesn't that make you wonder about our system? It was just like when my uncle Eddie Whatley killed his wife in cold blood and only got six years in prison, although he was sentenced to twenty years. That isn't justice. Our system seems to have guidelines that will keep people from telling the jury the whole story, rather than just the part the lawyers want said because there may be objections.

I don't think any judge should have the authority to stop a witness, such as me, from telling the truth about how that nineteen-year-old boy was killed because of a drunk and letting them get away with it. If I would have persisted, I would have been held in contempt of court. I had six pages written down about what happened and how it happened. I was the only credible witness, and I would have been more than glad (and still would) to give a jury the true story instead of letting that drunk get away with killing an innocent young person. If that had been my son that was killed, the drunk wouldn't have been bragging in the court about which nightclub he was going to that night. When a judge can limit the truth you tell, like the judge did in that case, something is wrong somewhere. How did the judge know what evidence I had unless the defense lawyer told him in advance?

In another case that should have been an eye for an eye was when I had these two brothers working for my lawn care business in Mobile. Both were on dope. As soon as I paid them every afternoon, they would go get them some crack cocaine or marijuana. I fired one of them because he was not a good worker. He and another man were doing carpentry work with a third man who was from Ohio. The first two men killed the man from Ohio. The man from Ohio pleaded with them, saying, "Please don't kill me," and that he had

232

two children. They killed that man for $150. The one that used to work for me came back to the little motel while I was there and was bragging that he had just killed the man. He was wearing the boots of the man he had just killed and had the man's toolbox. He was talking about how they cut the man up and dismembered his body. He went to prison years ago after he admitted to what he did. It should have been an eye for an eye, and he should have been sentenced to death. He had admitted to the crime, so why keep feeding him for many more years and giving him several appeals? Things like that are one reason that the jails are overpopulated.

CHAPTER 9

ENCOUNTERS WITH THE KU KLUX KLAN

Some people think that the Ku Klux Klan (KKK) was formed to be a force against Black people, but that may be a misconception. My mother told me that the KKK was formed to deal with any man, Black or White, who did not take care of or provide for his family. I was told they were founded back in the prohibition days, but that may be hearsay. I don't know for sure. I knew my father and my uncle Eddie belonged to the KKK and a few more men that I knew. The men would be drinking sometimes and would say things that they shouldn't have. Even though my daddy was a member of the KKK, my mother told us when we were little that a cross may be burned in our yard some night. That meant someone thought that my daddy wasn't taking care of his family like he was capable of doing, but our daddy was trying to take care of eight people, including my grandfather. I guess that was pretty hard to do all by himself.

When I was in my fifties, I had some run-ins with the KKK. The people and situations had changed. I was cutting grass in Mobile for a KKK leader, and he was telling me that there was a power struggle to see who would be the top man running the organization. The top man had contributions coming in from all the members. The man that I was talking to was in trouble with the Internal Revenue Service. He said he had money in a Swiss bank account and that our government was trying to get some of it. He brought me into his house trailer to show me how many guns he had. He had knives and different things with KKK emblems stamped on them that he was selling. He had guns hanging all around the walls in one room, and he had one gun with a round clip that would shoot like a machine gun. In another room, he had fishing rods hanging on the walls, all around the room. He went on vacation one week, and his trailer "mysteriously" caught on fire. The voluntary fire department showed up to put out the fire, but the fire truck ran out of gas about one hundred yards from the fire. So they just sat there and watched it burn. The fire was so intense that it bent the barrels of those guns, doubled over. He was a nice guy but didn't save anything. He didn't know his house trailer had burned until he got back from vacation.

I had a bad experience with a stupid, ignorant KKK leader. At the time, I owned five acres of land with three rental properties on it. The KKK leader owned five acres across the road from me. He started building a house next to the house that he lived in, and every once in a while, my horse would get out of my fence and go over to his land. He had a horse also and made a remark to my neighbor that if my horse came on his land again, he was going to keep him. Well, my horse did get out again, and I went over to the KKK leader's neighbor's house, but I was on his land talking to the neighbor over the fence. The KKK man had a few of his friends with him on his porch and hollered at me to get off his GD land. The neighbors told me to come on their side of the fence, which I did. Then here came the KKK man down the hill toward us, popping of and cursing with his hand in his pocket. The neighbor lady told him, "Mr. Boyd, he is just looking for his horse." He popped off at her and said, "You ain't nothing but a niggar lover!" She asked her husband, "Are you going to let him talk to me that way?" But the husband told her to be quiet or else the KKK leader would burn their house down. I told them, "That is exactly what that SOB wants you to think." I don't get mad often, but I was pretty mad at that point. I told the KKK leader that if he wanted to step out into the road, I would be happy to whip his ass. He told me to come over to his land, and I told him no and that no one was scared of the little gun he had in his pocket. He was trying hard to be a big boy in front of his crowd, and I didn't really care what happened at that point. I told him he was lower than any Black person that I ever met and invited him a second time to step out into the road for his ass whipping. I really thought that he was going to pull his gun out and shoot me when I told him that. I never saw my horse again after that day. I guess he stole it, but I was tired of tending to the horse, and my daughter Cheryl didn't really like riding it anymore because it had kicked her one time. That idiot finally got his house built and his old house burned down. He told the insurance people that he couldn't save anything, but the insurance company came and looked inside the house and found some of his old furniture and got him for fraud.

They had a son that was as stupid as they were. The son said he and another boy went downtown to find a Black person to hang. They went down there and just got the first Black person they saw, and they did hang him. The son was put in prison right away, and he is still in prison as far as I know.

One night, I was on my way from my land going back home, and the idiot had a cross in a big field, next to a church, and he was trying to light it. I stopped to see what was going on. He had his KKK members trying to help get the cross burning. He was up there, yelling, "We are going to have to stop the Jews! They are trying to take over everything in our country!" All the rednecks were hollering and showing their ignorance, so I got into my car and left. They still didn't have the cross burning when I left. Later on, the man and his wife were put in jail for fraud, and the last that I heard, they were all still in prison: the father, the mother, and the son. Idiots like this used the KKK to promote their hatred against Black and Jewish people instead of what I was told it was started for, dealing with people who didn't take care of their families.

CONCLUSION

My beautiful wife Nettie Jo, who I was married to for forty-eight years, passed away on October 14, 2007. I continued my lawn care service until March 4, 2008, and then I decided to get out of the business and move back to West Blocton. I married Midge Reach on June 24, 2008, eight months after Nettie Jo passed away. Nettie Jo and I had double-dated with Midge and Gordon Reach when we were young. Midge and I were married for three years and nine months before we divorced. She was a very good and smart woman, but we were sort of going different directions in life. We were only married for nine months when I told Midge that I was tired of retired life and I was going to find a job. So I started looking. I called Murray Guard Security Services on March 29, 2009, and was hired. I only worked for them until December 21 of that year when another security service called Walden's Security bought out their contract while we were working at the Mercedes Benz plant in Tuscaloosa. I have been working full-time ever since, have not missed one day of work, have never been late, and have never turned down overtime. I got Officer of the Month in September 2014 and got a $50 bonus and a plaque to put on my desk.

Nettie Jo Whatley

When James Vaught was interviewing me for the job for Walden's Security, I was being sincere and said I would give him notice in advance. He looked at me sort of surprised, and I told him that I am not retiring until I am ninety. He laughed and hired me. I will work as long as I stay in good health, and God has been good to me so far, and I thank him.

I have had a pretty fascinating life so far. I finished high school and joined the air force, where I became an international Morse code operator and finished at the top of my class. I went to Tripoli, Libya, and was baptized in the Mediterranean Sea with several other airmen by a Louisiana preacher. I won a bowling trophy and a horseshoe trophy in the eighteen months that I was there. I went to Istanbul in Turkey; and Rome, Naples, and Pompei in Italy; Athens in Greece; and then back to Tampa, Florida, to finish my military service. I started pitching ball in 1955 while I lived in Libya and pitched fifty-three years straight until 2008 when I left Mobile. I played baseball with the great Joe Namath who won Superbowl III. My picture, working at O'Neal Steel in Birmingham, was put into fifteen industrial books advertising a radio-controlled overhead crane in 1964. I was put in a TV guide in Mobile in 1980. I was put on the front page of the sports section in *The Mobile Press Register* on June 19, 2000, with Tiger Wood (playing golf), Shaquille O'Neal (playing basketball), and me playing softball. They ran a TV news special on me playing ball in 2005 with men less than half my age. I have won a lot of ball and bowling trophies over the years. I bowled for thirty-three years on a regular team. There is a picture of me from when I was in the air force in the Woodstock Town Hall, hanging on the wall, and I am on the veterans' memorial in West Blocton. As you can see, I have had a pretty interesting life with God's help. This concludes my life's autobiography.

Left to right (Top): Carol, me, Nettie Jo, Teresa
(Bottom): Cheryl and Michael

Me with the Cahaba River lilies

Cheryl, Mike, Carol, me, and Teresa

Carol, Cheryl, me, Mike, and Teresa

Rail engine used to move Coke from ovens to load on trucks and railcars. The men produced 631 tons per day.

Old House in "Dago Holler"

Old Coke Ovens in West Blocton

ABOUT THE AUTHOR

Bobby Whatley was a resident of Bibb County, Alabama, until he finished high school. He then joined the United States Air Force and served for four years. After basic training in San Antonio, Texas, he was sent to Biloxi, Mississippi, for seven months to train and learn international Morse code. After training, he was then shipped to Tripoli, Libya, in North Africa for eighteen months. He stared pitching softball and baseball while he was there. Bobby was baptized in the Mediterranean Sea by a Louisiana preacher, along with seven other airmen. He finished reading his Bible on the Atlantic Ocean while coming home to the United States. He has been to Italy, Turkey, and Greece. He continued to pitch ball on different softball teams for fifty-three years. At seventy-three years young, he was playing on three different softball teams a week with twenty—and thirty-year-old men in Africa, Alabama, Florida, Tennessee, and Mississippi. He worked in a coal mine for one year and worked in different steel plants for thirty-three years. Mr. Whatley was a plant superintendent for twenty years. He has played baseball with the great Joe Namath and has been on the front page with Tiger Woods and Shaquille O'Neal. He was put in over fifteen industrial magazines while he worked for O'Neal Steel in Birmingham. His name can be seen on the veterans memorial in West Boston, Alabama. When he was sixty-nine years young, he appeared on a TV special, throwing a softball seventy-five miles per hour accurately behind his back. Bobby Whatley has that TV special on DVD.

9 781638 816447